"A humanizing, humble, and hard look at a life. Investigative journalism of the soul. Sari Botton's *And You May Find Yourself* is like the older sister of *My Misspent Youth* by Meghan Daum. You will absolutely find yourself in this intelligent, clever, and clear-hearted book."
　　—Chloe Caldwell, author of *The Red Zone: A Love Story*

"What you will find in here is a funny, honest, inquisitive, fearless, provocative, thoughtful, and generous new friend."
　　—Abigail Thomas, author of *Safekeeping: Some True Stories From a Life*

"*And You May Find Yourself* reminds us that the more specific and particular a person's story is, the more universal it feels. I'm glad Sari Botton solved the mystery of herself and gladder still she was generous enough to share the answer with readers."
　　—Laura Lippman, author of *My Life as a Villainess: Essays*

"Many women will find the best and worst of themselves in this compelling memoir—an honest, deep dive into a Gen-X self-described weirdo, who turns out to be all of us."
　　— V.C. Chickering, author of *Nookietown* and *Twisted Family Values*

"Sometimes, age really is just a number. The cultural touchstones and fashion trends might be different, but women across generations will recognize their experiences in And You May Find Yourself as Sari Botton charts her journey to embrace who she really is across a series of essays – writing with warmth, humor, and never shying from vulnerability about the mean girls of middle school, a therapist who gives the greatest dating advice, and the big questions around career, passion and children."
　　—Minda Honey, author of the forthcoming essay collection *An Anthology of Assholes*

AND YOU MAY FIND YOURSELF...

Confessions of a
Late-Blooming
Gen-X Weirdo

SARI BOTTON

Heliotrope Books

New York

Heliotrope Books LLC
heliotropebooks@gmail.com

ISBN 978-1-942762-99-7
ISBN 978-1-942762-98-0 eBook

Cover illustration and all interior illustrations ©Sari Botton
Designed and typeset by Naomi Rosenblatt with AJ&J Design

Dedicated to all the other
late-blooming Gen-X weirdos out there,
and the messy women of any generation
trying to find their own way.

Edited by Sari Botton

*Goodbye to All That: Writers on
Loving and Leaving New York*

*Never Can Say Goodbye: Writers on Their
Unshakable Love for New York*

CONTENTS

Part 3 • Blossoming

"Most people live their entire lives with their clothes on, and even if they wanted to, couldn't take them off. Then there are those who cannot put them on. They are the ones who live their lives not just as people but as examples of people. They are destined to expose every part of themselves, so the rest of us can know what it means to be a human."

—Sheila Heti, *How Should a Person Be?*

"The most subversive thing a woman can do is talk about her life as if it really matters."

—Mona Eltahawy, *The Seven Necessary Sins for Women and Girls*

"Because right now there is someone
Out there with
a wound in the exact shape
    of your words."

—Sean Thomas Dougherty, *Why Bother?*

"I know now, after fifty years, that the finding/losing, forgetting/remembering, leaving/returning, never stops. The whole of life is about another chance, and while we are alive, till the very end, there is always another chance."

—Jeanette Winterson, *Why Be Happy When You Could Be Normal?*

"It's never too late to be what you might have been."

—George Eliot

FOREWORD

Dear Readers,

First things first, so you know what you're getting into:

This is a work of creative nonfiction. The stories collected here are based on real life experiences to the best of my recollection—which, to be quite honest, is a little spotty in my mid-fifties. That's okay, because memoir is not investigative journalism.

Memoir is also not objective. It centers the perspective of the storyteller, which may differ significantly from the perspectives and recollections of others who were present for the very same experiences. Which is to say that I do not consider my versions of the experiences herein to be the sole, sovereign versions. They're just *mine*.

I heard one of my favorite anecdotes about this common discrepancy at the Woodstock Bookfest's memoir panel several years ago. Martha Frankel, the festival's director, talked about publishing *Hats and Eyeglasses*, her memoir of gambling addiction, and coming from a family of gamblers. When she was finished writing it, she sent the manuscript to her sister. "Let me know if I got anything wrong," Martha said. When her sister was done reading she called Martha and said, "None of it's true. But I don't have any problem with you publishing it."

〜〜〜

One of the great challenges of writing memoir is that you can't tell a story about yourself without including other people, for context at the very least, but other people aren't always thrilled about being included. With this in mind, I have taken great pains to omit unnecessary details and to blur people—changing names and other identifying characteristics—to the greatest extent possible, in some cases combining people into composite characters. I've also collapsed time in a few instances, in the service of more streamlined storytelling. (This is the "creative" part of "creative nonfiction.")

Furthermore, I recognize that everyone makes mistakes; that given the opportunity, most people will at least attempt to grow and change; and that none of us are merely the sum of our worst past behaviors. More than with individual people, I take issue with our culture and the long-standing systems of oppression that drive it, influencing (and limiting) people's choices. And so, I have strived in my telling of these events to give everyone mentioned the benefit of the doubt.

Reader, I ask that you do the same for me.

~~~

Regarding the format and genre of this book: Some of my favorite books are collections of essays and stories, and just like those, this is a *collection*, rather than a straight memoir with a single, linear narrative. I sold the book as a memoir-in-essays. But as I was working on it, I debated whether "essays" was an accurate category. While some of the pieces are true personal essays that make arguments and draw connections to universal truths, others feel more loosely like creative nonfiction stories from a life. I've come around to thinking of them all as "confessions."

Each story in here is meant to stand on its own, which in some cases has resulted in a bit of repetition. I also experiment in places by alternating between present and past tense—similar to the ways in which we speak to one another, conversationally switching to present tense when diving into anecdotes within a larger story. While the book is organized with a general narrative arc, the pieces lend themselves to being read separately, in any order. But don't let me stop you from reading them all, straight through from beginning to end, if that's what you prefer.

However you read this book, I hope you'll enjoy it.

~~~

A few words, more generally, about this endeavor, which has been hard-won for me: Writing this book has been a great privilege and joy, but it's also been challenging in ways, and something of an act of defiance. I anticipate a certain type of backlash, having witnessed as other writers were met with it, time and again. And so I offer this note as both a defense, and a declaration of intent.

As a woman born in the mid-1960s and living in a patriarchal culture, I have always struggled to feel justified in taking up space anywhere, most of all on the page. Writing about my experiences is my passion and chosen profession, but I have always wrestled with feeling entitled to it, especially since some deride this kind of work by labeling it "navel-gazing" and "over-sharing," which implies it's unwelcome information, especially when it comes from women.

These are the thoughts that dog me: *Who am I to think my story has value? Who am I to believe anyone will care about what I have to say—about my perceptions of the world around me, and my own particular experiences?* As crime novelist Laura Lippman writes in the introduction to her essay collection, *My Life as a Villainess* (William Morrow, 2020), "The question that hovers over anyone who dares to write personal essays, especially a woman, is, 'Who the hell do you think you are?'"

Among the many catalysts for my resistance toward writing this has been a certain negative attitude in our culture toward first-person writing.

For the uninitiated: Reliably, every few years some critic takes a massive dump on personal essays, memoirs, or both. One of the arguments that keeps getting regurgitated is that the authors (frequently women or others who are marginalized) aren't writing about an experience that's extraordinary enough, or that their lives aren't sufficiently interesting to warrant a publishing contract. The criticism catches fire and circulates on social media as if it's some new idea. Memoir-haters pile on. Then comes the backlash from first-person diehards like me.

My defense goes like this: While there's definitely room for sensational essays and memoirs by people who have had outrageous experiences, or who are famous for one reason or another, that's actually *not* the meat and potatoes of the first-person category, and it's not what dedicated fans of this kind of writing seek in it. No, the primary job of the essayist or memoirist is to use the craft of writing to illuminate and make meaning of *the ordinary*—to name or crystalize experiences that are incredibly common in such a way that readers understand their own versions of those common experiences anew.

There's more to it, though: It's the job of essayists and memoirists from marginalized groups to shed light on their experiences, even the average ones—*especially* the average ones—which have frequently been ignored by a culture and field long dominated by affluent white men. When women, LBGTQIA, BIPOC, and disabled writers dare to share their perspectives on everyday experiences, it is a bold, political act.

I offer you this mini-dissertation on first-person writing as a way to calibrate your expectations for this, my somewhat experimental, episodic memoir-in-confessions, and to apprise you of my mission with it. Let me confess right out of the gate that I have not lived an exceptional life. I did not survive some horrific accident. I did not win the lottery, or endure remarkably unfortunate circumstances. I've had my difficulties. I've been through my share of traumas and tough times, emotionally, financially, and otherwise. But we're not talking tabloid material.

I'm a writer, mainly of first-person nonfiction—a woman-writer, in my mid-fifties, an age at which American culture tends to deem us boring, invisible and disposable. This is work I feel naturally called to. I always have, from the time I was a young girl and I sequestered myself in my bedroom, recording my perspectives on my relatively average life. It's also work that feels imperative to me. I am staking a claim; it is my right to do this, to deconstruct my everyday experiences as a woman in

American culture, because I feel like it, because I enjoy it, and because frankly, while my work won't be everyone's cup of tea, I'm not bad at it. I'm writing specifically as a late-blooming Gen-X woman, but when I read this line of grafitti in a photo posted by millennial writer Chloe Caldwell on Instagram, it helped me recommit to my mission: "I just felt like writing something…"

~~~

I talk a good game, but there were moments as I was working on this when I was so daunted, I lost my nerve completely, and nearly gave up. Obviously, though, I found my way back to my sense of purpose. I remembered how hard I fought for this opportunity, and how fortunate I am to have been given it; it's not something to take for granted, or to balk at. I remembered how I've stood up for other women writers who've been derided, and called selfish and narcissistic, for writing about their own experiences. *Oh, yeah — right*, I recalled. *I've been an advocate for this kind of work. And, finally, it's my turn.*

I remembered how little I know about the lives of my grandmothers, who both died around my age, in their early- and mid-fifties. I know even less about one of my maternal great-grandmothers, who succumbed to influenza in 1919, at the age of 25. I remembered how much I relish reading books by women about their lives.

I remembered that my voice matters. I'm using it now, to take up space, to say, "I was here."

— Sari Botton

June 2022

INTRODUCTION: GREETINGS FROM WEIRDVILLE

People often ask me which books by famous writers made me want to become a writer myself. I always feel put on the spot by this question and worry about coming up with an impressive answer—mostly because I don't have an answer, not even an unimpressive one.

The truth is, I didn't become a writer because I was inspired by anyone else or their work. I became a writer because I felt like a weirdo, different in ways from many of the people around me, and out of step with my peers—a late bloomer in terms of when I hit certain milestones.

In my family, at school, in my neighborhood, at summer camp, at synagogue, and most of the spaces I inhabited as a kid, I was *just enough* unlike everyone else, on a variety of fronts, to feel like a misfit and be self-conscious about it.

For example:

I was more intense, introspective, and sensitive than most, crying often. Yet, I didn't embarrass easily, so I would take flying leaps publicly—like singing my heart out to the whole neighborhood from my front stoop—only realizing I'd made a weird choice once everyone was laughing at me. I've always had what can only be described as Resting Worry Face, which has made people feel concerned and a little nervous about approaching me. (A few have confessed.)

My dad was a teacher in my school system and clergy at my temple, and my mom later became my Sunday School teacher there (at the most cringy time possible, aka seventh grade)—all of which set me *just slightly* apart from the other kids. So did being Jewish in a town that mostly wasn't. In a sea of girls named Theresa and Jennifer and Lori and Susan and Jill, I had an unusual name that people weren't sure how to pronounce—both my first and last names being *so close* to more familiar names, that kids and teachers often instead landed on "Sara Bottom" or "Sally Buttons" or "Shari Barton." A late developer, I didn't get my first full period until I was 18, making me unlike so many of the other girls around me who talked about their "friend," or their "Aunt Flo," and complaining about pads and tampons and Midol. I didn't like sports and was bad enough at them to fail gym one semester in high school. I didn't like the same clothes, hairstyles, heartthrobs, or foods as most of my peers; I sensed it meant something was wrong with me that I wasn't at all into: satin baseball jackets, Sasson jeans, and Candies slides, David and Sean Cassidy (I swooned over Andy Williams and Frank Sinatra), feathered '70s hairstyles like Farrah Fawcett's, the most common dietary staples, including bananas, milk, any preparation of eggs in which the white and the yolk were separate.

The feeling of being an uncool weirdo followed me into college and beyond, through adulthood. Having grown up in a house filled with classical and liturgical music, opera, jazz standards, and showtunes (all of which I liked), I wasn't hip to the pop and rock music my high school and college friends listened to—not until friends and boyfriends started making me mixtapes, to help me keep up. With my offbeat tastes in things, I felt out of place in suburban monoculture, first when I grew up there and later when I returned, briefly, in my twenties. I had no real desire for children, nor much of an affinity for hanging out with other people's kids.

When I worked in offices, I struggled to find my place among my co-workers, always inept at navigating office politics. In my family, I was the observer. The black sheep. The one who questions everything, who has doubts about things everyone else accepts as gospel. The only one who couldn't get with religion—couldn't take the messages and strictures and history at face value, always needing to look below the surface and ask uncomfortable questions—who also didn't like living in houses (I have a strange affinity for dwellings that weren't built with the intention of housing people, like the former yeshiva my husband and I lived in on the corner of Eighth Street and Avenue B in Manhattan), nor living in the suburbs, nor various aspects of traditional nuclear family life...

There's more; I'll stop here.

Writing, from the time I was 8 or so, helped me sort out this being-a-weirdo business, and also make sense of behaviors I observed in others. I sometimes felt as if I were an anthropologist, or an alien from another planet sent to Earth to report back on my findings. I would hide in the bottom of my bedroom closet and scribble on a legal pad, or the smooth "ditto" paper I asked my teacher parents to bring home from their classrooms. Or, I'd whisper into my shiny blue Panasonic tape recorder. (Once, I accidentally recorded *my feelings* over the practice tape my dad made for my bat mitzvah; embarrassingly, I had to ask him to record it all over again.)

Expressing myself to myself was only so cathartic, though. From a young age, I longed to express myself to others, too—to be heard and read and understood. I wanted to be a writer. I found it satisfying and validating then, as an adult, when

I started publishing first-person creative nonfiction pieces. Readers frequently responded, letting me know that my experiences and perspectives resonated with them too. Lo and behold, I wasn't the only weirdo out there.

～～～

The stories in this book are mainly about feeling different, and being a late bloomer, and being a woman who has too often relied on the approval, validation, acceptance, and attention of men in order to feel even vaguely okay. I also probe what it means to be: an adult woman; a daughter; a "divorce kid"; a friend; a wife; a cool person; a non-mom; a New Yorker; and a "free spirit," who often doesn't want *what* she's supposed to, *when* she's supposed to. Taken all together, these pieces are about becoming and owning The Real Me after getting sidetracked away from myself for quite some time. Too often when I was younger, instead of accepting who I was, I would try to act "normal," and go along with what everyone else in my age group was doing—Generation-X being a demographic that in and of itself was known for being weird. Not always content to be *even weirder* among the weird, I often made choices that didn't fit me, trying on and tossing off versions of myself I desperately wanted to believe were real because I thought they would have made other people happy with me, or accept me. I'd live with those choices for as long as I could before waking up one day feeling as if I were living inside that Talking Heads song, "Once in a Lifetime." *And you may find yourself...in a starter marriage in the suburbs in your early twenties... And you may ask yourself... Well... How did I get here?*

～～～

As a woman born in the mid-1960s, during the first wave of Generation-X, I came of age at the intersection of two conflicting attitudes: "should" and "whatever." I internalized both, and as a result, have zig-zagged between those poles throughout my life, sometimes conforming, other times breaking out of what feel like confining prescribed roles. While so many of the people I grew up with have lived their lives in one straight line, the trajectory of my life has looked more like scribble-scrabble. It's been one messy adulthood, and a slow process of *becoming*.

I write this now from the peak of an anxious awakening that began in my forties: I've realized that for much of my earlier adulthood, I didn't really know what I stood for, or who I was. Discovering that I have strong feminist and progressive political leanings has been emboldening, but also perilous, in that once again there's something that sets me apart from a good portion of the people in my world.

In the middle of my sixth decade, I'm still working to fully know myself—and also, to belatedly feel like an actual adult, something that has long eluded me. A variety of factors have left me feeling like a perennial child, the biggest of which might be my bypassing motherhood, which has meant, in a big way, living off-script from the culture at large. A hysterectomy at 43 left me surprisingly, happily childless, and transported me straight from much-protracted adolescence to menopause. Other likely factors: being physically small—just under five feet—which often leads people to perceive me as a little kid; being a child of divorce and latchkey kid who's never quite recovered from the attendant requirement to act like an adult too young; being part of a generation very much identified with immaturity.

It's not lost on me that I'm awfully long in the tooth to still be "growing up." I'm quite self-conscious about that, actually. The incongruity between my chronological age and the way I feel takes on a whole other dimension when I remember that I'm roughly the age both of my grandmothers were when they died.

I think about my grandmothers a lot these days, and wonder about my own longevity. My father's mother died at 51, two years before I was born, of a brain tumor. My mother's mother died at 55, when I was six-and-a-half, of breast cancer. Thinking of them brings to mind that George Eliot quote: *It's never too late to be who you might have been.* For my grandmothers, that adage didn't hold true. In their fifties, it was too late. After raising families, sustaining retrograde marriages, then battling fatal illness for several years, neither of them got to become who they might have been. Their lives were over before it was their turn to live for themselves, to explore alternate paths, to break out of old roles.

All my life I've been afraid to land in their shoes—living a life cut short. And here I am, at 56, just figuring big shit out. How much of my life do I have left for this clumsy soul-searching? Now that I'm older, and family and friends keep dying around me with greater frequency, I can hear the clock ticking. How much longer do I have to truly *find* myself?

~~~

I know, I know—it's kind of an icky term. When I was a child in the '70s, I often overheard grownups talking dismissively about people who were "finding" themselves—other adults they knew who'd pulled up stakes and relocated to new cities, quit jobs, went back to school, joined an ashram, volunteered on a kibbutz—all with the objective of figuring out who they *really* were, as opposed to who they had mistakenly become, or who they'd been pretending to be.

When adults in my world referred to those searching for themselves, they did so with an air of derision; there was an implicit eye-roll in the statement, "She's busy *finding herself*…" It seemed as if there was shame in admitting that the life you'd chosen hadn't worked out the way you'd hoped—confessing that you needed to regroup, or embark on some kind of expedition, literal or figurative, toward self-rediscovery. Instead, you were supposed to quit complaining and lie in the bed you'd made for yourself.

I got the impression back then that there were only a few right ways to be a grown woman in my world, mostly involving getting married young, having children, living in a house in the suburbs, and doing a job of some kind (or two, like both my parents did), whether that job was a good fit for you or not. You had to stick with it all, even if you'd initially chosen badly for yourself—a kind of self-sacrifice and self-abandonment that seemed dreadful to me as a young girl, especially as a day-dreaming misfit who never felt truly comfortable anywhere.

Those assumptions and others led me onto a course that took me away from myself. Connecting the dots between the creative weirdo I was as a kid and who I honestly am as an adult has been my great project of mid-life. This book is my rear-view exploration of the bumpy ride between those two points—*so far*.

PART 1

Try to Act Normal

Lost

In August of 1992, two months before my 27th birthday, my life exploded.

Wait—that's deceptively passive. Let me try again.

In August of 1992, two months before my 27th birthday, I exploded my life. I took the gameboard of my small existence and threw it over, leaving behind a starter marriage, plans for making a family, my home, suburbia. It felt incredibly urgent and necessary. It was also messy and horrible. *I* was messy and horrible.

I'd been wed to my first husband, my college sweetheart, for just over three years when I woke from what felt like being asleep at the wheel, and realized I had no idea who I was or what I wanted. Everything felt all wrong: Having married the second guy I'd ever dated, whom I'd met at 19, and who was becoming increasingly traditional and observant as a Jew, while I began experiencing something of a feminist awakening and drifting in a more secular direction; That I was married at all, so young (I'd gotten married three months before my 24th birthday); Where I lived (the same bedroom community of New York City that I was born in); My job (reporter at an unsexy trade magazine covering the home furnishings industry).

Confronting the all-encompassing nature of my dissatisfaction was terrifying. Even scarier was realizing I had only the vaguest notions of what I'd prefer instead. I had the feeling of living a lie, without knowing what the truth was. I was certain, though, that almost everything I did have in my life, and who I was, felt utterly false. It was unbearable.

For a good while before my big reckoning, which looked awfully like a nervous breakdown, I was almost willfully oblivious to my own unhappiness. I didn't want to be unhappy. I didn't want to do anything that might upset the applecart, or my husband. Too defended against acknowledging any of it, too desperate to convince myself I was content with my life choices, I did everything in my power not to acknowledge what I was feeling. I continued going about my existence until I stopped being able to out-run the hard, inconvenient truth.

~~~

No one had coerced me into the life I was living. Far from it. I chose almost every detail—had desperately *longed for*, even *campaigned for*, many of them, including the genius idea of marrying almost criminally young. It was what so many others around us were doing—our siblings, and cousins, and college mates. At 24 and 23 respectively, Elliott and I were, shockingly, one of the last couples in our social set to get engaged and married. As I was embarking on adulthood, I somehow couldn't see beyond the confining parameters of my little world, or find the courage to consider other possibilities beyond it.

Toward the end of college I'd momentarily flirted with other possibilities, like seeking a reporter job I'd been invited to apply for at a small local paper in the Berkshires, where I'd freelanced during senior year, which would have put me a few hours away from Elliott after graduation. There was also a nagging dream of spending time traveling and working in Europe. But I was too insecure, in myself and in our relationship. Elliott was good looking and outgoing, a magnetic flirt who drew lots of women to him even when he wasn't trying. He was fickle and hard to hold onto, which irrationally made me hold on harder and make him the center of my world.

For a brief moment, I shifted my focus—although not of my own volition. Just before he graduated, at the end of my junior year, he'd broken up with me. After I recovered from the initial blow, the breakup turned out to be good for me. That summer—the summer of 1986—I had an internship at *New York Newsday* as a reporter on the arts desk. It felt good to put my focus on work, instead of wasting my energy trying to hold onto an elusive man, as I'd been doing for so long. I flourished in my summer job. I'd assumed I'd be fetching coffee for reporters on staff, but no, they threw me in the deep end and made me a reporter for twelve weeks. I published a couple of articles a week, and received praise and encouragement from the journalists and editors I worked with. My confidence grew in my own ability—something that had nothing to do with whether a man thought I was pretty or sexy or worthy of his love.

Then, after I returned to Albany for my senior year, just as I was growing strong and independent, and starting to date—just as I was beginning to achieve as a freelance writer, landing my byline here and there—Elliott returned. I took him right back, no questions asked. And instead of daring to grab hold of more power in the relationship now that he was pursuing me, I reverted to my old, weak position, and let Elliott remain, uncontested, in the driver's seat. I was so afraid to rock the boat, to risk losing this guy so many other women loved to flirt with. I reverted to making him and our relationship my number one concern.

At a time when I should have left my future wide open, I held onto the prospect of being with him forever, as if it were my only option. Our relationship was long-distance my senior year, with me in Albany, and him downstate. Coordinating weekends together in either place was challenging, and absorbed a tremendous amount of my time and energy.

After graduation, I moved back home to the south shore of Long Island to be near Elliott, and I applied only for jobs in Manhattan. I can't count the number of times that I've stopped to wonder how different my life would have turned out, how much stronger my career, if I hadn't gotten back together with him, had put myself into my work, and tried living somewhere other than where I was from. If only I'd had the self-confidence and courage and belief in myself. If only I could have seen the possibility of a different path.

~~~

But I couldn't. Once I had my B.A. in hand, I was on to pursuing my MRS. That's a reference to an old joke from my mother's generation, a supposed anachronism which sadly also applied to me. In my late-mid-fifties now, it seems bizarre recalling how much time I spent that first year out of college anxiously wondering whether and when Elliott would propose. It was practically all I thought about, as everyone else around us tied the knot.

How desperately I yearned for a diamond solitaire. A wedding. The security and validation of it all, beginning with his much awaited proposal. At the same time, I felt resentful that it was all up to him. I wasn't allowed to even bring up "the m-word," lest I freak Elliott out. I had no choice but to wait for him to decide.

I wasn't thinking expensive fairytale wedding. Not coming from money, I scoffed at those. *What a waste*, I thought. I didn't have much money, and neither did my parents. And even if we did, I wouldn't choose to waste tens of thousands of dollars on one day of my life. I wasn't about to hand over a wad of cash to Kleinfeld's for a puffy, white dress I'd wear for literally five hours and then never again. No, I went to J.C. Penney and bought a sample wedding gown off the rack for $250. When I called my mom from a payphone in the mall to tell her I thought I'd found my dress, my sister picked up, then called out, "Mah, Sari's buying her wedding dress in a lawn mower store..."

I didn't care what dress, or even color of dress, my wedding party wore. But they—all family—did, and an argument broke out about it at my bridal shower. Half the wedding party identified as Color Me Beautiful "winters," (Remember Color Me Beautiful?) and the other half as "springs." The winters wanted to wear pink; the springs, peach. The two groups were literally shouting over each other, at me, "Pink!" "Peach!" Finally I said, "Okay, *you* wear pink, and *you* wear peach! It will be fine!" And it was.

I really wasn't on board with making the reception any kind of fussy event. All I really cared about was the ceremony. For a clergy kid who struggles with religion, I have a strange affinity for ceremony, in general. I like deriving a sense of power from naming an intention and performing a ritual to make it so. I like to mark occasions with celebration. My favorite occasion to mark is the one where two people commit to each other.

~~~~~

I've had a thing for wedding ceremonies going back to my early childhood. It probably makes perfect sense that when I, a "divorce kid," grew up, I longed for the normalcy of happily-ever-after. I became hell-bent on succeeding where my parents had failed—at marrying young. Maybe it was a misguided attempt to repair the rupture in my family of origin. I don't know what gave me the impression that I, a person in her early twenties, involved in only the second romantic relationship in her life, knew how to make a marriage work and last. But that was what I'd been determined to achieve practically since my parents sat me down and told me they were separating, in the spring of 1976, a formative life event that forever altered me, and which echoes in my mind even still. Irrationally, to this day, I become grief-stricken when I learn of couples ending marriages or long-term relationships—even couples I barely know—as if it's happening to me again.

~~~~~

Three years after my splashy synagogue catering hall wedding, I woke up and discovered I had no idea what I was doing or why. I realized I'd been on autopilot, making choices based on what I *thought* I should want, and more concerned with other people's satisfaction than with my own. Each time I made a decision, I was guided by the unconscious motivation to keep others content—my husband, my parents, my bosses, anyone else with more power than me—so that they'd be pleased with me, and reward me with praise and validation, which would give me a kind of emotional boost I confused with happiness. I didn't know it, but I was pretending to be happy, to be the easy-going blank slate I somehow believed I should be—a nice, accommodating girl; a good little wife who rarely questioned or challenged her husband.

When the change occurred in me, it felt as if my entire nervous system had been replaced with a new one that caused me to see and feel everything differently. It didn't happen instantaneously—more like gradually and then suddenly, encroaching on my consciousness more and more loudly until I could no longer ignore it. I denied it to myself, tried to block it out, for as long as I could. But then, in the winter of 1992, I fell into a deep depression. A couple of friends urged me to find a therapist. During a three-week period when my husband was away on business, I found myself a shrink in Manhattan, so that I would have a reason to travel into the city each week.

I scheduled my first appointment with Dr. Bernice Blum for a day shortly before Elliott would return from his trip. Something about taking that action made me feel empowered and hopeful. It lifted my mood. Then, a shift occurred inside me that took me completely by surprise: instead of longing for Elliott's return, I began dreading it. That didn't stop me from lying to my new therapist. "The one thing that's right in my life is my marriage," I insisted at my first appointment. I was trying to uphold the myth of my happy marriage to my new shrink, and to myself.

~~~

Eight months later, I'd leave. It was a hell of a time, those final months. When I stopped being a docile blank slate and started being an outspoken person with opinions, we stopped getting along. It probably didn't help that in finding my voice after being silent for so long, I could be clumsy in expressing myself. Eventually we reached a point at which we couldn't agree on so much as the color of the sky. It was difficult and painful, but I felt alive and real in a way I hadn't before, and I wanted more of that. I didn't know how to stop moving in that direction, nor did I want to.

I began looking forward to Elliott's business trips—much-needed breaks from our endless arguing.

~~~

Shortly before the end of my marriage, on a night when both our husbands were traveling, my neighbor Suzanne and I accompanied two hot, young guy friends to a bachelorette party at a bar in the west end of Long Beach, where they were to be the unofficial "talent." Before she and I left our apartment building, for the first time since our wedding, I slipped my wedding and engagement rings off. It wasn't enough to be out at a bar, dirty dancing with two attractive younger men, neither of whom I was married to. I needed to test out what it might feel like to be *symbolically* free, to be a different me, even if this temporary version was not much more authentic than the version of me I was toying with leaving behind.

We didn't know the bride or her bridesmaids, but it didn't matter—it was probably better that way. It wasn't a formal party; they hadn't rented a private room at the bar or anything like that. It was just an evening of sweaty dancing to a deejay, with not only the wedding party, but a horde of other bar patrons as well. We hooted and hollered along with the crowd as our guy friends stripped down to their underwear. We drank, and danced, and flirted. On the ride home, I made a note of how ironic it was to have tried on the role of "unmarried woman" at a party meant to usher a different woman toward matrimony.

~~~

That first little taste of freedom was intoxicating. I wanted more. Soon I'd have it.

I thought setting myself free would make everything all better. It seemed so simple then: I had been lost, and, *I thought*, now I'd find my way.

I didn't know yet how many other ways there are to lose yourself.

Leaving the Land
of Make-Believe

I was four the first time I tried to publicly pass myself off as someone else. It was 1969, and my mother and grandmother took me along with them to Alexander's department store in Hempstead, Long Island. In the women's department, as they flipped through racks of clothes, I got bored and wandered off.

A little old lady spotted me in my peach-and-white-striped Danskin pants outfit. I was playing with a pile of needlepoint-covered decorative pillows in the home furnishings department.

"Hello, little girl," she said, stooping to greet me. "Are you lost?" I looked around and realized I had no idea where my mom and grandmother were. But I was enjoying exploring on my own. I felt free, and very grown up, and wasn't quite ready to find them.

"No," I insisted. "I am not lost."

"What's your name?" the woman asked. I paused for a second and thought before responding.

"I'm Andi Neuman from New Jersey," I said. "I go to Temple University."

The woman looked surprised, but played along. "Well, 'Andi Neuman from New Jersey,' let's take a little walk." She put my hand in hers and led me through the store to the customer service window. There she explained the situation to a clerk, who peered out over her desk to consider me.

"Tell me your name," the clerk said.

"I'm Andi Neuman from New Jersey," I repeated. "I go to Temple University."

"Oh, okay," she said, with a laugh, then turned on the microphone at her desk. "Good afternoon, shoppers...."

I was startled by the sound of her voice echoing out into the store. For the first time, I was scared. Still, I felt a little thrill hearing my assumed name over the loudspeaker. Within moments I saw my mother and grandmother come running toward me, frantic but relieved. They'd recognized my alias; I'd been pretending to be my uncle's sister-in-law, Andrea, my favorite babysitter, with whom I was enamored. She was pretty and funny and, at 20, very grown-up to me. Just a few weeks earlier, she'd taught me how to blow bubbles with chewing gum, and now I wanted to learn *everything* from her, and more importantly how to *be* her.

～～～

An ongoing challenge of adult life has been trying to recognize when I'm not being myself—when I'm slipping into an old habit of pretending to be someone else, usually in order to please people, mostly men or others who have more power than me. After too many occasions on which I woke up one day realizing I was living a lie, I've made it my business to truly know myself, and be myself.

I've come to learn I'm not alone in this; many women have told me their experience has been similar. I believe a huge factor is the way in which girls and women have long been discouraged from expressing their true thoughts and feelings, especially when they depart from the norm, or from what we've been told we're supposed to think and feel—especially if, heaven forbid, there's anger involved.

I suspect that for me, another factor was how much I loved make-believe as a child. Even before I began watching *Mister Rogers' Neighborhood* and became entranced by his wonderful Land of Make Believe, a magical kingdom he'd transport viewers to by way of electric trolley, I loved being able to slip into and out of other identities. It was an exciting and comforting means of escape from myself into someone more interesting, or more confident, or just plain different from the me I was unsure of.

I enjoyed playing make-believe so much, I clung to it past an age when it was considered appropriate.

～～～

I was so enamored with pretending that, early on, I thought I'd make a career of it. I was going to be *an actress*, and also a dancer and a singer. I wouldn't have my official debut until two years later, in the first grade play, but I was *determined*. I caught the acting bug at my maternal grandparents' apartment, where I'd sleep over on Saturday nights so my parents could go out. We'd watch Shirley Temple movies on Channel 11, WPIX, and sing along to songs like "Animal Crackers in My Soup." I was so excited to see a child performing on the small screen, acting, singing, dancing. I knew from the first time I saw her that I wanted to do *that*.

Later, as we got ready for bed, my grandmother, Nanny Clarisse, and I would costar in Ivory Soap commercials, like we'd seen on the television. I had my lines perfectly memorized.

"If my skin's fresh and healthy looking," I'd say to my own reflection with a smile and a twinkle in my eye, "I guess it's because I've gotten down to basics. You know—fresh air, sunshine, healthy food, and Ivory soap…" I had my whole career planned: I'd start off as a child star, then grow up into an Ivory Girl.

When we woke on Sunday mornings, Nanny and I would turn on the television again, and dance along to the *Wonderama* gogo, pretending we were on set with the other kids. I wanted more than anything to be on that show. I wanted to be on any show—on *all* the shows.

Back at home, I lost hours and hours to pretending in secret that I was the beautiful "Truly Scrumptious" character in *Chitty Chitty Bang Bang*, a corrugated cardboard box at the bottom of my bedroom closet standing in for the car that could float and fly. I'd also serenade the neighborhood using our garden hose as my microphone. I once woke the whole neighborhood, belting out songs from the driveway at 7:00 on a Sunday morning. My parents received an annoyed phone call from across the street. "Do you know where your daughter is??"

~~~

Where performing and pretending to be other people was pure fun in my early childhood, when I was 10-and-a-half, it became something else entirely. In June of 1976, at the end of sixth grade, my parents split up. I'd been worried about this happening, not only because I sensed my parents' unhappiness, but also because there was a whole divorce boom occurring around us.

Families were dropping like flies in our suburban Long Island community. I would stay up at night and pray to god that my parents wouldn't split up like so many other kids' parents had, that I wouldn't become one of those bedraggled "divorce kids" who always seemed a mess, emotionally and physically. Divorce stretched parents' finances, as they forked over tens of thousands of dollars to lawyers, and now had to pay for two households instead of one. That left less money for new clothes and haircuts for the children. Some of the kids in my midst whose moms and dads had separated or divorced came to school looking completely disheveled, with scuffed shoes and "floods," pants they'd outgrown, and messy hair. They were exhausted—emotionally and physically—from being dragged back and forth between two different homes. Sometimes they didn't have their homework because they'd left it, or their textbooks, at the wrong house. It was the saddest thing, and I was desperate for it not to happen to my family.

I became anxious and hyper-vigilant. For a Thanksgiving-themed essay assignment in my sixth-grade class, I wrote about how much I loved my family and hoped nothing would ever happen to it. Before bed, I bargained some more with god, promising I'd be extra-extra good if my family could stay together.

Obviously it didn't work. I became fractured and insecure. I stopped having any idea who I was, and started studying others for clues as to who I *should* be.

Who was I? Who was I supposed to be? After all, I could be anyone I wanted, according to *Free to Be... You and Me*.

~~~

For the uninitiated, when it was released in November, 1972, *Free to Be...* was a groundbreaking recording of stories and songs about gender and racial equality, and bridging the "generation gap" between Gen X kids and their parents and grandparents. It was produced by actress Marlo Thomas with funding from the Ms. Foundation, and featured now iconic performances by Diana Ross, Alan Alda, Mel Brooks, Harry Belafonte, Roberta Flack, Carol Channing, Dick Cavett, Rosey Grier, Chris Jackson, Thomas herself, and others.

Free to Be... was a rich compendium of liberal-minded allegories that strongly influenced me and informed my understanding of how the world worked—or how it *should* work. The story of the independent-thinking princess "Atalanta" let me know that girls didn't have to marry men they didn't love—or marry at all. (A message I seem to have ignored in my twenties.) Songs like "William's Doll" and "It's Alright to Cry" told me it was okay for boys to be sensitive. "Parents Are People" told me that "Mommies and daddies can be anything they wanna be," regardless of gender. The poem "Housework" made it clear that housework was everyone's job, not just women's.

One particular line in "When We Grow Up" (a song ostensibly about disregarding norms for masculine and feminine attractiveness) made the greatest impression on me: "When I grow up, I'm gonna be happy, and do what I'd like to do..." The whole record made a strong impression on me, but that one line gave me the notion that adulthood was going to be *awesome*. I would get to be *whoever I wanted to be*! Do whatever I wanted to do, whenever I wanted to do it!

My parents bought the record for my sister and me on a family outing to the Sunrise Mall. I took to it instantly, playing it day after day, singing along to its jangly, upbeat soft rock, absorbing its empowering messages. On *All in the Family* I observed Archie Bunker razzing his neighbor Maude and his daughter, Gloria, about "women's lib," and right there on this record was confirmation that Archie was a retrograde jerk, and that Maude and Gloria were doing the right thing, standing up to him. Things were changing!

I ate up this utopian vision of the world. Even at that young age I somehow knew it was revolutionary, different from the more constrained world my mother and grandmother had been raised in. I knew it had something to do with changes I was witnessing in my mother. It was all somehow related to my mom starting to go back to work as a teacher for the first time since I was born, initially as a substitute, then as a teacher with her own classroom.

After the job came my mother's own car, a tan '72 Dodge Dart. A few years later came her new, modern haircut. She returned home one day with her long locks cut off into a pixie, and instantly I cried. I was turning 11, and suddenly my mother no longer looked the way I had known her to look. At 36, she was evolving so rapidly in so many ways that I found it difficult to recognize her.

~~~

In the winter of '76, I didn't yet know exactly what was happening between my parents, but I knew something was off. That spring, on the night they told us they were considering a separation, I begged them to stay together. "If you get divorced, I'll be from a broken family," I cried. To me, that meant that *I* would be broken. When they ultimately separated, I felt myself begin to fracture. Though in ways I adjusted, and re-adjusted as my family changed again and again over the years—and always appreciated my parents remaining friends, sometimes even celebrating holidays all together with us—the truth is that I have never fully re-integrated. A part of me is always 11, the age I was one when my family of origin came apart. Even at 56, this remains true.

I hear this a lot from other "divorce kids" from the '70s, as we called ourselves then. Now, divorce is much more common; something like half of all marriages end that way. Then, it was a growing trend, and there was a stigma attached to it. What's more, no one really knew yet how to navigate divorce in such a way that emotional damage was minimized for the kids. It took a toll on many from my generation.

When my efforts to keep my family together failed, I became painfully insecure. But I found solace in *Free to Be...* and the endless feast of possibilities for adulthood that it promised. I clung to it, listening to it over and over, wearing out the vinyl, singing along to its optimistic songs that promised a better future, for the world, and for me.

~~~

Soon my father remarried and moved to Westchester, a whole new world where the houses were bigger and nicer than the modest home in a blue-collar town on Long Island where I lived with my mom. People wore starched, preppy clothes and pronounced their "R"s. Toggling between those two places marked the beginning of an identity crisis for me: I felt split in two, one version of me only able to fit in with my friends on Long Island, the other specifically engineered to fit in in Westchester.

My Long Island accent didn't survive the first year of this new arrangement. I hadn't even known I *had* a Long Island accent—didn't know what that even was—until I started spending weekends with my father and his new family in Westchester.

I took it as an opportunity for self-reinvention. I listened carefully, and then went to work punching up my "R" sounds, rounding my "A" sounds so that "can't" no longer sounded like "Cay-ant."

When I slept over at my friend Beth's house (on Long Island) one weekend, I received a great compliment from her aunt (now pronounced "ahwnt," like a New Englander). "You have the coolest accent," she said. "I can't quite place it. It's like you're a newscaster. Where are you originally from?"

Next, I felt compelled to dress like the Westchester crowd. My hip-hugger bell bottoms made by Luv-It—a brand for tween girls, purchased at Chwatsky's department store in Oceanside—were fine for Long Island, but they *would not* cut it up north. For my days there, I required 100% cotton chinos in neutral tones, with sharply ironed creases down the fronts of the pant legs, as well as Levi's 501s in denim and corduroy. The scoop-necked tee shirts in bright patterns would stay in my drawer in Island Park. On my Westchester days, I'd need starchy cotton button-down oxfords layered with wool crew-neck sweaters from a store in Rye called Rags to Riches. Bonus if the sweaters had professorial suede patches on the elbows. My kooky Famolare shoes with the wavy rubber sole were for Long Island; for Westchester, I needed no-nonsense Bass Weejuns and Sperry Top Siders. I was striving for authentication as a WASPy Westchester Jew.

It was complicated juggling my two identities, and also making sure I had the right clothes with me in the right places. But I was committed to maintaining the two distinct versions of myself because I so desperately wanted to feel as if I belonged wherever I was.

In addition to the charade around my identity, I was also engaging in make-believe wherever I went. In Westchester, my sister, step-sisters, and I would pretend we were stars of the stage and screen, working all weekend on musical numbers that we'd perform on Sunday evening, singing and dancing for our parents. On Long Island, I would play "talent agent" with a new friend, Melanie, whom I'd met in a musical theater workshop.

~~~

Most kids like playing pretend. But my affinity for it went far beyond what would be considered normal, and lingered until I was 14—embarrassingly old for that kind of interest. All my life, I was an odd kid who liked disappearing into my imagination more than most of my peers, sometimes engaging in that kind of play all alone, either by choice, or because friends were turned off by it.

The last time I tried to play "talent agency" with Melanie on a sleepover at the beginning of ninth grade, she looked at me like I had two heads, then essentially stopped talking to me. Things were already strained between us, because at the end of eighth grade, Melanie had participated in a Mean Girls affront that left me with no friends, as I describe in the next chapter.

In real life Melanie and I were both failed child actresses, clients of a local children's talent agent, who occasionally sent us on calls for commercials, musicals, and television shows, but not as frequently as she sent some of the other kids in the weekend musical theater workshops we were enrolled in.

We'd dreamt up the imaginary business "Stars, Incorporated" when we were 11 or 12, an age when such games were more appropriate. Our imaginary talent agency was meant to be an improvement upon the real one that had let us both down by not sending us soaring toward child stardom.

The last time I went to Melanie's house for a sleep-over, I had just begun ninth grade with not one single friend; she was in eighth grade, and had secured her place among the mean girls who'd ousted me. I was suffering emotionally in so many ways—socially, and also in my home life, as the "divorce kid" I'd wanted never to become. After dinner, I made the grave mistake of suggesting we play talent agency. I'll never forget the withering look Melanie shot my way. In all the years that I'd been trying to manage my identity between disparate suburban counties, I hadn't matured to the point where I recognized I was too old for make-believe.

The rest of the night was painfully uncomfortable. Melanie and I shared the pull-out couch in the basement like we'd always done, but this time she didn't stay up whispering and gossiping with me until all hours. In the morning, my mom picked me up. I said goodbye to Melanie, and we never spoke again. It was the official end of our friendship, and also the end of make-believe.

Mean Girls

I have a few recurring nightmares, the worst of which goes like this: I'm a full-grown adult who's lost my job because my boss discovered I failed to complete calculus and physics in twelfth grade, so I'm mandated to return to high school. There, in a crowded hallway, I panic because a) I can't find my classroom, and b) it's just dawned on me that I don't have my homework. *Did I even do the homework?* I can't recall, which further stresses me out.

Oh, another important detail: I'm stark naked. I juggle the books and folders I'm carrying to try and hide my private parts, but they don't provide sufficient cover. Everyone in the hallway points at me and laughs.

The sad/funny thing about this nightmare is that, save for the nudity, it's only slightly more harrowing than my actual high school experience.

～～～

One more important detail: the dream takes place in the *second* high school I attended, in Oceanside, New York. That's right. God, or Whoever Is In Charge Of The Universe, decided it wasn't enough for me to be haunted by just one set of horrible memories in an educational setting; I needed to be haunted by two. And so, in eleventh grade—*in the middle of high school*—after my mother remarried, I had the misfortune of being relocated to a new town.

Making matters worse, the closing on our new house kept getting postponed, so we couldn't move in until November of that year, 1981. Which meant that for the first two months I attended Oceanside High School, I didn't even *live* in that South Shore Long Island town. My newly blended family—my *second* blended family, this one on my mother's side—was boarded during that time at the home of my new stepfather Bernard's elderly parents in Flushing, Queens.

Suddenly a small Tudor-style house that had been a comfortable dwelling for two little old people had its population increased to seven, adding the following five new residents: my mom and stepdad, my 12-year-old sister, my 16-year-old stepbrother (his twenty-year-old brother, away at college, sometimes came for weekends, boosting the local population to eight), and 15-and-a-half-year-old me.

We were a weird, disjointed crew, made up of two separate factions who hadn't even known each other a full year. And now we were all crammed together, all the time. *Seven* people at every meal. *Seven* people (including three teenagers) sharing one telephone line. *Seven* people sharing two bathrooms, one of which was located in the basement. In that windowless, cinderblock chamber, I slept on a cot positioned two feet away from another cot occupied by my stepbrother, a year older than me but in my grade.

Every day my mom drove my sister, my stepbrother, and me forty-five minutes each way to and from school, fetching us just as the dismissal bell rang. So, ix-nay on after-school activities. It wasn't terribly conducive to making new friends in my new town. The thing was, I desperately needed new friends.

~~~

It's a testament to how horrible my freshman and sophomore years had been at my old high school that I was initially excited to move and start my junior year somewhere else—even just one town over from Island Park, the South Shore Long Island town where I'd grown up. Despite struggling to adjust to life with my new family, I was happy to be moving—to be starting over.

I'd had the most miserable time at West Hempstead High School, where students from Island Park were bused thirty minutes each way because our town didn't have its own high school. It was the standard dork-in-high-school routine—not being welcome at most tables in the lunchroom, getting picked last for teams. I wasn't just bad at sports, I was fearful and timid, on top of being incredibly uncoordinated. I tried hard, I really did, but received a failing grade in gym in ninth grade, anyway. In order to earn a passing grade, I had to stay after school for remedial exercises, ie: having an Amazonian teacher who hated me basically hurl a dodgeball at my head over and over, as the cheerleaders practiced at the other end of the gymnasium. (See? Almost as bad as the recurring nightmare.)

But I owed the greatest portion of my misery to something that happened the year before, at the end of junior high: a socially fatal falling out with a clique of smart/popular girls I'd been part of. In the fall of 1979 I entered ninth grade at West Hempstead High School with *not one friend* because the school year before that, in the second half of 8th grade in Island Park, I'd been ousted very publicly by that clique.

It was one of the defining social experiences of my life, one that would make me wary of friendships with girls and women, especially groups of them, and one that would play out again and again, even into adulthood—in my thirties, forties, and fifties. (Lord, if you're listening, please help me steer clear of this phenomenon in my sixties, seventies, eighties—however long I live. I *do not* wish to deal with this bullshit in assisted living.) The circumstances would be different in each instance, but the dynamic the same—some of the girls or women in a group I'd become close with would bond separately, then close ranks and triangulate, leaving someone on the outs, either passive-aggressively, or plain old aggressive-aggressively. Sometimes I was the one who got pushed out. Sometimes it was a different girl, and in an instance or two, I'm ashamed to admit, I was complicit in her misery.

No matter how far along in life I get, I keep meeting other women who tell me they've had almost the exact same experience—in childhood and adulthood. This phenomenon of women and girls being aggressive toward one another, and competing for the top spot in their social hierarchy, would eventually get a recognizable name, familiar shorthand for something nearly universal: "Mean Girls," after the Tine Fey movie by that name, based on a book, *Queen Bees and Wannabes*, by Rosalind Wiseman.

～～～

I shouldn't have been as surprised as I was by the *Mean Girls* affront in junior high, because I'd experienced and witnessed it before. The first time was when I was just five and playing with my nextdoor neighbor, Charly, who was a year older. With blonde curls and blue eyes, Charly looked like a perfect little angel, but she was anything but. She had one hell of a mouth on her, and it both terrified and mesmerized me. I hung around Charly in part out of convenience, and because my mom would sometimes drop me next door when she did errands, but also because I was completely taken by her sass and confidence.

One day we were playing and getting along just fine when Jill, a mutual friend Charly's age who was tall and pretty and popular, walked up to us and said hi. As soon as Charly spotted Jill, out of nowhere she pushed me to the ground in front of her—as if we'd been fighting, which we hadn't. "You're nothing but a piece of soap!" Charly shouted. I cried and ran back home. It was textbook Mean Girls triangulation, an attempt to turn one girl against another to secure her place at the top of the social hierarchy.

When it happened in eighth grade, I was perfectly poised for that particular type of fall because, for the first time, I stood close to the top of the food chain. I'd been riding kind of high when the school year began. At the end of seventh grade, at 12-and-a-half, I'd played Lola in *Damn Yankees*. Dancing and singing onstage in a halter top and short-shorts (what can I say; it was the '70s) elevated me a bit, socially, from a prissy "brain" to a tween with a bit of a mystique. With boys starting to like me, I held more currency with everyone.

Also, in junior high we were divided into academic tracks, non-inclusive nonsense that happened to be socially advantageous for me— briefly, anyway. Being relegated to "Track One" made it so that I was in classes exclusively with other kids who were studious, as I was. It was within these ranks that the clique formed. School-wide we were hardly popular. We were all short and sort of cute, but not conventionally attractive like the more popular girls. Our status was recognized only among the studious set. Still, it was very heady after being considered an all-out dork in elementary school.

In the middle of eighth grade, my entire social life came crashing down when I became "the main character," to use current internet parlance, of an escalating tween drama and a series of betrayals—some theirs, some mine—led the clique to turn against me. Karmically, I sort of knew I had it coming. I'd been fearing it since a few months earlier, when I'd failed to stand up for Nina, another girl in our group, when our clique's ringleader, Shira—a tiny, angular, dark-haired girl, whose image came to mind when I tried to picture the Lila character in Elena Ferrante's Neapolitan novels—corralled us all toward ostracizing Nina.

I'd been a coward. Actually, I'd been worse than that; when Shira initially focused her hatred toward Nina rather than me, not only was I relieved, I allowed myself to feel superior to Nina. Still, I didn't feel totally secure on my rung of our little social ladder. Eager to hang on, to keep hold of what shreds of popularity I'd managed to attain, I kept my mouth shut as Shira bullied Nina to her face and smeared her behind her back. Eventually, I even took part in the back-stabbing. We all did.

~~~~

Nina was a sweet, innocuous girl with light brown hair and gray-brown eyes who didn't make a very strong impression. She was timid and parent-fearing, and the best student in our group, which put Shira second, grades-wise, and Shira did not like being second at anything.

Poor Nina didn't need a classmate to bully her. She was already being bossed around at home by her mean older brother and her overbearing parents. She was rarely allowed to join us for most of the weekend activities we engaged in together, which were rather wholesome—movies, bowling, shopping. The less Nina hung out with us, the more we naturally grew apart from her, and the more that made her a target for Shira's cruelty.

In a short amount of time, Shira started saying nasty things behind Nina's back, and trying to get us to agree. "Have you ever noticed that Nina has bags under her eyes at only 13?" Shira would ask. Or: "Did you notice Nina was wearing the same underpants in the gym locker room as she was wearing the other day? Ew!" Or: "Nina thinks she's smarter than us, but with all the studying she does, she doesn't have a life!"

It didn't take much effort to get us to pile on. We went right along with Shira, mercilessly cutting Nina down when she wasn't around, rolling our eyes in unison as we picked her apart. When Shira said Nina was prissy, we all agreed. When she made fun of Nina's clothes on a particular day—more prim than our more casual dress of tee shirts layered over long sleeves, with Levi's—one of us would say, "Oh, god, did you see what she wore *yesterday*? That shirt buttoned all the way up to her chin?" And we'd laugh. When Nina said she didn't feel comfortable going to one of the frequent "boy-girl" parties where we played Spin the Bottle and other kissing games, to her face we'd say, "No problem," but behind her back, one of us would call her a prude, and the others would giggle diabolically on cue.

This toxic strain of triangulation, enlisting others to alienate and unfairly build a case against another party, is horrible, but it can also be irresistible, especially when you're 13 and insecure and eager to be accepted. It can be tempting when you're much older, too. These days I try to make it my business to forego taking part as soon as I recognize that someone's trying to sway me against someone else, or involve me in cutting them down—despite the admittedly recognizable allure. (Try as I might, in all honesty, I don't always succeed.) It's a hallmark of the *Mean Girls* offense, recruiting others to help ostracize a weak target. The smear campaign might begin with a real, specific complaint about the girl in question—maybe she said something that got the ring-leader in trouble, or she flirted with the wrong boy. (I can't recall what Nina did, other than act meek, making her a natural focus for Shira's budding meanness.) But whatever the initial complaint might be, it's likely not enough to turn everyone in the group against a girl. The ring-leader needs more ammunition, and so she scrutinizes every little thing the girl does, every article of clothing she chooses, every word that comes out of her mouth, until she has enough to build a convincing case.

I believe you should get a pass the first time you're seduced by the ringleader of a clique into a smear campaign like this, especially if there isn't a second time. Presumably you're young, like I was. You're flattered she's choosing to share a secret with *you*, that this popular, discriminating girl has let you into her inner circle. At first you think you're just taking part in gossip, which is mean, but not nearly as mean as what comes next: The ring-leader starts talking about her target *a lot*. What she says is *all bad*. Most of it's true, although some is greatly exaggerated and twisted, or out of context, meant to portray the target as just horrible. Then she baits you into shit-talking the girl she hates. Or maybe you don't need to be baited; maybe you volunteer some nasty comments to keep yourself in good standing with the ring-leader. In short order, you, the ring-leader, and whoever else is in on the kill, has created a complete cartoon villain, a version of the person being ousted that barely resembles the girl you used to be close with in grade school, who came to all your birthday parties, who one year gave you the frilly nightgown that was once your favorite (but which you of course would no longer be caught dead in). A bogeyman whom everyone will easily agree deserves the heave-ho.

When I let myself become an accomplice to Shira against Nina, at first it felt electrifying—being chosen, realizing with great relief that I wasn't the target. Taking part feels shitty, but secures your place in the social order, at least momentarily. But I felt ashamed each time Shira or another girl in the group uttered something mean, each time I laughed along, each time I retorted with my own distorted comment about Nina to keep up with the others—each time I realized I could someday land on the other end of this.

A knot would form in my stomach. I'd think, *Did I really pile on like that? Did I really say those awful things? Did I really laugh along as the others said cruel things?* Then I'd think, *I bet I'm next.*

~~~

So, yes, of course I was next. It wasn't just karma that visited the *Mean Girls* business upon me. It was a series of choices I made to try and counteract my complicity in Nina's ouster—to try and have it both ways.

It all hinged on a growing friendship I had with another girl a year behind us in school, a petite redhead named Melanie, who was on the outside of our clique, and not happy about it. She and I got to be close because we were in an after school musical theater workshop together in the next town over. There's something incredibly bonding about rehearsing and performing together. I look back now at photos of us singing and dancing in a winter holiday revue in those days, the late '70s, and we look so innocent. There we are in pigtails and tap shoes, step-ball-change-ing to "Take Me Out to the Ball Game." There we are, smiling as we do a synchronized dance number to "The Most Wonderful Time of the Year." You would never know that away from the stage, in our social life, there were cruel machinations going on, and we were part of them.

Melanie didn't bother to hide her jealousy of Shira and other girls in the clique— of their relative popularity, and of their hold on me. She would test my loyalty often. One morning after a sleepover at my house, she sat sulking in a rocking chair in the corner of my bedroom.

"What's wrong?" I asked.

"You don't like me as much as I like you, or as much as you like Shira and your other friends," she said. "Like, I think of you as my best friend, but I don't know if you think of me that way."

I was stunned. I didn't realize I had that kind of power, that kind of advantage in our friendship.

"No, you're totally my best friend," I insisted. As I said this, feelings of guilt and disloyalty toward the clique came over me, but I overrode them. Melanie didn't seem to believe me. She kept testing me, and I kept trying to prove that she had nothing to worry about. I even made a Certificate of Best Friendship, and "laminated" it with shiny Scotch Tape.

Sometimes our back-and-forth about Melanie's friendship status relative to the other girls was exchanged in person or by phone. Other times, it was through hand-written notes on loose-leaf paper, which we decorated with hearts and flowers using our clunky blue Bic four-color pens, and left for each other through the slats of our lockers.

In my notes, I tried to bolster Melanie's confidence in our best-friendship by informing her of my misgivings about Shira and the other girls. I told her they were mean. I described what they'd—*we'd*—done to Nina, and how conflicted I felt about it. I provided blow-by-blow details of the cruelty, and what I was now secretly doing to try and counteract it: how, after Shira told Nina that she was no longer welcome to eat at our table, and Nina cried right there in the lunchroom, I'd gone to console Nina privately, after school.

"Shira's a monster," I'd said to Nina. "You shouldn't want to have anything to do with her." I didn't say I was sorry and admit to my part. I didn't say, "I'll be your friend." I just tried to make Nina assign less blame to me, by telling her she shouldn't like Shira and the other girls. I did this while at the same time trying to maintain my stature with those girls, and also simultaneously appeasing Melanie by insisting I didn't care about the clique at all. It was quite a high-wire juggling act, attempting to be in everyone's good graces while behind the scenes participating in various conflicting acts of shit-talking.

Somehow, though, it didn't *feel* like shit-talking, not the way talking behind Nina's back had. It didn't feel like triangulation, like building a case against someone. It felt like some kind of *corrective*. I had the misguided impression I was being *helpful*, behaving somewhere in the ballpark of *virtuous*, fighting against Mean Girl-ism by snitching on a bunch of Mean Girls. I was trying to put at ease two girls who stood outside of the clique—both Nina and Melanie—all the while trying not to draw the ire of Shira and the others—to keep sparing myself from becoming a target.

~~~

I thought I had it all figured out, that I'd succeeded in keeping everyone reasonably happy, or at least *happy with me*. I'd done the best I could do, I believed, short of turning my back on the clique altogether, which seemed impossible if I was going to have any kind of a life in my small town. I felt stuck, but given my limited options, everything felt if not exactly *right*, then at least sort of *okay* in my little tween world.

Then one evening, when Melanie called, she sounded different. There was a teasing tone to her voice when she asked, "Remind me, what do you think of Shira?"

"You know what I think," I said. "She's mean." (The recollection of this is so painful, I've blocked out many of the specific details; I probably really let my description of Shira rip.)

Then I heard giggling. Not one person—two.

"Oh, really, Sari?" It was Shira, on a second extension in Melanie's house. "I mean, why don't you say that to my face?!" More sinister laughter. Then Shira quoting out loud the notes I'd written to Melanie and left in her locker. Then *click*. Then hot tears running down my face.

The next day there was a confrontation with the rest of the girls, plus Melanie, in front of my locker. They handed me some of my notes, and taunted me to my face, calling me names, before walking away together and laughing as what seemed like the entire rest of the school watched.

So, Melanie hadn't in fact hated the girls in the clique, as she had attested. No, she was envious of them and wanted in. Maybe she wanted to be the ring-leader herself. She was definitely proving herself to be ring-leader material, cunningly baiting me for incriminating evidence, then using it to secretly bond with Shira.

In what felt like an instant, five girls I'd become close with but had always been somewhat wary of became my arch enemies. They never again invited me to join them at the movies and bowling and for sleepovers. I was no longer welcome at their table at lunch. But it went much further than that. They began tormenting me loudly in the hallways, and in whispers during class. They made fun of everything about me—what I wore, what I ate, how I walked, my lack of a training bra when we were in the gym locker room, when at that point, I honestly needed one like a benefit. (I avoided getting one because I was afraid it would make me feel more grown up than I was ready to be. Also, I had absorbed a cultural message that big boobs, like the women in my family had, were gauche.)

In English class one day, Shira stage-whispered to the others, "Did you see her bright red patent leather rain boots with the wedge heel?!" I'd just gotten them on clearance at Times Square Stores, a local discount department store, and adored them. "She thinks she's so stylish," one of the girls stage-whispered back, "and she's not!" The whole gang broke into laughter so loudly, our teacher called them out into the hallway and scolded them. A few weeks later, they were so cruel to me after I was cast as Sister Sara Brown in *Guys and Dolls*, making fun of the way I'd sung at the audition, that I quit the play.

When spring rolled around, I felt afraid to go on the eighth grade trip to Washington, D.C., a school tradition I'd been looking forward to since I was much younger and a friend of the family told me stories about her trip—bunking with friends, kissing boys, being on her own without her parents for a few days. Our English teacher heard I canceled my reservation, and took me aside after class.

"Don't let them keep you from this," she pleaded, with tears in her eyes. "You'll regret it for the rest of your life. Go anyway! Room with different girls." But I couldn't.

Our English teacher was my only real support that year. I stayed after school one day to tell her everything that had happened, and she was incredibly sympathetic, while also admonishing me for my part. For the rest of the school year, now and then she would check in on me, asking how I was. I'd lie and say, "fine," but just her asking meant something. It made going to school bearable. In the final week of junior high, she forced the girls to apologize to me. She insisted I attend the eighth grade dance, and that the girls sit at a table with me.

~~~

I trembled as I entered the gym that night in my imitation Gunne Sax skirt and top, with Carber brand rubber-wedge sandals. Donna Summer was playing on the loud-speaker as Shira and the others came right over to me and offered a cursory apology. "It's okay," I said. We all did our best to get along that night, and to act as if there was no bad blood between us. It was forced and artificial, but it felt better than the alternative.

But nothing had really changed. The following fall, in the hallways and class-rooms at West Hempstead High, I drew nothing but dirty looks and more pointed whispers from those girls. I got bullied by tougher Island Park kids, too, who'd had my father as a fifth grade teacher. They apparently felt emboldened to lash out once we were several towns away from my dad's classroom in our old school district. One girl would regularly jump me in the hallway and challenge me to a fistfight. Not by any stretch the fist-fighting sort, I would essentially freeze and play dead until she got bored and left me alone.

How I hated going to school those years. I tried to find my people in musical theater, and I made some acquaintances in the casts of two plays I took part in. But because West Hempstead was so far away from Island Park, and there were only a few late buses you could take after extra-curricular activities, it was difficult to socialize af-ter play rehearsals. I couldn't bond with people the way you usually do around a show.

I gave up on trying to have real friends in West Hempstead, and instead put my energy into friendships with kids from summer camp, mostly other theater geeks who lived in other towns on Long Island, or in Westchester. I also stopped eating for a while. I'd sit alone at lunch, starving, and writing letters to camp friends. I'd call them at night, and get together with them on weekends, when I could. Alone in my bed at night, I'd pray that something would change that would allow me to move to a different town, and a different high school.

Enter The Widower, Bernard.

~~~

Despite being adjacent to one another, in the late '70s and early '80s at least, Island Park and Oceanside were very different towns. Island Park was rougher—like, with actual gangs—and largely blue-collar. Oceanside was more affluent, with newer homes, and higher-end stores. I had it in my mind that we were moving up in the world by moving there, which in and of itself was a bit exciting. But more than that, I was excited to get away from the mean girls of my past, and embark on a new beginning.

Then we were cursed with that layover at Bernard's parents' house in Flushing for September and October, 1981. When we finally moved into our new house that November, I found it hard to fit in, socially. This despite the advantage of dating my first real boyfriend, Jason—a tall, handsome, sandy-haired kid a year older than me, whom I'd met the prior summer when we both worked at a sleep-away camp, and who happened to be a senior at Oceanside High.

When we started dating at camp, Jason and I lived in separate towns; at the end of that summer, my newly-remarried mother announced she and her new husband, Bernard, had sold their respective homes and bought a new one together in Oceanside.

Moving to Jason's town was a mixed blessing. It meant I knew someone there, who could introduce me to other people. But we were hardly an organic match. We had little in common—he was an athlete and I was a thespian—and neither of us was terribly interested in what the other enjoyed. We got together by way of process of elimination mid-summer of '81, after everyone else had paired off, and had just enough chemistry to ignite something between us.

We started out with a lukewarm connection, but a bond formed, and over time it grew. It became burdensome for Jason, though; I was unsure of myself and desperate for his acceptance and affection. I became clingy, and it made Jason understandably eager for me to have more people in my social life than just him. A member in good standing of Oceanside High School's smart/popular clique, he encouraged me to make friends with the girls in the group. I was terrified. But I let him introduce me.

~~~

Once I met the girls from the smart/popular clique, I didn't have terribly high hopes for connecting with them. But I tried. When a bunch of them invited me to go to a popular dive bar with them on a weekend night, I said yes, even though I had never been to a bar before, save for the bowling alley near summer camp that served drinks.

When we got there, the bouncer wouldn't let me—*and only me*—in. The bar was overcrowded and there was a line out the door. They couldn't allow everyone inside. My baby face and unconvincing fake I.D. made me an obvious choice for exclusion.

We were all a year or two underage—16 and 17. (The drinking age in New York State was just 18 then, so it wasn't too much of a stretch for some 16-year-olds to pass. It would be raised to 19 a couple of years later, right after I turned 18, and then to 21, just after I turned 19. The State Liquor Authority clearly had it out for me and my ability to socialize.) With an October birthday, I was even younger than the rest of the bunch, and looked notably less mature; starving myself for a year had minimized my curves, sunken my cheeks, kept me looking child-like.

After the bouncer showed the four other girls in, I had no choice but to wait outside by myself for a couple of hours—unless I wanted to call my mother and have her come get me at a bar I wasn't supposed to be at in the first place, which, no, thank you, I very much did not. The girls—young women I'd just met—hadn't even entertained the option of leaving and going somewhere else after I was bounced. A bunch of the smart/popular boys from school were inside, and some shy, weird, new girl wasn't going to stand in the way of a prime weekend socializing and flirting opportunity. For a second I considered suggesting we decamp to Dev's Place, a hippie coffee house with board games that didn't serve alcohol, yet had a boîte-like vibe—a place I'd gone with camp friends, mostly fellow theater geeks. But before I could open my mouth, the girls all floated into the bar, giggling, without me. All except the tall, dark-haired one named Ivy, who'd driven that night. Ivy led me back to the powder blue Chevy Caprice she'd borrowed from her mom, put the key in the door, and unlocked it.

"We won't stay too long," she promised as she opened the car door for me.

I froze my butt off on the hard, fake-leather front seat while Ivy and the others got wasted on pitchers of kamikaze. Humiliated and alone—and disappointed no one would see me looking cute in my mauve angora sweater and factory-second Calvin Klein jeans—I soothed myself the pathetic only way I knew how: singing quietly to ease my fears in a relative stranger's cold car, as traffic whizzed by on Sunrise Highway.

My first social outing with new "friends" in my new town had gone even worse than I'd imagined in the hours before the Chevy Caprice pulled up in front of my house to get me. But while I felt cold and scared in Ivy's mother's car, one piece of me was relieved I hadn't gotten into the dive bar, that I didn't have to feign liking to drink, or exhaust myself for two hours pretending to be blithe and upbeat and good company. I wasn't up for trying to make friends with a new clique of girls, for being constantly on the lookout for shifting dynamics and loyalties so I wouldn't fuck up and get burned again.

I wasn't like those girls; they were socially adept, carefree, a bit sophisticated, affluent. I was intense, overly sensitive, insecure, immature in some ways, precocious in others, and embarrassed about being from a broken family that was struggling financially, and in every other possible way. I was emotionally at loose ends, and lousy at covering up that I was going through a hard time—in therapy once a week to deal with the eating disorder I'd developed in part as a way to adhere to ridiculous beauty standards as my body began to change, and in part as way to control some aspect of my life divided between two different blended families. I *wanted* to *want* to be friends with those girls. I wanted to become the kind of girl who easily made friends with anyone, who knew how to be lighthearted and fun, the life of the party. Who wasn't wary of groups of girls. If I were any of those things, it would have made moving in November of 11th grade, while school was already in full swing, a hell of a lot easier.

To be fair, the smart/popular girls hadn't seemed terribly excited by the prospect of hanging out with me, either. I'd been foisted upon them by Jason, and them upon me. Needless to say, I never hung out with those girls again. I didn't make many other friends at Oceanside High, either—a few studying buddies only—nice kids, one of whom became more of a real friend when we went to the same college, the next year.

In the end, my family only lived in the Oceanside house for six years. My mother divorced Bernard just as I was graduating from college. We moved to another nearby town and once again started over.

~~~

I didn't expect to see any of the junior high mean girls ever again, especially not after I moved upstate to the mid-Hudson Valley, in 2005, at 40. Then came Facebook.

It's kind of hilarious to recall how special I felt in the summer of 2007 when I received an *exclusive invitation* from a friend to join. I wasn't on the site long before it started suggesting old acquaintances I might want to "friend," turning a noun into a verb. Whenever I logged on, in the middle right side of my screen, I'd see their smiling faces assembled in a grid of tiny boxes.

Only one of them, Melanie, sent me a friend request. It weirdly lifted my spirits. I didn't realize how much of the pain from that time I was still carrying. I surprised myself by accepting her request instantly. Melanie sent me a private message. "Remember when we were in the musical theater workshop together?" Of course I did. "Remember that spelling bee?" We went on like this a bit. *Remember this? Remember that?* Only the happy memories. It was a light exchange that didn't go anywhere deep, and I was fine to leave it at that.

Two years later, at an informal school reunion at a bar on Long Island, I spotted Melanie. Perhaps against my better judgment, I went straight toward her to say hello. Propelled by decades of feeling rejected and mystified by what happened, I felt both an inability to stop myself from approaching her, and a certainty that later I'd regret doing so.

After saccharine hellos and air kisses, Melanie offered something vaguely in the ballpark of an apology. Over blaring classic rock, she yelled, "Remember when I turned on you, and made your life a living hell?!" Then she laughed, exaggeratedly. *Ha ha ha.* I was stunned. I didn't know what to do other than fake laugh along with her. *Ha ha ha.* Then she turned and started talking to someone else, and together they moved away from the bar.

That was it. That was all I was going to get. It felt hollow, and disappointing. When I got home, though, I felt more generous toward Melanie. I realized it must have been hard for her to even see me all these years later, and to say anything at all about what had happened. Sure, what she said was vague and barely registered remorse. But she did at least acknowledge her part. I, on the other hand, have never apologized to Nina. Although, there's the added factor that Nina became a mean girl herself in high school. She joined the rest of the gang in tormenting me in the hallways. So maybe we're even?

I realize now how hard it is to own that kind of shitty behavior—*any* kind of shitty behavior—and make amends for it. How many of us actually possess the self-awareness and fortitude for that? It's rare. It makes me especially appreciative of the apologies I've received after more recent Mean Girls pile-ons. And it makes me feel good about an apology I delivered in my early forties after a woman overheard a conversation I had with a friend, in which we said unkind things about her. The friend and I had begun by enumerating legitimate reasons we didn't want to collaborate with the woman on a project, but somehow it turned into an all-out bitch-fest. Unfortunately, one of us had butt-dialed the woman in question at the beginning of the conversation. Our entire conversation about her was recorded on her voice mail.

~~~

So, news bulletin: high school doesn't ever end. Those social dynamics keep showing up. (Maybe that's why, to this day, I keep having that recurring nightmare about it.) I suspect it's partly because as a culture, we haven't developed acceptable, non-hostile ways of confronting grievances with one another, or modes of kindly moving on from friendships we're no longer interested in, other than either having a blow-out fight, or ghosting.

Collectively, we're averse to having uncomfortable conversations with the specific people we need to have them with. When a friend says something that offends us, or that conflicts with our point of view, most of the people I know would never have the courage to speak up directly to that person. It's considered impolite. Ironically, instead we often take a more damaging turn, talking about our grievances to other people, hoping an outside third party will assure us we're justified. But that which isn't said directly, which is instead turned into exaggerated, warped gossip, is always more hurtful than any truth bomb delivered to the right recipient. And it can be nearly impossible to recant, because a) good luck getting ahead of the gossip mill, and b) few of us have the tools to do an about-face once we're in full-on attack mode in concert with others. Once an unholy alliance like that is formed, a combination of schadenfreude and burgeoning shame make it nearly impossible to continue being friends with the person we've bitched about.

Part of the problem is that in the telling, we tend to blow those grievances up to outsize proportions, just in case anyone had any doubt that we are 100 percent right and the other person 100 percent wrong. That lands us in the region of betrayal, and from there, there's no easy pathway back. Even if we're not willing to admit we've committed a betrayal, some part of us knows we have, and I'm sad to report that this is the point at which most of us are inclined to double down. A small fissure in a friendship grows to an unbreachable chasm. We won't find a way back toward resolution or repair until either we're caught and confronted, or until enough time passes for the whole thing to blow over, and for us to reflect, and maybe laugh at ourselves.

I've been through this kind of thing enough times, from enough angles, to have some understanding of it—how seductive it is to bond with someone by picking apart a third party, a common enemy; how destructive it can be; how difficult it can be to repair a relationship damaged that way; how devastating to find yourself on the receiving end—but I seem incapable of permanently escaping it. Maybe it's an unavoidable aspect of human nature, of group dynamics.

Even as an adult, I've often found myself on the outs, and I *think* I know why...?: I grew up to be the indiscreet dummy who will say that hard thing no one wants to hear—out loud. I will speak up about my disagreement with a popular point of view, sometimes too bluntly. I can deliver a platter of truth—well, a platter of *my* truth—a bit gracelessly, not because I want to be a jerk, but because it's a difficult thing to do, and I haven't mastered a graceful way. But even if I did, just on its face the information would be hard to take in, because those kinds of conversations aren't customary.

I am also the friend who won't tell you what you want to hear after you lay out the case for why you should give that asshole you were dating another chance. (Even though in the past I was guilty of giving entirely too many assholes too many chances.) I will be brutally honest, telling you what I think you need to hear, and often that's not what people seek when they're confiding in you. So, they go to a mutual friend and say, "Can you fucking believe what Sari said???" And things get triangular from there.

Another possible factor is my daring to challenge dominant personalities when things get tense, surprising them by stepping out of the submissive role I generally default to. A dominant person can smell the submissiveness in me a mile away, the way dogs often immediately know whether they like one another based on scent and disposition alone. In pushing back against the established hierarchy, I break an unspoken agreement regarding who has the power, who is in charge. It's a non-BDSM version of "topping from the bottom," and so-called tops do not appreciate being taken off guard and challenged in this way.

~~~

When a Mean Girls affront happens, I no longer take it personally, although it still hurts. In the end—after spending too much of my life pretending in order to please people—I'd rather be honest and suffer the consequences than act fake to get along. If this makes people think I'm weird and ostracize me, so be it. In my late fifties, I can take it.

I've also come to realize that longstanding friendships can be cyclical, that it's natural to go through phases when you are closer, and phases when you aren't—sometimes punctuated by phases where you're completely on the outs with one another. You know a friendship is real and worth maintaining when you can eventually come back from that.

New friendships feel harder to gain traction with, the older I get. A few women I've come to know in recent years have become close companions, but many more have come and gone (especially those I've only known online, where it's difficult to get a full picture of who someone is, and easy to get the false impression that you and a stranger are compatible). One minute it's seemed a new friend and I have great synergy, and then the next, one of us does or says something that turns the other off, and, like that, it's over—although no one will ever say out loud what the offending thing was. (I really wish we could normalize saying what the offending thing was!)

I remain skittish when it comes to befriending groups of women. I'm more comfortable being a satellite member of several groups than a fixture in just one. I'm not part of an ongoing group text, not someone who's automatically invited to everything. It can get a little bit lonely. But every now and then I hear about some big Mean Girls style blow-up in a group I'm only tangentially part of, and feel relieved to not be going through that once again.

Ironically though, as an adult, I often find myself drawn to mean women. Fortunately I have several good friends who are not at all like that, women who are kind and thoughtful and reciprocate my friendship. But there's almost always at least one bossy bitch on the periphery of my life who has been salty toward me at some point, and whom I desperately want to convert into my adoring friend. I will exert endless energy trying to placate those women and earn their acceptance, even though I'm not sure I actually like them. Maybe I admire their outspokenness, their fearlessness, their lack of concern over what anyone thinks of them. But then I'll witness one of them being mean to someone who doesn't deserve it, or cruelly ostracizing another woman from a friend group just for sport, and I'll ask myself why I give women like them any power over me.

Reject me, insult me, and I'm forever yours? Sadly, it sounds familiar. I learned in therapy years ago how to stop re-enacting bad romantic relationships with mean men, how to let go of the misguided hope that one day the same scene would play out differently. But I still haven't learned to stop re-enacting my unhealthy dynamic with girls who pride themselves on bullying and being jerks, nor to exclusively choose those friends who also choose me.

I guess I've still got work to do.

Confessions of a Closet Vocalist

Most 17-year-olds cut class for socially acceptable reasons: to smoke pot, or to have sex while their parents aren't home. Me, I had a very different reason for occasionally skipping gym in twelfth grade: I would sneak home to secretly sing. Mostly show tunes.

It was the fall of 1982, and I was miserable. My boyfriend, Jason, had gone away to college, and we had begun to drift apart. I had no real friends in what was my second high school, after moving to a new town in the middle of eleventh grade. Life with my new blended family was not going terribly well.

I didn't drink or smoke or do drugs; singing show tunes by myself was the only way I knew how to self-soothe.

~~~~

I love to sing. It's my all-time favorite activity, my escape, my drug. It has been since I was a small child. I'm a sucker for karaoke to the point that if I'm visiting Manhattan for work, I will go to an empty karaoke bar all by myself in the middle of the day, order a seltzer, and trade songs with no one but the bartender. I throw myself so wholeheartedly, so earnestly into each number, it's as if I were competing as a soloist at a NYSSMA (New Yorks State School Music Association) competition.

I'm not a bad bad singer. I also happen to be the daughter of a professional—a cantor and opera singer who, when he taught elementary school, made up song parodies to many of his students' names. A man who walked around the house vocalizing, testing and conditioning his voice at all hours. Which is why I never really learned when it was and wasn't appropriate to just break out into song publicly. If it weren't taboo to walk around singing our hearts out to everyone everywhere, I'd do it every single day.

There was a period in my life, though, when I figured out that singing publicly was social suicide. It began in junior high. I performed in musicals then, in school and at summer camp. I was good enough to repeatedly get offered lead roles, and it thrilled me. But while it seemed acceptable then to sing in that context, it suddenly became uncool to sing in others. For example, Sunday school.

For as long as I'd been attending Sunday school at my local synagogue, from the time I was in first grade, there'd been a guy with a guitar visiting our classroom each session, to teach us Jewish folk songs. It was something that I and many of the other kids looked forward to—if only as a break from the more dry historical or linguistic lessons. We'd all happily sing along, *Bim, bam, bim bim bim bam...Shabbat shalom, shabbat shalom, shabbat shabbat shabbat shabbat shalooooooom...!*

But suddenly, in seventh grade, when Guitar Guy would show up and start strumming, no one would join in. I absolutely would have, if anyone else did—*anyone*—but if there were others interested, you'd never notice. Guitar Guy would start singing, and no one would sing along. He'd stop. "Come on guys. You love this!" He wasn't wrong. He'd known us all for years! He'd start up again, slowly, hoping one or two kids might be persuaded. I'd look around to see if anyone else might be considering singing along, but everyone had their eyes down, gazing at the floor. There was something about singing, something about the way it revealed emotion, that made it taboo for an age group that was suddenly grappling with lots of new, conflicting feelings. Singing had the power to expose what you were trying to hide, and so there were no takers.

"Sari will sing! Sari loves to sing!" That would be my mother chiming in. She was my Sunday school teacher that year. "Come on, Sari! Sing!"

If there'd been any chance before that I might open my mouth, now I definitely wasn't going to. I shot my mother a look. "You love to sing," she said. "Why won't you sing now?" The whole class was gawking at me. The wiseasses in the back of the classroom started snickering. I thought I would die of embarrassment.

~~~

The mortification of my mother pushing me to sing in class was compounded by another factor: to my child stardom-obsessed tween mind, she was the primary person standing between me and success. Each Saturday I took acting, singing, and dancing lessons at a local children's theatrical workshop, where the proprietor, Marie, was a talent agent. Marie wanted to send my sister and me on "calls," or auditions, for musicals, movies, television shows, and commercials. Every time Marie called, we'd go crazy, begging for my mom to take us out of school for the day and bring us to the city to try out. Most of the time she said no. Once in a while she'd say yes. Sometimes she'd let us go on a first audition, but then, when we got a call-back, she'd have second thoughts about being a stage mother, and letting us be child actors. And so she'd remove us from the competition.

As an adult now, I know she was right. Taking time away from her work as a teacher, taking us away from school, dangerously inflating our egos at a young age—none of it made sense. And we all know now how child actors tend to turn out. But at the time, my mother's interference with *my career* was a primary conflict of my life. Adding to the frustration, despite standing in the way of my professional ambitions, now she wanted me to sing in Sunday school, and for "company," when family and her friends came over. I was incensed.

Feeling thwarted, I tried to take matters into my own hands. I secretly subscribed to *Showbusiness!* newspaper, splitting the cost with a close friend from across the street, who a couple of years later would enroll in the High School of Performing Arts using a Manhattan-based relative's address. I'd mail a "professional" photo of myself that my friend had taken, along with a resume I wrote myself, that included lines such as, "I always face the audience and project."

During eighth-grade Christmas vacation, I took a trip to Los Angeles by myself, to visit my aunt, uncle and cousins—my bat mitzvah present from them. While I was there, I was determined to get discovered. I told my aunt and uncle about this, and they made a reservation for us at a piano bar restaurant.

All week I looked forward to my performance. I believed dinner at the piano bar was my big chance. I had a vision of what would happen: I'd sing something from *Annie*, or *Damn Yankees*, shows I'd performed in. There'd be an agent in the audience who was so taken with my performance, they'd sign me on the spot and start casting me in shows and movies right away. I'd of course have to move to L.A. So long, frigid New York winters!

But we got there and learned the pianist knew only Top 40 pop tunes. And the only one on the list I knew the words to—how did I know the words??—was "Feelings." *There are no bad songs, only bad singers*, I chided myself, recalling something I'd heard in the children's theatrical workshop.

When it was my turn, I put down my fork, stood up at my place at our table, and belted my 13-year-old heart out. *Feeeeeeeelings. Whoa, whoah, whoa, feeeeeeeelings....*

Everybody clapped. A couple of people cheered—I was the only child performing that night, and some in the audience seemed charmed by that. I felt amazing.

But then it was over, somebody else's turn. A guy got up and sang Elvin Bishop's "Fooled Around and Fell in Love." No agent came up to me. My big chance was over. I flew back to New York, and my boring life as an unfamous teen-ager resumed.

~~~

In high school, although I had small parts in a few musicals, I mostly stopped singing publicly. *Privately*, however, there was no stopping me. Except that it was difficult for me to find the privacy I needed for my little solo performances. And so I started cutting gym now and then, and sneaking back to my house, which was around the corner from Oceanside High School.

I'd sing along to records, or accompany myself, badly, on piano. I'd sing show tunes and old standards. The song in heaviest rotation was "But the World Goes Round," a world-weary Kander & Ebb number that my idol, Liza Minnelli, performed in Martin Scorcese's *New York, New York*. I lost count of the number of times I snuck home to sing the shit out of that song. But one time in particular stands out.

The house was perfectly quiet when I got there. I sat down at the piano and began to play and sing. After the first few verses, I felt like doing a little dance, so I got up from the piano and started moving. I didn't really need the instrumental accompaniment—I could get higher off of the song without it, if it meant I could move my body, too, boosting my endorphins.

I was perfectly lost in song and dance when I heard it: my step-brother's signature galloping down the stairs. I was caught—mid-kickline, jazz hands shimmying, voice ringing through the entire house.

Why was he home? How had I not realized he was?

"Are you staying home for lunch?" he asked, breaking the awkward silence. "Cause, I was planning on using the kitchen."

I was so stunned at being busted, I struggled to find words. "No, no, I'm going to go back to school soon," I said, then ran up to my room and slammed the door shut. I don't think I've ever been more embarrassed.

But that humiliation didn't put an end to my secret singing habit. Decades later I'd get busted again, by my upstairs neighbor in the East Village. As a freelancer working at home, I assumed it was safe to sing my heart out during the day, while other people were away at work, in offices. But then Richard from apartment eighteen popped down at 3pm one day to ask, "Do you think we can move the Joni Mitchell Hour to a time when I'm not home?" Turned out he was a copy editor at a law firm, on the graveyard shift, and he was stuck listening to me warble in the afternoons. *Oops.*

～～～

Eventually, as a grownup, I got back to singing in public, but mostly for people I didn't know. That seemed to be the only way I could find the courage. For a time in my thirties, I would go to jazz open mics at cafés and jazz clubs like Cleopatra's Needle on the Upper West Side, and Rue B in the Alphabet City, and sing standards to strangers. I never let my friends know I was doing it. Singing made me feel too exposed to share it with most of the people close to me. But it also cured whatever ailed me the way nothing else could.

At 38 I met my husband Brian, and one of our many places of overlap was our love of singing and playing music. Brian had been a singer and drummer in a number of bands in the '90s, and he owned (still owns!) a lot of recording equipment. I had started writing songs just before I met him. Early on in our relationship we started making and recording music together, and it was *the most fun*. To this day, we still do. We have a little ukulele duo act we call "Loveypie," a mutual pet name we came up with when we were...making fun of pet names. We play out here and there, but just for fun. (I harbor no delusions about our getting discovered like I did at 13 in L.A.)

But Brian is not a show tune or old standards guy, although he doesn't mind when I break out into song at home, as I tend to do. Mostly, though, I spare him and still sing those songs by myself. When I'm working at home, I take breaks from my writing to belt along to karaoke tracks I find on YouTube. Sometimes I listen to that music while I'm out on walks, and don't realize until someone looks at me strangely that I'm singing along, rather loudly—and that they can't hear the track I'm singing along to, so they only hear me, belting *a capella*.

Recently I was heartened when I "caught" two different neighbors of mine singing out loud themselves, thinking no one else was around. One man, who lives three houses down, immediately apologized when I walked past him as he belted "Two Occasions" by The Deele.

"Do not apologize," I insisted. "Sing it!" It made me happy when he stopped being self-conscious and turned up the volume. I'll have to return the favor some time.

The Weight: A Manifesto

You're not supposed to complain when people compliment you. But not all compliments are created equal, and two that I received in the spring of 2017, at 51, really hit a nerve.

The first came from an older woman, let's call her Gerry* (*not her name), who famously has no filter. Everyone who knows her has a Gerry story (or three) to tell, times when she was brusque and impolite. Usually they're examples of when she lodged brutal insults, but in this instance, it was a comment intended to flatter.

"Have you been working out?" Gerry asked after giving my body a few head-to-toe glances. "Because you look…" and here she paused, "…better."

Better. Apparently, before then I didn't look so hot.

The second came from a family friend at a wedding—another older woman, this one very nice. (God help all women when it comes to body image, but especially the women of my pre-Boomer parents' generation.) We were clustered during the cocktail hour with four or five other people when she gave my body a top-to-bottom scan similar to the one I'd received from Gerry, then issued her evaluation. "You're skinnier!" she shouted, as if responding to a game show quiz. I visibly froze, which seemed to make her doubt her conviction. "You're skinnier now…did I…get that right…?"

My face flushed. Too many pairs of eyes were now literally sizing me up.

"I try not to think about that," I lied, smiling nervously, hoping it would put an end to the discussion.

"Are you kidding?!" the woman shrieked. "My weight is *all* I think about!" Everyone laughed along with her. *Ha ha ha.*

"You shouldn't do that to yourself," I shot back, like some snotty teen. "It's bad for you."

I felt terrible the minute the words left my mouth, worse when I saw them land. The woman's eyes narrowed and her expression became pained, revealing a woundedness that cut right through me, for which I knew no antidote. Everyone stood in stunned silence until another family friend ambled over to say hello. The group shift-ed into greeting mode, hugs and kisses all around. I was grateful for an opportunity to slink away, but my night was ruined.

The problem with both compliments was that the women had gotten it right. I *had* been working out. I *had* lost a little weight. And I hated everything about that.

~~~

Like just about every woman in America—plus plenty of men and people across the gender spectrum—I've got issues with body image, weight, food, eating, and exercise. I know. *Shocking!* Who doesn't?

In my teens and early twenties I struggled on and off with anorexia, and it warped my relationship to my body and its appetite. When I was young and starv-ing myself, I thought it was just another way in which I was weird and different. But since then I've become an unofficial student of this subject, and arrived at the conclusion that our culture has a massive, collective eating disorder. I've now read and heard countless stories about other people's experiences, which on the one hand depressed the hell out of me—the sheer ubiquity of these issues!—but on the other helped me realize I'm *not* weird in this way, or alone. After twice considering trashing this piece (is there any way to tell the story of an eating disorder that isn't cliché and boring?) I've decided to share my version and perspective, on the off chance it might be helpful to someone.

So, yeah, I had an eating disorder, which started when I was around 15. But long before that, as a small child, I learned to hate my body, its size, its contours, even though I was pretty normal-sized—fit and slim, actually. Like everyone else in Amer-ica, the adults around me had been taught to hate their bodies, and as a result they innocently, unintentionally passed that along to me. In recent months, I've heard a couple of them, now in their seventies and eighties, articulate their body hatred, past and present. It's been shocking to hear them speak about this so directly, but also strangely validating. It confirms for me that my own body hatred didn't come out of nowhere. When I was growing up, they telegraphed those messages more obliquely, through constant dieting, worrying aloud about carbs and calories and ketones, and making body-shaming jokes about their weight as well as other people's. Obliqueness notwithstanding, the messages came through loud and clear, anyway.

Even though I've worked through a lot of that over the past few decades, some of the sickness remains in me, and even more so, in our thinness-obsessed culture. Our collective eating disorder is so pervasive, many don't even realize they're living inside of it, the way a fish doesn't know it lives in water. To me, though, at this point, it feels like a prison I might never be released from. It makes me angry, and I do not enjoy being angry—because you know what I've been taught is even less acceptable, and less attractive than a woman with a few "extra" pounds on her? *An angry woman.*

Intellectually, though, I know my anger is justifiable, and maybe even necessary, psychologically, so I'm going to attempt to own it here. Here goes.

When I said I hated "everything" about those compliments I received in 2017, and what I'd put myself through in order to receive them? I meant *everything*:

- I hated the idea that the size and shape of my body, and my eating and exercise habits, could be construed as anyone else's legitimate concern.

- I hated that I'd felt compelled to slim down and firm up in the first place. Honestly, I'd already been pretty normal-sized to begin with, although that shouldn't have mattered. Life-long body dysmorphia makes me a somewhat unreliable narrator about the state of my "figure," but to the best of my understanding I am not, nor have I ever been, overweight, nor any kind of "over-eater." I'm petite (a hair under five feet; a size 4 or 6, depending on the brand) and curvy—soft-bodied, with a full bosom (34D or 32DD, depending on the brand) and an ample behind. But I'm not at all fat. (Not that there's anything wrong with that...if you'd like to argue with me on that point, please allow me to refer you to the wonderful Maintenance Phase podcast.)

- I hated the way people have always treated me most favorably when I've been especially thin—even more so when I've been *too* thin. This is particularly vexing when it comes from family and old friends—some of whom have commented on feeling "proud" of me when I've been super skinny—considering they know I struggled with anorexia in my youth. (More about that in a bit.)

- I hated my entire history of being too concerned about my weight and appearance, and the many ways I've hurt myself in the vain, hollow interest of being "thin enough," whatever that means. I hated that I didn't (and still don't) know what "thin enough" actually means, nor "normal," nor any of the relative terms used to describe people's sizes.

- I hated that it's become difficult for me to tell when limiting certain kinds of food and engaging in exercise are instances of me being healthy, and when they are instances of me hurting myself. Often it starts out the good way, then turns the bad way. Related: I hate the way the weight loss industry has more recently adopted the language of wellness, using words like "body positivity," making all of this even more confusing.

- I hated how fine the line was between what many people considered fat and thin. How many times in my life had men uttered stupid shit to me about my weight or my size or my shape, when I was actually pretty damn slim? (In the first three weeks we were together, my otherwise wonderful husband called me "full figured" while I was at my dating skinniest.)

- I hated that my level of thinness at the time—the thing people were noticing about me and commenting on—didn't feel quite thin *enough*, not for me, and probably not for the peanut gallery, either. *You can't be too thin, or too rich.* How many times had I heard that dumb adage growing up?

- I hated our patriarchal, capitalist culture, which has frequently made me hate myself for not living up to its unattainable ideals of femininity—which is the whole point. Capitalism creates problems that are impossible to solve and then tries to sell you solutions that in the long run don't work. That's how we wound up with a $71 billion diet industry. Diets don't work, not long-term. They make you feel deprived, which leads to over-eating, which leads to more dieting, which makes your body think it's starving, which slows your metabolism. After weight loss regimen upon weight loss regimen, you also lose your natural ability to know when you're hungry and what you're hungry for, which happens to be intrinsic to a little thing called *survival.* I would like back all the time I've had to invest in reacquainting myself with my natural appetite, and trying to learn "intuitive eating."

- I hated that in this sick, misogynist culture, I've always been the most visible to men exactly when there's been the least of me, my body taking up the smallest amount of space possible. There's a metaphor in this that's just a little too obvious, don't you think?

- I hated that I'd been inculcated with fatphobia, and taught to silently scrutinize other women's bodies, too. How merciless I can be when silently judging other women's shapes and sizes! Not to mention their food choices.

- I hated that if I *hadn't* lost those few pounds in the months leading up to that wedding I attended, my evening likely would have been even shittier. I would have noticed other people registering exactly what had bothered me about my body—the "saddle bags" of cellulite on my thighs, the too short distance between my boobs and my hips, my pronounced hind quarters—and felt just as eager to disappear.

- I hated that no matter what I did—whether I lost weight or I didn't—I couldn't win. And that despite such futility, I almost always erred on the side of starving and hurting myself.

This time was no exception.

~~~

Two months before that wedding, I'd gotten the brilliant idea to once again, for the millionth time in my life, restrict my eating in an extreme way. I figured I had sixty days to lose ten pounds before I saw family and friends-of-family, people who love me, but who are critical of bodies—mine, theirs, everyone's. (Again: I can't blame them; they're victims of this sick culture, just as I am.)

I devised this plan despite countless instances in recent years in which I swore off dieting altogether, insisting it was unhealthy, physically and psychologically. It would be my fifth or sixth gambit at cutting out carbs entirely, even though Atkins and similar high-protein diets had by then fallen out of favor for being hard on the kidneys, and the environment. I was back to the same old same old: *so* much fish, chicken, turkey, ham, beef, cheese, and veggies of course, but none of the starchy ones. A granny smith apple here and there. Maybe some berries. I also returned to the gym after about a year away—a series of upper respiratory infections had made it difficult to exercise without coughing incessantly and worsening my condition.

This regimen was additionally triggered by a visit to a new general practitioner. During my examination, the doctor said *not one word* indicating that I needed to lose weight. No doctor ever has. But at the end of my appointment—*shudder*—I inadvertently learned how much I weighed from a sheet the receptionist handed me on the way out, cataloging my diagnostic test results: blood pressure, urinalysis, reflexes, Body Mass Index (BMI)—that bullshit indicator that neglects to take into account one's proportioning—and of course, height and weight. During the exam, I'd tried in vain to keep myself blissfully ignorant. "Please don't tell me my weight," I'd said to the nurse, as I turned my back to the scale, something I've done by default in that situation for decades now. (My old doctor's office knew the drill, and they didn't hand you a sheet with your test results. I wanted my old doctor!)

Listed just below my height, the sheet read "122 lbs"—more than I'd ever known myself to weigh, and a number I was very much not okay with. I had no idea how much more it was than the last time I was weighed, or the time before that, because I had neither allowed anyone to share that information with me, nor found it out on my own, since September, 2009, when I was briefly super-skinny—109 pounds—in the wake of a major surgery.

Stepping on a scale of my own volition is an act I've typically reserved for times when I've been particularly thin. Even then, I've usually tried to refrain, because I've found that the number is rarely as low as I'd like it to be, or if it is, I become obsessed with maintaining it—no, *besting* it. Next I become hooked on the scale, and no matter which direction the numbers move in, I'm fucked. If they go up, I hate myself and restrict my food further. If they go down, I want them to keep going in that direction.

Despite eating-disorder-specific therapy as a teen, and all other kinds of therapy as an adult—despite several rides on the body acceptance merry-go-round, at the end of which I'm always one-hundred-percent certain I'm cured—no number on the scale ever leaves me content. Every number is a slippery slope back in the direction of food-restriction and over-exercising, so I know better than to ever weigh myself.

Shortly after it was released in 1990, I watched Henry Jaglom's pseudo-documentary, *Eating*, and about (mostly white) women and their fraught relationships to food and their bodies. It takes place at a 40th birthday party where, among other conflicts, no one wants to partake of the cake. After the candles are blown out, the first slice gets passed around the entire room with not one taker. Over the course of the movie, women in attendance share their stories of starving themselves and being bulimic. An older woman in attendance is surprised by this, but then confesses to some of her own disordered perspectives on eating. A young woman in the mix finally decides to eat a piece of birthday cake after all, but reveals that she can only enjoy it privately, locked in an upstairs bathroom, with no one watching. I think about that film a lot. When I first saw it, it seemed like an exaggeration, a bit of a parody. Now I think it might as well have been an actual documentary.

Do you know one single woman who has a healthy relationship to her body, eating, and exercise? I do not. (I know plenty of men and people elsewhere on the gender spectrum who are pretty screwed up about those things, too.) Every time I think I've found the one woman with a completely healthy body image, she says or does something to prove me wrong—a self-hating comment about her thighs or butt, an apology for eating something "fattening," a promise to "work off" her dessert at the gym the next day. A refusal to schedule getting together during mealtimes, because she can't eat in front of other people. Most of those willing to talk about it with me admit they've been struggling with weight and body image for most of their lives, and that they were taught by our culture to hate their bodies.

〰

How old were you when you learned to hate your body? I was 15 when I launched an all-out assault on every ounce of fat on my small frame, but I was in kindergarten the first time I thought I was bigger than I should be. My body size and shape were within a standard, normal range, according to my doctors, and photographs bear this out. But I somehow was convinced I was fat.

I vividly recall the day I determined this. My mother brought me to visit my aunt at her home, farther out on Long Island. There, with me on her lap, my mom showed both of us proofs of professional photos she'd had taken of me, and I got upset when I saw them. I was wearing a red cotton summer outfit, a matching top and bottom set, with a white floral pattern on it. My cheeks and arms seemed too full to me, too soft. I didn't want my mom to show the pictures to anyone else, and begged her not to. I look at those photos now and I can't at all see what I saw then; I'm just a normal girl with no extra padding on her. I say this about so many other photos taken of me in the past; at the time the photos are taken, I believe I'm "fat." When I return to them even the following year, I can no longer see it.

Fifty-one years later, I think I look just lovely in those photos from when I was 5. My mom was right not to listen to me, to share the photos with the family anyway. But I was distraught about it at the time.

A year after, in first grade, I was bothered terribly when it became clear that I'd gone up in clothing size, from a girls' four to a six. My mother bought me some clothes and underpants in my new size, and I was relieved to discover that they were a bit too big on me. I remember the first night I wore new underpants and a new night gown. After I got out of the bath, my mother handed them to me.

"Where are my old ones?" I asked.

"They're gone now," my mom insisted. "You have to wear these."

The underpants were white cotton with yellow flowers and green stems. They extended up nearly to my rib cage, and the unwashed fabric was stiff and uncomfortable. In bed I cried about moving up to the bigger size. I didn't want to in any way be associated with that higher number. I knew my parents and grandparents and friends of the family were always trying to fit into smaller sizes, and now I was moving in the wrong direction. It was lost on little me that children were supposed to do the opposite of adults, and keep increasing in size, at least for a while.

All the adults around me dieted constantly—family, friends-of-family, neighbors, teachers, babysitters—and talked about it a lot. Our cupboards were filled with Tab and Sweet 'n Low and all manner of artificially-sweetened foods, the freezer with a low-cal ice cream substitute called "ice milk." We also had a fully-stocked cookie jar and other regular desserts and snacks for the kids, but when the adults ate them, they expressed guilt over it. Their dessert after dinner was often a sad baked apple topped with cinnamon and a low-fat, sugar-free whipped cream alternative. I was surrounded by grownup women who made excuses if they "allowed" themselves a cookie, or a pat of butter on a baked potato, and men who were chronic yo-yo dieters, cycling from Weight Watchers to Weigh-of-Life to Atkins to Pritikin, to binge-eating and putting all the weight back, in between. Very early on, I must have absorbed their shame, and their disdain for their bodies, and applied it to my own.

When I was 7, an adult commented on my ample butt, the part of my body that, more than any other, I have struggled to make peace with. Whatever positive regard I still held for my body evaporated. I am a small woman—when new people meet me, they use words like "tiny"—but my behind has always been disproportionate to the rest of me.

Shortly after that, on a day when I was home from school with a stomach virus, I experienced a weird sense of empowerment from my ability to go most of the day without eating. I was overcome with nausea and vomiting, but I saw the whole ordeal as a stroke of luck. When my babysitter brought me a plate of Saltines with jelly, I could barely hold down a single cracker, and I remember thinking that was a *good* thing. After my queasiness subsided and my appetite returned, I tried to resist eating for the rest of that day, and the day after. I wondered, *How long can I go?* Maybe if I stopped eating for long enough, I could lose my big butt.

That day marked the first time of many that I stared intently at my reflection in the mirror. I climbed up onto the edge of the bathtub so I could see myself from head to toe in the large mirror behind the sink, and turned sideways to assess how far my tush and belly protruded. My stomach was pretty concave in the wake of the virus. I sucked it in, holding my breath, to see what I'd look like even thinner, and decided, *Yes, I'd prefer to look like that.* This became a daily ritual until we moved out of that house, when I was 15 and battling anorexia.

In fourth grade, my friends and I began comparing our bodies. I had one friend, Lucy, with juvenile diabetes, who would go through periods where she was rail thin. At night, I would pray to god to give me diabetes, too—along with glasses, braces and a cast. I craved the attention Lucy got, along with the other kids who possessed those other accouterments. (When kids gathered around to make bright magic marker drawings on one another's casts, it barely registered that there were painful broken bones beneath the plaster.)

That year, Lucy and other girls I knew started "humblebragging" about their doctors declaring them "underweight." Suddenly it was fashionable for your weight to be in a low percentile for your age group. The girls reported this in a way that made it sound as if it was an unfortunate situation, and beyond their control. *Woe is me—underweight again! I just can't keep the meat on my bones.*

The worst offender was a girl named Jeanine. She and I were the exact same size, but she wouldn't shut up about how underweight she allegedly was. One Sunday morning, after we'd had a sleepover at my house, she joined me on the rim of the bathtub for my daily ritual of thinness assessment. We both turned sideways and looked at our reflections.

"I'm so much skinnier!" she said, laughing, teasing. I looked and looked, but she seemed to be the exact size I was. "I can't help being underweight," she added. "My doctor says I should eat more, but I get too full!"

That morning, I picked at my breakfast.

〰〰〰

As I write, this, I sift through boxes of photos from my childhood, for reference. Through fiftysomething eyes, I'm trying to understand how as a girl and a young woman I came to view my appearance so inaccurately, and so ungenerously. Yes, there are slight variations in my body size—slim, skinny, a little fuller—but still, throughout, *pretty freaking slim.* Making things more confusing is that some people around me have always reflected back to me what I was seeing in the mirror. If I put on three pounds of premenstrual bloat, I got noticed less. After my period, when I was at my monthly thinnest, suddenly everyone wanted to know my weight loss secrets, and men flirted with me. Until my hysterectomy at 43, I gained and lost the same three goddamned pounds every month, and people treated me so differently before and after.

As I consider pictures from different times in my life, it's interesting to observe how my comportment changes here and there. The most marked change: in photos taken when I was 14 or 15, I begin to hide myself. I achieve this by wearing baggy clothes, but also by trying to let the camera see less of me. I always have my face in semi-profile, because it looks slimmer that way. No full smiles—they make my cheeks and chin look fat (er, "fat"). I turn my body partially sideways for the same reason, or cross my legs for a sleeker silhouette. By contrast, in photos from the time just before then—my tween years, from 10-13—I appear perfectly unafraid to be seen. I'm smiling, with my whole body front and center, for the world to see.

The tween years were sort of golden for me. A fucked up part of my brain says, "Oh, yeah—you peaked at 13." It would be funny if it wasn't in keeping with our sick fascination with teen and tween girls. The bottom line is, in junior high I liked how I looked, and in pictures, you can see that. I'd grown a few inches to basically my current height, a hair under five feet, and as a result of the growth spurt, was temporarily even slimmer than I'd been before. I still hated my butt, and felt incredibly self-conscious about what people saw when they walked behind me in the hallways at school. But I mostly liked the rest of me.

I thought of myself as "pretty." Staring at my reflection in the bathroom mirror then became more about admiring myself than tracking my thinness, although there was still some of that going on. And there were still moments where issues with eating arose. Like the summer I was 12, between seventh and eighth grades; something weird happened after visiting day at summer camp.

It was my first summer at sleepaway, and it was a hard transition for me. I worried all the time about my still-single mom being alone, and lonely. On visiting day, she brought me a bag of ripe peaches and plums, and after she left, I misplaced it. Somehow it never made it from the blanket my family sat on during the visiting day festivities, into my bunk. I felt absolutely horrible about it. I was so overcome with guilt, I felt undeserving of food, and completely lost my appetite. I couldn't bring myself to eat a single thing for two days. The longer I went without eating, the more empowered I felt. But I also felt scared. How far could I go with this? I was pretty sure you needed food to live. By the end of the second day, I began eating again.

For the next year or so, I was fine, eating-wise and body-image wise—until, at 14, my body started to more rapidly develop. Suddenly my clothes fit a bit tightly, and I didn't like it. In photos from that time, my face is a little rounder than before, my body more curvy, though I am still very much *not fat*. But I'm clearly a few pounds heavier than I was before, and I'm not the only one who noticed.

"You don't eat the cakes and the candies, do you?" At a shiva gathering after my grandfather's funeral, his widow asked me this in her European accent. She gave my body the once-over as she was asking. Mortified, I nodded, "No." I would have liked something sweet, but after her comment, there was no way I was going to be seen serving myself anything from the dessert table. Besides, I didn't want my body to keep filling out.

I did not want to get any bigger, and I also wasn't ready to feel older. I wanted to remain a child, small and slight, and carefree. My childhood had felt abbreviated. I wanted a do-over. I resisted getting a training bra until I was a full B cup, and it became embarrassing. Again—I look back at pictures from this time, and I seem absolutely normal for a kid of my age, if a little softer than I'd been before. But at the time, my self-perception was distorted, my impression of my size and shape greatly warped. I couldn't stand my body, and the way it was "massing out," as I'd heard a friend's mother refer to the phenomenon.

〰〰〰

Everything got ratcheted up a few notches in the middle of 10th grade, the winter of 1981, when I was 15. I decided that I needed to take some action to control this body that insisted on growing and changing in ways I had no say over. First I embarked on something called "The Stewardess Diet," a four-day plan I learned about from a girl at school. Breakfast was nothing but black coffee—something I didn't drink yet— and a half grapefruit. Lunch and dinner were basically eggs or different kinds of meat with plain, undressed vegetables. It's a testament to how desperate I felt that I ate the two hard boiled eggs prescribed as dinner for day one, because I hate hard boiled eggs with a passion. I gag at the mere thought of them.

After four days of that boring regimen, I didn't feel nearly thin enough, and I grew impatient. Getting skinny as quickly as I wanted was going to require drastic measures. I'd watched adults crash-diet many times, dropping massive amounts of weight. But I didn't have access to liquid amino acids, or Weight Watchers, or diet books. I went to the library to see what I could find, and there, instead of diet books, I was drawn to a young adult novel called *The Best Little Girl in the World*, by Steven Levenkron.

It was the story of a teen girl who develops anorexia and bulimia. Clearly it was meant to caution young readers *against* starving themselves, but for me, it had the opposite effect—it became a blueprint. (I pray my own story doesn't become a blueprint for someone else's self-harm.) I learned all the tricks from Francesca/Kessa, the main character, who develops an alter ego for her new thinner self: how to move your food around on your plate, hiding some of your dinner under other parts of the meal; how to leave evidence of your having eaten breakfast without having taken so much as a bite; the kinds of excuses that would work on overworked, tired parents, and on and on. I read the book twice. It destroyed my relationship to food and my body forever.

Within days of reading the book, I began literally, stealthily starving myself. In the morning, while my mother showered for work, I put cereal crumbs in a bowl, which I placed in the sink, to give her the impression that I'd had breakfast before heading to the school bus. (I have always eaten cereal dry. Add milk to the list of "normal" foods I have always gagged at even just the thought of.) At school, I'd skip lunch, and brisk-walk the grounds of the school to burn fat off my body. At dinner, I would put a small amount of whatever meat was served into a large portion of salad, but eat only the lettuce and vegetables, and at the end of the meal, quickly toss the meat at the bottom of my bowl into the garbage. I went on like that for weeks.

Initially, starving myself was hard. I filled myself up with water, Tab, diluted orange juice, and tea, and it helped distract me from my hunger. Each time I peed, I imagined fat pouring out of me. A couple of days in, something shifted, and I felt the equivalent of a runner's high from not eating. It was utterly exhilarating to feel so in control. To feel empty and light. To have a secret I kept to myself.

There was something dangerously powerful about the whole thing. I had so much energy! I expended it in the evenings, dancing vigorously to the more upbeat songs on Springsteen's *The River* album. I say "dancing," but it looked more like awkward aerobics, kicking and punching the air, twisting and turning, with the objective of working all the fat off all my parts. Every evening, the same moves, the same songs. A ritual. A pact with myself. Words of inspiration (my own words) written in calligraphy and posted to my bulletin board: "And the inside cried to the outside, I want to be thin!" Every time I felt hungry, I thought of those words, and I would remember my mission.

That commitment to myself made me become even more of a weird loner than I already had been. As it was, I had no real friends at school, because of the Mean Girls afront at the end of eighth grade that I never recovered from, socially. I had some friends from summer camp, but none of them lived in my town. None of them were around to witness this first phase of my eating disorder. Making a pact with myself, being sneaky about avoiding food, walking around the school grounds during my lunch hour, putting my body through the ringer at night—all of it made me very *intentional* about being all alone, where before, it hadn't felt like a choice.

A month or so in, though, I became scared. In a short time, I had gotten myself down to 90 pounds from 112. I was very thin. My parents became alarmed. I became alarmed, because even though I knew, definitively, that I was thinner than was considered healthy, I only wanted to keep losing weight.

I was afraid of myself. I didn't trust myself. I confessed to my parents that I'd been starving myself, and that I wanted to get some kind of help. They found the name of a therapist who specialized in childhood eating disorders, and I started going once a week.

~~~~

My therapist, Evelyn, was a nice woman about my mother's age—in her early 40s. She was attractive, with a blond shag, and wore bourgeois-bohemian outfits that combined hip or hippie-ish pieces with preppier ones—think prairie skirts and dresses made more serious with Talbot's blazers. I was supposed to like her. I *wanted* to like her. Sometimes I felt like it was my job as her patient to make her feel liked. But as nice as she was, our connection, our relationship to each other, didn't feel natural or easy to me.

The first problem was that Evelyn herself was pretty skinny. I got the sense she was naturally so, but what if that wasn't the case? What if she had chosen eating disorders as her specialty because *she had one*? Conversely, if she was bony by nature, how could she possibly understand what it meant to be afraid to gain weight? Some of her choices suggested this was the case.

First she made the grave mistake of having me keep a running list of everything I ate each day. It put me at odds with myself—the part of me interested in getting well wanted to let this exercise help me; the part of me interested in staying sick wanted to use it in an obsessive way, or to lie about what I had and hadn't consumed. Next, she ridiculed me one day when I told her I'd stopped myself from having a corn muffin when I was really hungry, because I thought it alone would make me fat.

"Oh, come on," she said. "What would happen to you if you ate a corn muffin? *Nothing.*"

These choices of hers made me feel uncomfortable talking to her. My mom would drop me off at Evelyn's office, and I'd sit there, mostly not saying anything, and worrying about what I *should* say. I knew my parents checked in with her, and didn't know how much of what I said would be confidential.

Complicating things, I felt split about wanting to get better, and so didn't fully trust someone whose only objective was helping me stop being sick. I didn't want to feel scared, I didn't want to die like some of the anorexic kids I'd been told about. But I also didn't want to weigh any more than I currently did. No, I wanted to weigh even less. Some internal monster kept trying to convince me to keep going down in weight. I was terrified of that monster, while also terrified of going back to a weight in the normal range.

Despite all that, after a few weeks, Evelyn became familiar enough for me to let my guard down a bit. I began opening up to her—only to realize that once my fifty-minute session was over, I left feeling cracked open and raw. I didn't know what to do with all the feelings that had come to the surface, all the stories I didn't get to finish telling, and it stressed me out.

The whole time I was in treatment with Evelyn, I wondered whether she had any real insight into the mind of an anorectic. But there were other doctors involved in my treatment who were worse. For instance, the arrogant male physician in the eating disorders unit at Long Island Jewish Hospital who told me I hadn't lost a high enough percentage of my body weight—25%—to warrant being clinically categorized as anorexic. He practically sneered at me after weighing and examining me, as if to say I was only a wannabe anorectic, not worthy of his time. One part of me knew even then, in my compromised psychological state, that he was an idiot. The other part only heard, "Try harder, girl." And so I did. (Presumably, there have been innovations and improvements in eating disorders treatment since the early 80s!)

In 11th grade, after my mom remarried, we moved and I switched high schools. I welcomed a fresh start. Then the reality set in of being an odd girl to begin with, and now an odd girl with the added weirdness of an eating disorder. *Good luck making friends, kid.* I tried, and found a few acquaintances. But my obsession with diet and exercise kept me emotionally distanced from those few I was coming to know.

I don't know how I managed to focus hard enough on my schoolwork to earn mostly Bs and some As. My mind was so preoccupied with staying skinny. That and my first real boyfriend, Jason.

Jason and I started dating the summer before, at camp. It was only once I'd gotten super-thin, my jaw and cheekbones becoming more prominent, that he and other boys noticed me. Receiving male attention made me feel validated. It also made me want to be as thin as possible, forever. *Nothing tastes as good as thin feels*, an emaciated older woman, one of Jason's family friends, said to me knowingly one time when I was at their house. She let me know I was a member of her club, and I was proud to be admitted.

Despite my preoccupations, somehow I did well enough in high school to get into college. There, the battle continued, and became complicated by the slowing of my metabolism, apparently a homeostasis response to starving. I started putting on weight while consuming under 1,000 calories per day. I didn't get "fat"—my body moved in the direction of normal. But to my sick mind, this qualified as fatness, and *it would not do.* I tried to combat the weight gain by spending more time exercising—I bought a rusty used exercise bike at a yard sale and rode it in my dorm room daily, sometimes twice or three times daily—but it didn't help, and I was exhausted all the time.

Soon the added factor of hormones—both my own, and synthetic—would make everything more challenging. I didn't get my first full period until I was 18, while away at school, and it was a doozy. Then the next one was a doozy, and the one after that, too. At the end of my freshman year, I'd have laparoscopic surgery to diagnose severe endometriosis. That would lead to hormone treatments that would make me gain weight, and develop acne. I felt bloated and pimply, and I hated myself more than ever before.

But there was something useful about having a whole other condition to deal with, the treatment of which made it impossible for me to be impossibly thin: it made me feel as if I had no choice but to let go, at least somewhat, of the need to be super-skinny. It was the beginning of becoming a bit less vigilant about my weight, which was something of a relief.

I wasn't all better by any stretch of the imagination. But it put me on a path toward *a little bit better*, and then *a little bit better than that*, then a slip, followed by *a bit better than before*, then a slip, and so on, mostly moving me in a good direction with all of this nonsense that still affects how I feel about myself, and still makes me fucking angry.

~~~

Yeah, this shit doesn't just go away. You can heal some, and grow in a healthy direction. But it seems it's never truly done with you, nor you with it. It helps to accept that, instead of fighting it. I used to be hard on myself about not being over it all. But lately, I am more compassionate toward myself, just as I am toward the adults who passed this on to me, I'm certain without intending to.

Again and again, it has returned. Throughout my twenties, thirties, and forties, I alternated between briefly accepting my body at a normal weight, and seriously restricting. From time to time, I gave up carbs entirely, over-exercised, and became waifish. Still, I never again went nearly to the extremes I had as a teen. But even when I *wasn't* in harsh dieting mode, I was still hard on myself when I ate desserts, or too many carbs, or too much fat.

I'd fight with myself every day about exercise, too. I'd feel compelled to commit to an hour of vigorous aerobic activity. Sometimes I really enjoyed running, or using cardio machines at the gym. But the experience was tainted by the punishing attitude held by my internal task-master. She believed I needed to *earn* my food for the day with sufficient exercise, preferably done in the morning, before work. Another part of me resented the task-master for making these calorie-burning activities *required*. It ruined whatever endorphin boost I experienced. Also, it seemed impossible for me not to become compulsive about exercising. If I was on board with exercising, I was ON BOARD, and vigilant, to the point that I'd come to hate it, and then stop. Forever in an internal conflict with myself about my workouts, I would go through periods where I'd put exercise off all day, then hate myself if the rest of the day got away from me, or other things came up, and I didn't get a chance to sweat.

At 33, I unwittingly adopted a slightly different flavor of eating disorder, one disguised to look like a smart approach to eating: orthorexia, which conflates restriction of certain foods with being "healthy." I'd been struggling with a host of ongoing health issues—frequent upper respiratory infections, nausea, thrush—and got re-diagnosed with celiac, as I'd initially been as a two-year-old, in 1967. I saw an MD who was into complementary medicine, who put me on a three-month elimination diet to try and figure out what other foods might be making me sick. Then, in the middle of my diet, he closed his practice and moved across the country. The elimination diet—no sugar, dairy, meat, gluten, alcohol, vinegar—put a temporary stop to my recurring symptoms. It also seemed to help regulate my very irregular period. Best (read: worst) of all it made me feel in control, and "healthy." So I just stayed on the diet...for the better part of four years. In my late thirties, when I was dating and trying to have some normal sense of a social life, I eased back into eating everything, other than gluten, mostly without incident.

In my late forties and early fifties, another shift occurred: Injuries I'd incurred while jogging, plus frequent respiratory illnesses, made it difficult to engage in vigorous aerobic exercise. It turned out to be kind of a blessing in that it forced me to switch to less punishing activities, like walking and low-level hiking, and also to accept my body a little bit fuller and rounder.

Still, every now and then, something triggers a regression—as happened in 2017, before that wedding.

～～～

I write these words in the spring of 2021, in the midst of a global pandemic that forced me to close down the small coworking space for writers that I used to operate and do my own work. I've been "sheltering in place" for fifteen months and counting. These days I am mostly okay, when it comes to body image and eating. But remnants of this stupid disease remain inside my head. Maybe they always will.

One of the "problems" with working from home now, in isolation, is that I have constant, unfettered access to my refrigerator and cupboards, and for hours at a clip I fight to ignore the siren song of their contents, even though just about everything we stock qualifies as "healthy," including the reduced fat organic cheese popcorn I sometimes like to snack on. Even though I'm not generally prone to overeating, and never have been. It makes me realize I've let the overeating tendencies of those who came before me convince me that it's my problem, too. By exposure, or epigenetics, I've absorbed their anxieties and their shame. Ironically, I feel *weighed down* by their anxieties and shame, and my own. The shame might be worse than the anxiety, and I have so much of it. *I'm ashamed about having had an eating disorder. I'm ashamed when I gain weight. I'm ashamed when I become obsessed with weight loss. I'm ashamed when I concern myself with other people's bodies and eating habits.* It's all a lot to bear. Sometimes I feel as if I might collapse under it all.

Most mornings, at 11:30 I feel hungry, but won't allow myself to eat. No lunch until the clock strikes noon! No, 12:30! I want to revolt against this baseless decree, but the unreasonable despot I'd be rebelling against is yours truly. Where did I get this dumb rule from, anyway? I have a lot of food rules, by the way. For instance: I'm allowed one square of chocolate per day, or one small gluten-free cookie, likely one that I baked, or a tablespoon of ice cream, to keep me from feeling too dessert-deprived. (Friends who bought me a special black licorice ice cream as a gift were shocked to learn that I'd made the pint last for months by eating only a spoonful each day.) That's it for sweets, unless it's a special occasion. No full desserts more than once a week! Preferably not more than once a month! No, per quarter! If I have a carb-heavy lunch, aka a sandwich with bread, I can't also have a carb-heavy dinner, like pasta or rice. Etc. I keep these rules and others to myself, in my head, and know them by rote.

When the mid-morning hunger pangs beckon, I think about how the British serve "elevenses," a mid-morning snack, and take comfort in the implication that enough other people get hungry at the same time as I do that it's *a thing.* Okay, then! Not content to leave well enough alone, though, I then switch gears and bring to mind questions a Certified Nutrition Coach once taught me to ask myself any time I *think* I'm hungry: Do I *have appetite,* or am I, in fact, *hungry*? Might I be *angry, lonely,* or *tired,* instead? She gave me an acronym by which to remember this line of questioning: H.A.L.T. This is supposed to be "wellness": making you doubt your own hunger. Analyzing my impulse to eat in this way doesn't reduce my desire to eat, it just makes me feel more confused and self-conscious about it. And it is a tremendous waste of time, energy, and headspace. It's incredibly inefficient, too. I'm not as productive as I need to be because I'm afraid to gain weight, afraid to feed myself when my brain and body need feeding.

Sometimes I think, *Maybe a teaspoon of peanut butter will hold me over,* but that only buys me 15 minutes of relief, 20 minutes tops. This is a problem that could easily be solved with a bigger breakfast, but the unreasonable despot in my brain lets me have only small rations of fruit, yogurt, and gluten-free muesli for the first meal of the day. Another ridiculous rule of my own making, which I'm afraid to break.

I wish now that I could un-remember H.A.L.T, along with everything I was ever taught about calories, "good food," "bad carbs," anything having to do with the moralization of food and body size, Weight Watchers "points," and all the other nonsense that contributes to the tabulation forever running in my mind: How many units of which kinds of foods have I consumed today? Have I moved my body enough to burn it all off? Don't get me wrong, *I know* there are legitimate concerns regarding nutrition and exercise, and probably legitimately healthy ways of approaching both. It's not advised to eat just bacon and pizza and ice cream, and never move your body. *Duh.* But my history and that of my forebears renders me incapable of separating healthy approaches out from harmful ones, or from turning the healthy approaches into modes of harm.

My god, I'm so sick and tired of this. I wish I could finally, permanently let it all go.

〜〜〜

I mean, who knows—maybe someday I *can* let it all go. I'd like to remain hopeful. I've come a long way, and maybe incrementally, over time, the rest of it will fade from my consciousness. In the meantime, the best thing I can do for myself is realize I have deep imprinting and trauma around this, and treat myself with as much gentleness and kindness as possible. That means I need to go easy on myself in whatever mode I find myself—obsessed with my weight and appearance, or relaxed about it.

Just as necessary is having compassion for everyone else—those who infected me with this sickness; the people who insulted me, either directly, or through back-handed compliments. Every one of them was taught to hate their own bodies—and mine and yours—by a culture that wants to sell you what you can't have by making you feel bad about yourself.

I've also made a choice to only be a force of good in the world when it comes to this matter. In my late forties, I swore off writing service journalism about weight loss for women's magazines and lifestyle sections of newspapers, something I had been only too willing to do in the past. My editor at a women's glossy called me then, asking if I wanted to write an article on some supplement that was catching on with celebrities, which helped them to "naturally" slim down by "optimizing" their own hormones, and before I could even consider the assignment I heard myself say, "No."

Now I can't even bear to read those articles, nor the ones that are ostensibly about some aspect of nutrition or body maintenance, but are really weight-loss articles in disguise. Initially I'm drawn to them. *Ooh, what's this new get-thin-quick scheme?!* And then as soon as I get to the page and see the article, something in my gut shuts down my engagement with it. Any references to slimming or trimming, or dissatisfaction with the body the author is living in, and I'm not interested in the least. *Nope. Next.*

I've stopped joking about weight loss. In my twenties and thirties, I frequently referenced a Rhoda Morgenstern joke: someone would offer me something "fattening" to eat—a dessert, cheesy nachos—and as I ate it, I'd quip, "I don't know why I'm putting this in my mouth. I should just apply it directly to my hips." *Ha ha ha.* Now that joke makes me feel sick. All the jokes about weight and dieting do. My poor hips! My poor butt! My poor body. My poor psyche. What I've put myself through, on so many levels.

~~~

Speaking of humor…I wanted to write this as a funny piece. I tried and tried, and then I realized I don't think there's anything funny about it. Instead, I decided to let myself be angry and sad. And you know what? It feels as if a weight is beginning to be lifted off of me.

PART 2

The Boys of My
(Second) Youth

The Joy of (Not) Skiing

1.

February 1979

I'm a ball of nerves when I tag along with a relative a year older than me for a day-trip on the slopes with her high school ski club. I'm terrified of skiing, which I've never done before. But as a lowly eighth-grader, I'm excited to be invited along to do something with older kids, so I can observe them and learn how to seem cool.

On the bus ride to a mountain in northern New Jersey, I hear Dan Hill's *Sometimes When We Touch* coming from someone's bright yellow hand-held transistor A.M. radio and I think I'm going to barf—*god, that song is embarrassing*—but then I notice a cute boy and pretty girl across the aisle singing along quietly and holding hands in a very particular way, their fingers interlaced, and I decide that I want *that* when I'm old enough—a boyfriend to interlace my fingers with.

Another thing I must have: a collection of beat-up chairlift tickets from prior trips hanging from my jacket zipper, like so many of the kids have—a symbol of both privilege and casual sportiness that eludes me, a klutz from a humble background. Though I haven't tried it yet, it's difficult for me to imagine skiing frequently enough to accrue a collection of tickets.

The closer we get to the mountain, the more nervous I become. I'm not even vaguely inclined toward sports, or anything that requires significant coordination—always among the last picked in gym class, always falling down the same short flight of stairs in my own house. I figure that at least the teachers leading the trip will help me.

But when we get to the mountain, the teachers tell us we're on our own. "Go have fun!" I literally tremble. With absolutely no idea where to begin, I follow the other kids who don't have their own skis to the area where you rent them. Then I follow some of them to a hill where an instructor is talking about how to "snow plow," *verb*, by pointing the tips of your skis inward, forming the shape of a slice of pizza.

The next thing I know, I'm up in the sky on a chairlift, all by myself. The person operating the lift forgot to put down the bar meant to secure me in my seat, and I can't reach it myself, making the whole gambit even more precarious. Up in the air, I watch people quickly gliding off the lift when they get to the top, and realize I don't know how to do what they're doing. The lift pauses for a minute, and I'm just hanging there, swinging slightly with the rhythm of all the other chairs bobbing from a cord in the sky. My heart pounds. *How will I get off this thing? How will I do it quickly enough that the next person behind me doesn't trample me?*

I try looking down and am glad to see I'm not *too*, too far from the ground—not as far from the ground as I'd been a few minutes before. We're just a short distance from the sloped mound of snow you're supposed to disembark on. One minute I'm looking down and imagining what it would feel like if I fell. The next, I am in fact tumbling from the lift. I crash land, hard, crying on impact. Suddenly there are so many people running toward me, and I'm mortified.

"Are you okay?"

"Don't move! Stay still."

"We need to make sure you haven't broken anything, and don't have a concussion."

Miraculously, I'm unscathed, although a little achy. The only thing broken is the binding on one of my rented skis. I'm worried I'll have to pay for it, but the resort lets it slide.

I spend the rest of the day drinking cocoa in the lodge by myself, counting the minutes until we can return home. On the bus, everyone asks if I'm alright, and I'm so embarrassed. One girl says, "Next time, you should sign up for lessons before getting on a lift!"

I'm not so sure there'll be a next time.

2.

Winter 1992

My first husband, Elliott, loves to ski. Each winter, from the time we meet in the mid '80s he prays I will miraculously fall in love with skiing, too, and stop being so clumsy at it, while I pray he'll miraculously forget the sport exists altogether.

I'm not at all direct about my lack of interest, for the same reason I'm not vocal about most things I'd prefer not to do: I believe I'm *supposed to* feel differently. As a general rule, any time I have an instinct that runs counter to most other people's instincts, I almost instantly try to override it. I want to be perceived as up for anything, and low-maintenance! Like the kind of effortlessly sporty person who always has one of those old, beat-up chairlift tickets hanging from her zipper.

And so, a couple of times each year I find myself reluctantly stuffing weekend bags with mismatched, borrowed ski garb, hauling those bags from the apartment to the car and, a few hours later, from the car to a hotel room in some snowy town north of our Long Island home. This time it's South Fallsburg, in the southern Catskills.

I'm particularly resistant to this trip after another chairlift calamity the year before, when we'd gone to a mountain in Vermont with a bunch of friends. I'd accidentally stayed on the chairlift after the rest of my beginner class (filled mostly with children) knew to get off at the midway point, and found myself utterly terrified at the top of a "black diamond"—typically the steepest and most treacherous trail at any ski area. Our instructor saw what happened and stayed on, too. He found me at the top, then had me hold onto his shoulders as he walked us both down the mountain, backwards. I nearly died from the annoyed and pitied looks other skiers shot at me.

I'd secretly sworn off skiing at the end of that last trip. But I lost the nerve to stick to that when winter rolled around again, and Elliott started planning this trip to the Catskills.

So, here I am again. I don't want to do this, but more than that, I don't want to *say* I don't. The minute I arrive, Friday evening, I resort to Creative Visualization, envisioning lousy weather. Somehow it works; buckets of dense mountain rain come pouring down after dinner. I flick on the weather channel to make sure I'm not hallucinating. The local forecaster is nearly as surprised as I am. I could very well be off the hook.

"I'm sorry, Elliott," I say, although I'm only slightly remorseful about having psychically willed away his weekend pleasure. "Maybe we'll go skiing out west for a whole week next winter," I offer cheerfully. Yes, and maybe we'll go to Pluto the winter after that.

But my luck, Saturday morning it's sunny—and cold. There's no avoiding it. Ski Ordeal '92 is here.

At breakfast, I hear a woman who looks like an avid skier tell a friend she wouldn't dare ski on a cold morning like this one, after a night of hard rain. I tuck this information away in my Last Resorts file as my stomach nervously kicks up a forkful of instant oatmeal.

We shuttle to the mountain and begin the whole annoying business of getting set up: filling out a rental form that looks like a tax return and asks nervy weight and height questions; waiting on one long line after another, for boots, then skis, then poles; figuring out how to carry the skis and poles the cool way and how to click the boots into the bindings without falling over every time. Inside, I'm wondering why this process alone doesn't scare more people away; outside, I am the smiling, willing ski partner Elliott is wishing for.

"Sit now!" Elliott shouts as the chairlift scoops us up. Before we got on, Elliott asked the man in the booth to warn the guy at the landing to stop the lift when our chair arrived. I cringe at the thought of what chairlift man #1 has probably radioed to chairlift man #2: "Let the nervous wreck and her overprotective husband off easy."

But I'm touched that Elliott wants to make this easier for me, and so I want to find it in my heart to stay positive, just for him.

My attitude adjustment has a short slope-life, though. I'm weaving my way down the novice trail in wide, unsteady S's when I spot the first huge ice patch. Seeing no way around it, I stop short, shifting my weight up the mountain—okay, fine, *bunny hill*—and freeze in place. What if it's icy all the way down? I suddenly forget how to move, let alone ski.

"What happened?" Elliott calls up the slope, his tone caught somewhere between concern and disappointment. I wait a few minutes to speak, because I'm trying not to cry. But as soon as I open my mouth to explain, the waterworks start. I don't want to be afraid. I want to be a good sport. I want to tell people I like skiing instead of becoming a grouch at the mere mention of the word. After all, skiing is great fun! Everybody knows that! Why, after seven winters and even more ski outings with Elliott, have I never been able to truly convince myself of that? Or learn to ski? Today, the ice patches aren't helping.

I pull myself together and Elliott talks me through a slow procession down the rest of the relatively shallow incline, and it's not as bad as I thought. At the bottom, I consider calling it a day, but we've only been there twenty-five minutes, which means the $36 lift ticket and rental fee breaks down to more than $1 per minute. For some reason I decide that leaving will not be justified until I get the rate down to at least 50 cents.

So, up we go again, and again and again. I tense up at the same points, where the frozen ground glistens. At the end of each ten-minute run, Elliott praises my improvement and beams with pride while I try to calculate the current cost-per-minute ratio. How much longer before I can quit without that sinking, giving-up feeling?

Just when I've gotten comfortable with the novice slope, Elliott suggests we advance to the next level. I can't speak again—I'm fighting back more tears. I'm scared, I can't feel my toes, but above all, I don't know how much longer I can fake enthusiasm, especially on a more challenging slope. (I don't yet know this is a metaphor for where I'm at in our marriage.)

I don't want to let Elliott down. But do I have to like everything he does? I begin to realize that's not always possible. Apparently, so does Elliott.

"How about you go into the lodge and get warmed up while I ski that other trail and you watch me through the window?" he suggests.

It sounds too easy. But something tells me Plan B would make Elliott happier than dragging his reluctant, unathletic wife down a more difficult trail.

"Alright, go ahead, twist my arm."

I settle into a booth with a full view of the mountain's most difficult slope and carefully sip the cup of hot chocolate I've hardly earned. Each time I see the fluffy red down jacket and the big smile approach the bottom, I can't help but smile too. I cheer out loud for Elliott and forget about ice patches and frozen toes and chairlifts, and even spring and summer.

It turns out to be our last ski trip together. Also, our last winter. Our last everything. I'm a couple of months shy of 27 when I move out. As I do, I swear off skiing *forever*.

3.

Winter 2002

You know..."forever" is an awfully long time.

Did I ski again? Reader, I skied again—once more, to try and keep a man happy. (I do not recommend this approach to relationship sustainment. *Do not try this at home.* Or at a ski resort.)

That's right, nine years after the end of my marriage, at 36 years of age, I am back on my bullshit, doing a thing I hate to please someone I like—in this case Zach, a man younger than me by six years.

Incidentally, in the intervening years, I had done plenty of other things I hated because I thought they would make a man like me, including but not limited to: spending my birthday helping one boyfriend paint his apartment; camping and hiking [way beyond my skill level] in the high peaks of the Adirondacks and Catskills in treacherous weather, in one case, the day after a hurricane that had caused avalanches; becoming a gossip columnist so that I had a legitimate reason to stay out late in nightclubs with a paparazzo I was dating; "learning" to play poker [I had a mental block when it came to card games, not unlike the one I had around skiing—I could never seem to improve] so that I could join a weekly game with cute guys who worked in film; attending AA meetings with three different men, standing by them no matter how many times they fell off the wagon—including one man who cheated on me prolifically.

When I tell the story of Zach and me, I refer to him as "my 9/11 boyfriend," someone I met in the throes of post-terror-attack anxiety and loneliness, at a vigil in Union Square a few days after the towers came down.

Zach is too young for me, not so much chronologically as emotionally. Even at 30, he is in many ways still a boy, living half the year traveling in a van with his dog. In a key way, though, Zach is a better choice than prior boyfriends: he is sweet and kind. I am being treated by a therapist who is helping me overcome my long-standing allergy to nice men, and so in that way, choosing Zach is a sign of progress.

Zach works six days a week, and on the seventh, just like god, he rests. And by "rest," I mean he goes skiing on Tuesdays at Hunter Mountain. Yes, that's right:

skiing is now a weekly affair for me! The person who had sworn off skiing forever. I do not suggest to Zach any alternative activities that I might enjoy on a Tuesday, or ever—although I do once bring him to an experimental dance performance a musician friend has written the score for. When he invites me, I do not state, accurately, "No thank you, I do not like to ski." There is a man to be held onto—a younger, attractive man, which means I have limited time before he will naturally move onto someone younger than me—and so I do what I have always done: pretend, enthusiastically.

No matter how many times I go skiing with Zach, no matter how many runs down the bunny hill he takes alongside me, coaching me, shouting, "Make wide S's and you won't fall!" I do *not* get any better at it. I miserably spend every Tuesday with Zach at Hunter, mostly killing time in Hunter's beginner school with a bunch of 10-year-olds while he cruises down black diamonds. This goes on for the greater part of two winters, until the inevitable comes to pass, and Zach finds someone younger, and no doubt sportier than me.

4.

October 2003

The following fall I meet my husband, Brian. I've now been through four years of therapy with a crackerjack shrink, who's been encouraging me to unlearn pretending to be who I'm not. On an early date, Brian tells me the story of his most recent ski trip—during which a close friend collided with a tree, breaking his neck and a few limbs. "Yeah, stories like that are part of why I don't ski," I reply. "Also, I just don't like it."

We've been happily married for seventeen years, so far. He has skied a few times since we met. But I have never skied with him. I've assured him I never will.

Hurricane Tim

It was a big deal when I told my two sets of parents that on Yom Kippur, instead of attending either of their two synagogues, I'd be hiking and camping in "the sanctuary of the woods." It was the fall of 1999, and I was turning 34—certainly old enough to make my own decisions with regard to religious observance. My two sets of parents weren't too happy about it. They thought I was "rebelling," but that wasn't at all the case. It wasn't something I was doing *to them*, it was something I was doing *for me*.

From the time I was 11 I'd had issues with the divisions religion could cause, and all the violence committed in the name of god. I'd recoiled in Hebrew school when teachers would express anti-Palestinian sentiments, and was told that to question or challenge that was to be a self-hating Jew. But it sounded to me like bigotry, and didn't jibe with the golden rule or other tenets of Judaism I'd been taught. Also, as with just about all religions, there were sexist aspects to Jewish law that sat at odds with my nascent feminism. In my mid-thirties, it felt like high time I retreat from this thing that had troubled me, and was so deeply enmeshed through every layer of my existence that I couldn't get any perspective on it.

Calling the Adirondacks "the sanctuary of the woods" was spin, not just for them, but for me. I half-believed myself when I said that the object of my trip was some sort of spiritual communing with nature to soothe my troubled soul. At a deep level, though, I knew there was going to be nothing soothing about this weekend adventure. I was going with Tim, an emotionally unreachable man ripped straight from the pages of Pam Houston's *Cowboys Are My Weakness*, whom I'd been seeing on and off for close to three years. And we were hanging by a thread.

∞

Two and a half years before, in January 1997, a few months after I'd turned 31, Tim appeared as if out of nowhere. The night I met him, I almost hadn't gone out. A jazz singer I liked and hoped to interview for a profile was performing at a bar called Arlene's Grocery on the Lower East Side. But I was feeling down, and resistant to braving the cold. I knew some of why I felt down was that in the midst of a six-month dry spell in my dating life, I was lonely; ironically, in winter, when you most need to seek out others' company, you are least inclined to leave the house to do so. Somehow, as if some external force was leading me, I pushed myself out the door.

Tim and I were the only two people in the audience. It was a wintry weeknight, and the clientele at Arlene's tended to be more into rock than jazz. I'd spotted him when I walked in—a slight guy in worn chinos and a plaid shirt, his shaggy brown hair framing a striking, chiseled face. "He's like a brunette Gary from *thirtysomething*," I would tell a friend the next day. I was seated at a table far from his, and minutes after I felt his piercing blue eyes on me, he moved in my direction with his half-finished pint.

The main reason I ventured out that night was to meet the singer and set up an interview. But once male attention was on the table, I forgot my intentions. I also forgot my manners, largely ignoring the singer I'd come to hear as I joined Tim in conversation.

Tim had the gift of gab, peppering me with questions and telling me all about himself, at a mile a minute. He was a science teacher, he told me. When I said I was a writer, he started talking books—turned out he was a reader, too. *Not bad,* I thought. He talked in a hyper-animated way that struck me as slightly off, as if he'd just emerged from the desert and hadn't spoken to another human in years. He seemed like one of those New York City lonely people, who despite being surround-ed, wall-to-wall, by humans, rarely interacted with them. *Why on earth does this cute, smart guy seem so intensely lonely?* I wondered. Only in hindsight would I recognize it as a red flag.

"Have you read *The English Patient?*" he asked. I hadn't. He had, and was plan-ning to see the movie that weekend. "Would you like to join me?"

Before the movie he made me dinner at his place, a crammed, claustrophobic two-room studio in a run-down tenement on the Lower East Side. Another red flag: Tim owned only one plate. We shared it that first night, and many others, after that.

∞

Having been on a few prior hiking and camping trips with Tim, I knew that this one, to the Adirondacks, would be challenging. It had become an established part of the deal that these endeavors were always at a level way more difficult for me than for him. These were Tim's adventures. I was always "welcome to join" him, even though we traveled in my car. In the fall of 1997, we'd camped in a different area of the Adiron-dacks, and in 1998, we'd spent a weekend backpacking through three Catskill peaks.

The last day of that Catskills trip, we descended in a major thunderstorm, and the path was treacherous. As we approached the last quarter mile of our hike out, I slipped on a wet tree root and pitched forward, my 25-pound backpack intensifying the impact when my forehead made contact with stone. The pain was instant, but it was mitigated significantly by how concerned Tim seemed. Tired of being patient with my slower pace, he'd gotten a bit ahead of me. But when he heard me fall and scream, he came running back.

"Are you okay?" he asked, helping me up, then embracing me more warmly than he ever had before. I'd been trying not to cry, but the hug cracked me open. I melted into him, enjoying a taste of what I'd been holding on for, all that time. (Some feminist I was.) When we got to our nearby cabin, he applied ice to the egg-sized welt on my head and was tender toward me.

∽

This trip, there was an added danger factor: the week leading up to our outing, a major hurricane had ripped through the Northeast. I caught something on the news, then read in the paper about how it had devastated many Adirondack trails. There'd been mudslides, and many trees were down, blocking major paths. I assumed we would be canceling our plan.

"Are you kidding?" Tim said. "This is great news. It means fewer other people will go. We'll have our pick of campsites!"

As the owner of the car we'd be using, I should have realized I had the power to shut our plan down. Or I could have loaned Tim my car, and let him go by himself, which he likely would have preferred. But things between us had been so rocky, I was afraid to make waves. He'd recently broken up with me for the fourth time in less than three years. Shortly afterward, he'd returned to me, and I took him back, more desperately than I ever had before, even though I was fully aware of how miserable I was with him. I was in a low place, self-esteem-wise, and work-wise—I'd been bullied by a misogynist boss into quitting my last job.

As soon as Tim was finished with work that Friday, we jumped in the car. The plan was to spend the first night at the home of his friends upstate, then leave early Saturday for "the 'Dacks" as Tim and the other initiated outdoorspeople called them. As soon as we arrived, his friend voiced his concern. "You're still going, even though the hurricane has made a mess up there?" he asked. "I've heard some of the trails are completely washed out. You might want to cancel your trip, buddy."

I took a breath and looked to Tim, hoping he would be able to recognize a voice of reason when it was coming from someone other than me. *Please cancel*, I thought. *Please cancel. Please cancel. Please cancel. Please cancel. Please cancel...* It became a mantra in my head for the long 20 seconds it took him to respond.

"No way," Tim said, with a devilish laugh. "This is going to be the best. We'll be the only ones. We'll have it all to ourselves."

Great, I thought. There'd be no one around if anything bad happened, no one to alert rescuers if we got hurt. I still could have shut the whole thing down, or taken a bus back to the city, letting Tim take my car on his own. That I didn't is a testament to how desperate I felt, how much power I'd given Tim, how oblivious to my own power I was.

∽

I've read that addiction is established through intermittent gratification. When you've been gratified by something or someone, and then the source of that gratification is withdrawn, you naturally become consumed with recapturing it.

Tim and I had interlocking addictions: he chased the fleeting gratification of being numbed by booze, cigarettes, and weed. I chased the fleeting gratification of getting Tim's attention in the rare moments he wasn't completely numbed out—or pushing me away. I lived for whatever crumbs I could get from him, any vague expression of affection. Although, increasingly the only attention he gave me was snide criticism, couched as good natured teasing.

Tim seemed incapable of drawing me close without also counteracting that in some way, to create distance. Every kind gesture was tempered with a broken promise—he wouldn't call or show up when he'd said he would—or an off-putting "joke" about the shape of my body, petite with a more than ample behind. When we began hiking together the first year we dated, he came up with another term for my backside: he called it my "third foot," because often, when descending frighteningly steep passages, I would resort to sitting and sliding at least part of the way down on my butt. "Are you just gonna hike the whole way down on your third foot?" he'd ask, dismissively.

∽

"Frighteningly steep" was pretty much the default setting for the hiking Tim and I did together, most of it far out of my league—and far outside the realm of what I would have chosen to do with my time if I weren't trying to seem like the kind of person Tim would choose. I am uncommonly clumsy. Prior to meeting Tim, I'd only engaged in hiking so tame, at so little of an incline, that it was hard to distinguish it from plain walking. I'd been to Harriman State Park with a prior boyfriend, and again with some friends, but only on short trails with the lowest grades of elevation. I'd been on short hikes up something called "Rattlesnake Hill" with a writing mentor who lived in the Adirondacks, but it was, in fact, a *hill*. I thought that was what hiking meant.

I'd also never camped out overnight before, despite having attended sleepaway camp. Every year, the nature counselor would bring each age group into the woods with tents and sleeping bags, and I was always glad that my being cast in musicals, which rehearsed on those nights, rendered me exempt. Back in my bunk, I'd count my blessings that I wasn't sleeping on the ground, fighting off insects, snakes, and wildlife.

Don't get me wrong—I enjoyed being out in nature, preferably at the beach, where I grew up. I also enjoyed being in the woods, although preferably under less death-defying conditions. Years later, I would move upstate and happily hike up and down a small mountain in town most mornings—but I'd steer clear of the steep, unwieldy scrambles over boulders in nearby mountain ranges, even though they were much easier than the scrambles over boulders in the high peaks that I'd agonize through with Tim. At my mom's apartment, I spent many summer nights sleeping out under the stars, on a chaise lounge on her small terrace overlooking the Atlantic Ocean. But I was no one's idea of an outdoorswoman. Certainly not Tim's idea of one. I was merely who was around, and I had wheels, so I was "welcome" along.

That vague offer was all it took for me to make a beeline to Paragon and Camp-moor in search of serious hiking boots, a sleeping bag and mat, a backpack, polypro-pylene and fleece clothing, and other outdoor gear. The first year I was dating Tim, when I told my parents that for my birthday I wanted money instead of any other gift so that I could stock up on gear, they looked at me as if I had grown a second head. In fact, I'd grown a whole new persona. Like that, "Outdoorsy Sari" was born—a rugged, unfussy, low-maintenance version of myself I very much wanted to believe was real. She not only eclipsed Regular Sari for a few years; she nearly got Regular Sari killed.

∝

I didn't invent Outdoorsy Sari, or go hiking and camping, solely for Tim's benefit. I also wanted to see myself in a more rugged light. Like Ralph Lauren (nee Lifschitz), and so many other Jews before me, I wanted to be accepted into a cool, anti-chic milieu I'd never been exposed to in my suburban Jewish world.

When I heard my WASPy writing mentor, or Tim, toss off names of Adirondack and Catskill peaks they'd "bagged," I wanted to speak their vernacular. I wanted en-trée into their club. I felt like the stereotypical clumsy, fearful, frail, pale Jewess, and I eagerly wanted to transcend that. See, I didn't just become Outdoorsy Sari because I aspired to be with Tim; to a degree, I aspired to be with Tim so that I could *become* Outdoorsy Sari.

Once I began hiking and camping with Tim, I took pride in casually tossing off the names of the peaks I'd "bagged," too (for the record, I've got six peaks in the Ad-irondacks, and five in the Catskills), along with naming from rote the various kinds and brands of gear. It made me feel tough and sexy in a one-of-the-boys way that had previously seemed off-limits to me.

I'll admit that I also learned a lot on those adventures, and grew from them, in ways. I discovered I was much more agile and capable than I'd previously known myself to be. I figured out how to get through the hardest stretches by staying in the moment and simply putting one foot in front of the other. At the end of each backpacking trip, I felt surprisingly strong, accomplished, empowered. Still, I didn't so much enjoy those times in the woods with Tim as I endured them.

I always approached adventures with Tim with a mix of excitement and dread, a balance that had shifted more toward dread the longer we were together. A nice thing about hiking and camping with him was that it usually occurred when he was going through a dry period, drinking-wise. Tim wasn't a falling-down drunk like another man I'd dated; he was a mean drunk, though, throwing out nasty quips about whoever was around him, which was often only me. (Mystery solved: *this* was why he was lonely.) That's not to say that when he wasn't drinking he was exactly *nice*. He was still rarely warm, but at least his nastiness in those sober times was tempered.

The dread I experienced before camping trips with Tim was about wondering whether the person sharing a tent with me would be relatively kind, and also about my fears as a newbie hiker traveling with someone much more experienced and naturally athletic than me. Tim was never willing to alter our course to take into consideration my level of ability, or lack thereof.

I also wasn't keen on sleeping out in the cold. Even on unseasonably warm fall days, the temperature in the mountains would drop drastically after sundown. The only good thing about that was it meant Tim would most likely be especially snuggly in our tent. Oh, the irony of me shivering through the night, sometimes even risking frostbite, for just a little bit of warmth from a cold man.

∝

The ground was soaking wet when we arrived in the area of the Adirondacks where we would be hiking and camping, and the sky threatened more rain. We parked the car and hiked a marshy path until the sky opened up. Fortunately there was a big lean-to nearby, and we made a beeline for it. There was a park ranger there, and he was surprised to see us.

"You sure you're up for hiking in this?" he asked, gesturing to the area around us. "This place got hit pretty hard by the hurricane. Lots of trees down, and it's pretty slippery."

In my head, I thought: *Please listen to the ranger. Let's turn around and go home.* But I couldn't find the courage to say those words out loud.

"No, we're good," Tim said, and my stomach grew a knot.

∝

When the rain let up, we set out again. I took a deep breath, and went into being-in-the-moment mode, negotiating one step at a time. We'd be taking the Gothics Loop Trail over three peaks, one per day—Upper Wolf Jaw, Armstrong, and Gothics—setting up camp in a different spot each night.

As we began to ascend Upper Wolf Jaw, I slipped on a wet tree root, falling in such a way that I badly bruised my left shin. I cried on impact, as I tend to. Tim was a bit ahead of me, and I called out to him. "Tim, I fell!" When he didn't respond, I called again, this time with more alarm in my voice. I was so afraid he'd gotten far enough away to lose me. I had a shitty Nokia cell phone, but there was no cell service. I called out a third time, "Tim, I fell, and I'm scared! Where are you?" Now I was crying hysterically. Three minutes later, Tim was running toward me. I was on the ground, my heavy pack by my side, holding my shin.

"What's the problem?" he asked, coldly.

"I fell, and I hurt my shin, and I'm so scared. I don't know if this is safe."

That's when Tim lost it. He began jumping up and down and screaming, "This is joyful for me! Why can't you be joyful!" He sounded anything but joyful, by the way. He sounded like an overgrown toddler having a tantrum.

This set the tone for the rest of the weekend. Tim was annoyed by my presence, by the sound of my voice, by my every need, by the difference in our abilities. Whether we were hiking or cooking or setting up camp or sleeping, he gave me the silent treatment. I followed him quietly from place-to-place, counting the hours, looking forward to our three-day trip being over. With the ground still saturated, it was slippery and dicey at every turn. And I was terrified by what I'd been told about the third peak we'd be ascending, Gothics, which was bald at the top.

∽

I woke up in a panic the third morning, knowing that Gothics Mountain was ahead of me. It was either go over that dreaded peak, or go in reverse, back over the other two peaks we'd already perilously ascended and descended, and there wasn't enough time for that. I had no choice but to face the challenge.

The closer we got to the top, the scarier it became. The mountain was literally bald. And steep. The terrain was like nothing I'd ever seen before—like being on another planet. For much of the way, there was nothing to grab onto. At a certain point, I had to stop standing upright because I was sure I was going to fall to my death. If I sneezed and lost my balance, that was it.

I got down on my hands and knees and prayed. That's right; on Yom Kippur I prayed to the god I wasn't sure existed, the one I'd left behind in synagogue. I prayed and bargained for my life. What did I need to do to get myself inscribed in the Book of Life? To survive "bagging" this peak? Was god punishing me for not attending synagogue? For having issues with religion? For leaving my suburban first marriage for a less conventional life? It would be many years before I realized that no one was punishing me but *me*.

Tim had gone ahead—way ahead—again. I was all alone with a heavy pack on my back, and in a state of terror. When I got a little further up, I was happy to spot a cable affixed to the mountain face, which I could grab onto and use to pull myself to the top.

When I finally got there, Tim was waiting for me. "You made it," he said. "You didn't know you could do that, did you?" He was a bit warmer, but not by much. We stopped long enough to eat lunch. Then we descended, made it to the parking lot, and drove the five hours back to the city, mostly in silence.

∝ɔ

It was in this painful phase of my relationship with Tim that I made a fateful phone call. To a 1-900-phone-psychic.

I've done a lot of embarrassing things in my life, and calling a phone psychic is right up there at the top of the list. I've also handed over my hard-earned cash to more than my share of in-person psychics, witches, astrologers, carvers of "magical" candles, and other practitioners of the esoteric arts—which, I'll admit, is a little weird for a person who rejects religion on the grounds that, among other issues, it seems like a bunch of unfounded hocus pocus. But there's something extra sketchy and dubious about a pay-per-minute seer you find through a late-night infomercial while watching *thirtysomething* reruns, when you can't sleep because your whole life is out of whack.

When I made the call—not my first, mind you—I knew it was a sad and desperate act, but I felt pretty sad and desperate, and didn't have much shame left. It was the late '90s, and I was kind of a mess. In my mid-thirties, I was struggling to find enough freelance writing work after a traumatic ending to my last job. I was divorced and single, and I was convinced that was inherently bad. Like most of my generation, I'd been raised in a culture that centered marriage, which turned my struggle to find *the one* before I aged out of the possibility of childbearing into the central problem of my existence.

Looking back at who I was choosing in those days, it occurs to me that maybe I didn't really *want* to settle down just yet. Otherwise, what was I doing dating one emotionally unavailable, non-committal, temperamental man after another? At that early stage in my becoming a feminist, I think on some level I only knew how to maintain a level of independence with men who were even more resistant to commitment than I was. Whatever it was I was doing, at the time, I couldn't figure it out. All

I knew was that the men I was going out with were withholding and difficult to hang onto, and that for some inexplicable reason I wanted to hang onto them. Instead of seeing their inconsistent responses to me as a sign that I should look for someone actually available and interested, I believed it was a problem I could solve by becoming someone else—someone they would more likely be interested in.

Oh, how many ways I've repackaged myself to appeal to different men! I'm not sure where I learned it, but being something of a chameleon in relationships had actually been my standard modus operandi long before I transformed myself into Outdoorsy Sari for Tim and other men—from the time I started interacting with boys as a tween. When my junior high crush told me he hated the color green—one of my favorite colors—I lied and said I hated it too, then promptly threw my favorite green gingham shirt in the garbage. When my first husband and subsequent men in my life wanted to take me skiing, instead of saying, "I'm sorry, but skiing terrifies me and also I've tried it enough times to know I don't like it," I went along and endured miserable, cold hours upon hours in beginner school.

∽

It's a wonder I made the call that night, after prior calls to the 1-900 number had been so disappointing—usually women "psychics" on the other end with exaggerated, seemingly fake Southern or Midwestern accents, throwing out wild guesses about my future based on whatever information I gave them. I'd try to bend my mind to believe what they were saying could be real, but it was always a stretch, and always a letdown. After each reading—and after seeing the charges on my credit card—I'd swear off 1-900 calls forever.

But then, after three miserable years on-and-off with Tim, I arrived at a dark, lonely place. I felt hopeless about the future not only with him, but in general. I didn't have a therapist—couldn't afford one, and even if I could, I was too emotionally exhausted to consider unspooling my whole backstory again for a new one—and didn't want my friends and family to know how sad and lonely I was. So I picked up the phone and dialed.

This time a man answered. "How can I help you this evening?"

"Well," I said, "I wonder if you see things working out between me and this guy I'm dating. Or, if I end it, whether you see someone else on the horizon for me."

"I'm hearing you say you're thinking of ending things with him," he said. "What's that about?" I recognized this as the psychological "mirroring" prior therapists had engaged in with me. Was this guy a psychic or a shrink?

"I kind of want to break up with him," I admitted. "I mean, it's definitely not working out. But what if I give up, before I've tried *everything*? Or, what if I give up and don't find anyone else? Or—what if I *do* find someone else, but run into the same problems? Maybe all relationships are hard. Maybe all guys are bad, and every single one that I meet won't be attentive or kind enough. Maybe I should just make it work with this guy. I don't know..."

I told him about the backpacking trip we'd just returned from—about all the backpacking trips—and about how, every time I was sure Tim just didn't like me, and it was over, he'd suddenly be warm and attentive. But it never lasted.

"Okay, I'm going to share with you my key to relationships," the phone psychic said. "Get a pen and paper, because I think you should write this down."

I grabbed a pen and paper.

"It's really simple, but a lot of people don't realize it. You ready?"

I was.

"Okay. Here it is: Not everyone is going to 'get' you. Not everyone is *supposed to* get you. That's just how it is. When you're interested in someone and not getting back what you're giving, stop for a minute and say to yourself, 'Well, this person just doesn't get me. And that's okay.' And then just let them go, so you can find someone who *does* get you. It's the only way to find a person you can be happy with. Someone you get, who gets you."

It sounded ridiculously simple.

"That's *it?*" I said.

"That's it."

I thought for a second about what he'd said, and realized that as simple as it sounded, the concept was also utterly foreign to me. Recalibrating myself to appeal to someone who had the power to choose or reject me was all I knew how to do in relationships.

"Write these words down," he said, "and put them somewhere that you'll see them: 'Not everyone is going to *get* me, and that is okay. Not everyone is supposed to get me. When someone shows that they don't get me, I accept it, then move on to free myself up for someone who will.'"

As I wrote the words down, even though on a fundamental level they made so much sense, I found I had to fight my resistance to them. I put the piece of paper in my top desk drawer, where I could easily see it. To my surprise, the more I read those words, the more they sank in.

Still, it would take me a long time to fully integrate the concept. I still need to remind myself of it today, when I meet new people and friendships don't quite take off. My initial instinct is to try and become someone else, a version of me they'd likely prefer, at least in my mind. Then I think of my conversation with the 1-900-phone-psychic—my last of those—and remember to just be myself and let the chips fall where they may. *Not every potential friend will* get *me. And that's okay. Not everyone is supposed to get me.* (I also stop and wonder each time, whether the man I spoke with was disgraced journalist Stephen Glass, who admitted to falsifying most of his *Harper's* story about working for a phone-psychic outfit in the late '90s.)

∞

It would take a few more months after the weekend in the Adirondacks before I found the nerve to say goodbye to Tim. I thought I'd never hear from him again, but then, years later, he reached out a few times. In each interaction, he exhibited signs of what appeared, unquestionably, to be mental illness—not new behaviors, but old ones, now more exaggerated and obvious. Or, who knows, maybe exactly the same as before, except I can see more clearly now.

Over lunch one day, he mused aloud, "I wonder why I pushed *so-and-so* away," and also *so-and-so*, and *so-and-so*, and *so-and-so*. "Why do I push people away?" The unasked but implied additional question was why did he push *me* away, again and again, most perplexingly almost immediately after he drew me in close. Now I know the answer: the guy is unwell. Pushing people away *is what he does*. He wasn't just doing it *to me*. (Perhaps that's why he had in his possession only one dinner plate?) The whole time, I'd been taking someone else's fucked up psychology personally, and tailoring a version of myself to accommodate it.

A lot of other questions went unasked over lunch that day. Tim was utterly incurious about my life, my work, my marriage. It was a relief not to really care, or to have even the slightest inkling that I should try to change that.

The Sweet Smell of Excess

Al-Anon is incredibly helpful for many people, but for me it sucked. If I hadn't been too broke for therapy, I'd never have taken a friend's advice to attend those meetings. I found them to be worse than the AA meetings I'd been to over the years in support of my string of actively alcoholic boyfriends—three, if you're keeping count. The AA people, when they finally hit bottom, were brave, copped to shit, and took responsibility for all the bad choices they'd made when they were drinking. The "Al-Anonics" seemed victimy and whiny. Everything was someone else's fault.

Many of the people in Al-Anon were "addict addicts," who needed others in the worst possible way and yet would counterintuitively go for only the most unavailable, most uninterested, meanest people around. I, of course, could not yet see myself that way.

Joey, my friend in AA, suggested I try his meetings instead.

"I'm not an alcoholic," I pointed out.

"Here's what you do," he said. "Lock yourself in a room with a case of Jack Daniels and don't come out until it's all gone. Then go directly to AA."

I thought about it. While I was at it, I might try writing, too. I'd always wanted to try writing under the influence; I imagined it would free me from my arresting good-girl inhibitions.

I couldn't, though. I'd sworn off drinking nearly four years before, ostensibly for holistic health reasons. But also for a guy named Matt. I kept my vow of sobriety as I moved on to Tim, and then to Chris.

How vital I imagined I was to another's well-being. What power I could have. All while appearing saintly and superior. Trade that in for the occasional glass of wine? No way. This was much more intoxicating.

Except the buzz never lasted long. In a matter of time, each boyfriend would return to drinking, and I'd feel like a failure for my inability to prevent that. The relationship would bust apart—sometimes for a while, sometimes for good.

∽

Chris wasn't new to me. We'd known each other a long time. He and I went back and forth a few times over many years. Of all my men, Chris had the hardest time staying sober, and I had the hardest time walking away from him. A handsome artist, he was always surrounded by women and had difficulty being faithful.

I could have avoided my last go-round with him, beginning in the fall of 2000, when I was 35. It had been five years since I'd seen him, and in my mind, whatever appeal he possessed—the powerful sway he'd once held over me—was long gone. I thought I'd finally learned my lesson. But it turned out I had overestimated my recovery from that particular addiction.

∝

We made plans on the phone to meet at his studio space in Chinatown. His deep baritone had previously seduced me, but now it came with the memory of the way he'd get by the end of most nights—the verbal nastiness followed by incoherence, followed by his nodding off midsentence after so many beers and vodka shots. Not to mention the memory of his hitting me, and shaking me, hard, while gripping my neck one time, my shoulders another. It was hard to believe I ever wanted to be anywhere near that.

I didn't even think of the sex, the amazing sex. That always eventually fell by the wayside anyway. Every time we'd get together again, the sex would be a regular feature for a while, and it would be *good*. He knew how to make me feel just the right combination of beautiful, special, sexy—even if I saw myself as a mousy good girl. Probably *because* I was a mousy good girl. He had a full retinue of insecure girls just like me. But once the sex wasn't new anymore, his drinking would pick up. He'd lose interest and eventually switch his focus to another fawning fan of his artwork, another mousy good girl desperate to catch a glimpse of her inner sexpot in the mirror of Chris's flattering attentions, and his paintings of me.

I was getting together with Chris that night, I honestly believed, to clear the air after five years of silence following a fight we'd had. I'd gotten sick of his shit and moved on to someone else, and he had hung up on me. I figured enough time had passed. Enough with the cold war already.

Okay, maybe I was also interested in trying on—and showing off—the mantle of just how over him I was. I was on the rebound from a relationship with *another* active alcoholic—one not nearly as far gone as Chris.

∝

When I walked into the studio, the attraction/repulsion ratio shifted the tiniest bit. I was put off by the sight of the forty-ounce Budweiser Chris swigged. The man was

37 now. He came from Upper East Side affluence. Time to stop posing as a kid from the streets of Chicago, where he went to college. Realizing he was still stuck in that groove made me feel sorry for him. But in that detail alone—the feeling sorry for him—there was danger for me. Somehow, somewhere along the way, brokenness in men had become my kink.

He smiled the warmest, most welcoming smile when I entered. It was probably the nicest reception I'd gotten from him in the many years I'd known him. I felt something inside me, my resolve maybe, loosen and resettle at a slightly different angle.

Remarkably, despite his continued drinking, Chris looked good. He still had some of his summer tan. He was fit—an indication that he was likely still rising at five most mornings to get on his exercise bike and sweat out the rest of the booze from the night before. He still wore his dirty blonde hair long. It swung back and forth each time he rocked on his feet to the music he was listening to as he painted. He caught my eye, once, twice, again, again, smiling warmly each time, and that's when I started to feel it: *the love*. In that moment I was of the opinion that it was a *friendly love*, the innocent love of acceptance and mutual forgiveness between old friends.

One potent ingredient of that love was pity. Unfortunately, that night I didn't recognize what a slippery slope that presented for me. It was a key component of my attachment to one "beautiful mess" after another, this feeling sorry for them. It nudged me to absolve them of all responsibility and opened the door for me to wrest control—a subtle, unspoken transaction. My internal superhero emerged from the shadows to save them, whether or not they wished to be saved. Often they stated their preference not to be, which had the opposite of the desired effect: I only became more insistent.

Even though I was feeling warmly toward Chris at his studio, I still thought I was safe. But then we went—where else?—uptown to a bar in Hell's Kitchen, his neighborhood. I was not drinking, a habit I still maintained post-Tim. I'd assigned myself the role of "the nondrinker girlfriend to drinker boyfriends," apparently even when I no longer had a boyfriend.

At the bar, Chris downed many glasses of house white. He said he'd recently replaced vodka with wine, to good effect—it didn't get him completely blotto. That was something he'd figured out after an unsuccessful stint in rehab.

Chris told me about the ex-girlfriend he'd been involved with when he went to rehab—Sheila, a drug and alcohol counselor who had driven him to the rehab facility in the lush hills of the Hudson Valley and then dutifully showed up to get him at the end of his much abbreviated stay with the forty-ounce bottle of Budweiser he'd requested. As he relayed this story, Chris became visibly and audibly tipsy. He pronounced a few words just slightly incorrectly. His eyelids got heavier. As he got drunker, I got illogically, emotionally intoxicated myself—most likely a by-product of my competitive feelings toward Sheila. *She brought him beer after his time in rehab? Amateur!* I could do so much better. I could really save him, cure him of his addiction, given the chance. A tragic, codependent drug and alcohol counselor was no match for me and my virtue, my selfless love.

Chris must have noticed this shift taking place in me, because he made his move. He took hold of my hand across the table. He gave me another of those smiles, and then we went back to his apartment.

What was one night for old time's sake?

∝

In the morning, Chris's stale white-wine breath filled the room and turned my stomach. I found the presence of mind to tell him (and myself) that more of this kind of thing would be a bad idea, especially if he was still drinking. He looked wounded, and as flattering as I found that, I was pretty resolved.

Whew, I thought when I left. *Dodged that bullet.*

But days later he did what I always thought I'd hoped he'd do: He begged.

"I need to do this—I need to get sober for you," he pleaded, and I was nauseated.

"But they say it never works when you get sober *for* someone," I reasoned. I also instinctively knew that he wasn't ready, and I doubted he ever would be. There were too many other women around him who were eager to make transactions similar to mine, to let him do whatever he wanted in exchange for his making them feel important and sexy and powerful, too.

"Please?" He was serious. Out of my mouth came the word "yes."

"And promise you won't leave me if I fall off the wagon? Promise you'll stick around and help me back on?" What he was requesting was the opposite of the much advised "tough love." But somehow, I agreed.

Things were great for a few weeks. Chris was eager to try, and he replaced his fixation on alcohol with a fixation on me. He painted my portrait, wrote love letters thanking me for being the only one courageous enough to insist he stop drinking. It probably didn't hurt that we were conducting our relationship long-distance while I was taking a break from the city and living upstate—intermittent absence naturally making things more exciting.

We devised a system of writing to each other in cheap pocket notebooks when we were apart. Chris didn't have a cell phone or email, or even a computer, and it was really expensive to keep refilling this MCI card that I had, which we used for speaking to each other on the phone. So we'd each write to the other in one of the notebooks while we were apart, and then swap books every time we got together. I found the whole thing romantic and, well, intoxicating.

Chris was sober, and I was higher than a kite, strung out on his intense adoration.

But right on schedule, he fell off the wagon. Hard. He'd never made it longer than a month, and we were rounding three weeks. Just in time, his last girlfriend, Sheila, the drug and alcohol counselor, sent him a Christmas card. He met her for a "friendly dinner." He called me that night and tried to hide his slurring.

"I can't talk to you like this," I said.

"But you promised you wouldn't leave me if I fell off the wagon. You said you'd stay and help me get up."

And so I did. I went to Al-Anon, bristling as people whined. When Chris stopped going to AA, I dragged him there myself, holding his hand the whole time. After meetings, he'd sneak off. He always had to be somewhere. *I knew where.* In 2000, cell phones were not yet ubiquitous; Chris called from pay phones, and the names of the bars they were situated in came up on my caller ID. Often they were bars in Sheila's neighborhood.

Chris's drinking got worse—so bad that he passed out as we were eating dinner at a restaurant in Midtown, snoring with his head on the table as people tried not to stare. A person who was not addicted to addicts would have just walked away, left him there to awaken by himself. But I was not that person.

The next day I brought it up, but Chris turned the tables on me: the problem was that I wouldn't go to bars with him. "At least Sheila will drink with me," he argued on the phone one evening. "You're. No. Fun." He had this way of punctuating his words when he was sloshed, in what seemed like a pointed effort to *not* sound that way. "If you'd just come with me to the bar . . . " He fell asleep on the phone.

∾

Okay, fine.

I'd go with him to the bar.

Maybe sitting there across from him, sober, I could appeal to him. And get him to go back to AA. And change his ways. And save his life! And save our love! Because I was just that awesome and powerful.

For a guy who clung to the mid-'90s grunge look, Chris had weird taste in bars. He liked these shiny tourist traps on the ground floors of hotels, which especially appealed to high-class sex-workers and their businessmen-in-from-out-of-town clientele. One well-dressed escort appeared with two different men in the course of an evening as I sat and watched Chris down seven pints of draft beer, each one followed by a shot of chilled Stoli.

I stared as he pounded, wondering what it felt like inside his brain. I was fascinated by the idea of being blissfully anesthetized, but not quite tempted to go there myself. I found myself torn between wanting to be "fun" like Sheila and wanting to get serious and save Chris. One minute I was laughing at his stupid jokes, positioning myself *just so*, to receive his sloppy, fragrant, vodka-tinged kisses, and the next I was crying, pleading, "When will you be ready to get sober again?"

"This is just a bender, babe," he said, holding me tightly, alcohol fumes wafting from his mouth and off his skin, enveloping me, caressing me. "I just have to go all the way through this to get to the other side. Stay with me. We'll get there."

There was more drinking, more dragging Chris to meetings, after which he would run off. Then came the confession.

"I cheated," he admitted.

I punched him in the stomach. I stopped taking his calls.

"What about me?!" he shouted into my answering machine. "I want to kill myself, and you won't even pick up the phone. *Would you even cry if I died?*"

Somehow, I took him back. Like so many active addicts, he had a split personality—when he was good, he was very, very good. Kind and attentive, and vulnerable. In those moments, we would connect in a way I'd never connected with any other man, perhaps because we were creatively aligned. And it sold me, once again, on the idea of us. In those moments, I was sure I really loved him and he loved me.

But when he was bad, he was horrid. And he had already been horrid too many times. I should've been done with him then. Or the next time he grabbed me by the shoulders and shook me, hard. Or the night he grabbed me by the throat in a bar. But it wasn't until the night he canceled our plans so that he could stay at Sheila's and drink that it was finally over for me.

After we hung up that night, I was overcome with sheer agony. I couldn't think of anything else to do than try Chris's antidote for pain. I needed to know what it was like, what he and Sheila felt when they were knocking back shots.

I took myself to Detour, the jazz bar across the street from my East Village apartment. I hadn't had a vodka drink since my 18th birthday, when one-and-a-half screwdrivers yielded bed spins and a terrible hangover. But that night I wanted vodka. I knew the smell. But now I wanted to know the taste.

There was a woman about my age singing old standards, accompanied by a guitar and bass. I ordered a vodka martini. I liked the way it looked in the glass—clean, simple, all business. After four years with not a drop of alcohol, I sat at the bar and sipped it slowly. It went right to my head. I felt like I was in a bubble. The edges on the bar sounds softened. Everything moved more slowly.

Once I finished the drink, a man at the end of the bar sent over another. I smiled at him, not feeling the least bit flirtatious or amorous. *This stuff made people want to rip each other's clothes off?* The appeal was lost on me.

Sip . . . sip . . . sip. I felt out of it. Removed. Numb.

I stumbled back across the street to my apartment. As I lay down on the couch, exhausted, I noticed my journal on the coffee table. This was my chance to try writing under the influence. Inhibitions be damned!

The next morning I woke up with a crushing headache. The journal was on the floor. I picked it up. There were only two lines: "I drank vodka tonight. I can't feel my face."

∼

In the year after we broke up, Chris tried several times to reach me, including on 9/11. He called once after midnight, drunk, from a bar. I hung up on him.

I'd finally had enough of it all—most of all, my ridiculous sense of being powerful, and what it cost me. As painful as that last round with Chris was, I think I needed it to cure me, to kill any remaining romantic notions. I suspect that if I hadn't gone through all that with him, I'd have harbored a lingering curiosity all my life about whether things could have worked out between us. Now I know definitively that they couldn't. It feels good to have that knowledge.

It's now been more than two decades since I've spoken to him. Two years after our ending, I met my husband. Chris was my last active alcoholic boyfriend.

∼

According to twelve-step wisdom, you're never fully recovered from an addiction, only forever recovering. Maybe I'm naive, but this time I believe I'm truly, fully recovered.

The Fling

Of all the feelings the tragedy of September 11th, 2001 could have evoked in me, I wasn't prepared for this one: I was suddenly *in the mood.*

I was three weeks shy of 36 and had been recovering from a painful breakup with someone who'd cheated on me. For months, I'd had zero interest in dating and was revolted by the thought of being touched. Then, unspeakable tragedy not far from my East Village apartment sparked a rollercoaster ride through a series of overwhelming emotional states—terror, shock, rage, sorrow. What the hell was desire doing in there among them?

Later that week I informed my shrink: "Now that the world is ending and I'll probably never need it again, I managed to relocate my libido."

"Yeah," he said, shrugging, unfazed by my announcement. "That's normal." He proceeded to deliver a mini-dissertation on "post-disaster sex"—how humans are unconsciously hard-wired to try and propagate the species at times when extinction seems like a real threat. What an irrational impulse, I thought. When the world is utter hell, we feel driven to make more people so they, too, can be subjected to it?

When the evolutionary biology lesson was over, my shrink went back to being shrink-ish. "Lots of other people are probably feeling open now, too," he said. "Go out and meet one of them."

He was nudging me again, trying to get me to take the first steps toward moving on from my ex, as he'd been doing for a couple of months. My resistance immediately went up. "I'm sorry," I said, "but I still don't think I'm ready for a relationship."

"No, no, I'm not saying you have to have a *relationship*," he said. "I'm suggesting something lighter. Have a one-night-stand, or a fling. Just get laid."

Oh, sure. A fling was a great idea in theory. We'd been talking about this in some of my sessions—that not every relationship had to be long-term. How, in-between longer relationships, you could have some shorter ones with people you had some chemistry with, who maybe weren't your ideal long-term mate. Get some short-term needs met, then move on.

I had absolutely no idea how to do that. I mean, I knew how to choose men who weren't relationship material. At that, I was a champ. Most of the boyfriends I'd been with in the nine years since my first marriage had ended were clearly much better candidates for one- or two-night stands than for the year or three I'd invested in them—guys either without jobs, or effectively married to their jobs…recent dumpees very much not over their exes…active addicts resisting recovery…a musician whose manager, it so happened, did a good portion of her "managing" between the sheets. That's not to say that the only people you can have short-terms relationships with are those who are not yet the best versions of themselves. Plenty of people who have their shit together engage in short-term relationships as a matter of preference, or from time to time, as seems fit. But as a whole, the concept was foreign to me.

Growing up I got the impression that there was only one flavor of relationship on the menu: permanent. Those relationships that didn't go the final distance—even if they'd gone on for decades—were considered failures. There was no room for the possibility that a connection had just run its course—and that there existed shorter legitimate "courses" than forever-and-ever. Happily-ever-after was the primary goal.

When I found myself single at 26, after having been with only two men in my entire life—a high school boyfriend, and a college boyfriend, whom I married too young—I neglected to expand my perspective on dating and relationships. Despite very much needing some time to myself, I went back to looking for long-term love, and in all the wrong places. Regardless of whether or not a man was long-term relationship material, or vaguely suited to me in any number of ways—long before I could even know whether he actually was—I was auditioning for the role of the love of his life. I had no idea how to keep things light and unserious, not even in the very beginning.

How did you get just a little involved? Fall just a little in love? Care for someone only half-heartedly? Even more vexing, how could you stand someone caring only half-heartedly *for you*? I couldn't bear that. And so, if you slept with me once, you were basically my boyfriend, no matter how many ways you hit me over the head with the information that you just weren't that kind of guy.

Obviously this approach to dating and relationships wasn't working out terribly well. My therapist thought it was time for me to trade in my tired, dysfunctional routine for something radical: casual dating. Maybe he was right.

∝ゥ

I knew of a vigil that night in Union Square. I'd been meaning to attend. Existing for days in the same fragile emotional state as so many others, I felt the need to be both alone and among strangers—people I didn't need to individually interact with, and many of them. This is one of my favorite things that New York City offers, the ability to lose yourself in a crowd, to let the din of others' voices—their pulses and heartbeats—help your mind wander.

Maybe instead of putting on the same jeans and tee shirts I'd been wearing for days, I could pull myself together. It felt strange, that evening, applying makeup, tidying my long, unruly hair, choosing the more fitted jeans—efforts I'd foregone in the months since my breakup. Walking from my East Village tenement to Union Square, falling apart as I passed walls teeming with missing-persons photos, I became self-conscious about my mini-makeover. It felt like a sacrilege. I was hyper-aware of the blusher I'd applied to my cheeks, a blaring, Dusty Rose beacon of crass desperation.

Overcome with shame and grief, I aborted my half-hearted pick-up mission and was happy to disappear into the crowd. It was a big swarm of people, shoulder-to-shoulder—exactly what I needed. Someone handed me a candle. I waded through the sea of stunned but unusually friendly New Yorkers, and found myself near the statue of George Washington on a horse, where a demonstration was happening.

Hoping to climb up onto the low stone wall surrounding the statue for a better view, I bobbed and weaved until I reached it, and then looked up. Right above me was a cute young guy with dark hair, ice-blue eyes, and one of those khaki photojournalist-in-the-field kind of vests. He had a professional-looking Nikon pressed to his face, the lens pointing down at me. As I smiled nervously, he let go of the camera, leaving it to rest on the strap around his neck, and extended a hand to lift me.

"Who are you shooting for?" I asked awkwardly once I was standing next to him—assuming that like me, he worked in the press. It was also the most neutral, non-pick-up-ish thing I could think of to say.

He laughed. "No," he said, "it's just a hobby. I'm Zach, by the way."

We started talking—mostly about the attacks, and the aftermath, and how scared and sad we were. The conversation was warm and friendly, and it didn't end until he walked me home. At my door, he kissed me. It was the first bright moment in months of personal darkness. I had no idea where it would lead, but I went to bed that night feeling lighter and more hopeful. Who knew that in the wake of such devastation, it was possible to connect with another human?

∝

Zach called the next day to invite me to an exhibition hockey game at Madison Square Garden. He was a hockey and skating coach, he explained, a one-time NHL hopeful whose chances were ruined by a torn ACL mid-try-outs. Before the game, over Thai food, we exchanged more details of our lives.

Easy-going and comfortable as it was, a laundry list of obvious incompatibilities came to light. For instance, he was six years younger, almost 30 to my almost 36 (our birthdays were a day apart), which in and of itself wasn't necessarily a problem, but in the eight years since college, he hadn't established any kind of settled life. In the warmer months of the year— when he wasn't working twelve or more hours a day, six days a week—he traveled the country in his van, taking photographs, accompanied solely by his shedding Shepherd mix—the kind of dog I happen to be deathly allergic to. He also sometimes coached baseball, and had little interest in the arts, other than nature photography.

I, on the other hand—at the time, a freelance arts journalist— had failed gym in ninth grade and was known to some in college as The Girl Who Slept Through Game Six of the 1986 World Series, head down on the table, snoring, in a bar filled with cheering Mets fans.

We had a nice rapport, but in other ways, were a complete mismatch. *Perfect.*

"I found my fling." I announced to my shrink at my next session. I told him all about Zach and he gave his blessing.

Then the thing that always happened after my first night with someone inevitably happened. An invisible cement began seeping out of me, eventually filling all the gaps between us until I no longer knew where he ended and I began. This time the concrete set faster than usual.

In a matter of days, without any discussion, we were essentially cohabitating, alternating between his place and mine. Most of our relationship was spent sleeping together – literally *sleeping*, his shedding-allergen-factory snoring at our feet. Sure, there was some sex, but there wasn't a lot of time for that. Because of Zach's long coaching hours, most nights we'd meet up for a late, quick dinner, and then turn in soon afterward, so he could start the next day at 5 a.m.

I think it was all that slumbering that got me. Unlike most men I'd been with, Zach would wrap himself tightly around me, cradling me affectionately non-stop through the darkness until his alarm went off in the wee hours of the morning. Night after night, he lulled and comforted me in a way I clearly needed during that scary time in the world. In my oxytocin- (and Benedryl-) addled state, I slept more soundly than ever. I got hooked on it, and on him.

But quick dinners followed by six hours of shut-eye didn't afford all that much getting to know each other. And so it wasn't until Zach invited me to his mother's house in New Hampshire for Christmas, and we faced a pair of seven-hour rides alone together in his van, that more obvious details of our mismatch emerged.

Take the return trip from New Hampshire, when "Let it Be" came on the radio and I started singing along.

"Who is that?" he interrupted.

I stared at him. "You're kidding, right?" It was only one of the most popular songs of the twentieth century.

He nodded blankly.

"It's...*the Beatles*?" I couldn't believe he didn't know that.

"Oh," he said, after thinking for a second. "I think my step-mother likes them."

This was a fellow Gen-Xer, a man born in 1970. "Seriously? That's your only reference to *the Beatles*? What kind of music do you like?"

"Oh, no," he answered matter-of-factly, shaking his head, "I don't like music."

There wasn't a whole lot more talking the rest of the way. There was never a lot of talking, actually. We didn't have a whole lot in common to discuss! Did I take this as a sign, three months into my "fling," that I should be grateful for the sweet time we'd had in the wake of the terrorist attacks, cut my losses, and move on? No, I did not. Instead I adopted a new strategy: I would culturize Zach. I took him to dance performances, and to hear friends play music. I got him to sit—granted, baffled—through a Richard Foreman play at the St. Mark's Church.

I found ways to work with other clear incompatibilities, too. For example: each week Zach, an expert skier, ritually spent his one day off from coaching on the slopes. I, who never got over the time I fell off a descending chair lift at age 12, was "welcome to join" him, a familiar refrain from other non-committal men I'd dated. I ignored the part of my brain concerned with the lack of a proper invitation in "welcome to join" and became a regular in beginner school at Hunter.

When he wasn't skiing, Zach was practicing his flight skills in a tiny rented Cessna out of Teterboro. Lucky me, I was "welcome" there, too. And so I logged several flight hours in the passenger seat, my head thrown backward into the only position that precluded projectile vomiting.

Once winter and hockey season ended, it came time for Zach to spend half his year in his van with no one but his dog. Before we met, he'd set his sights on Alaska, and once he was no longer coaching, he got to work planning his trip. He once again informed me I was free to tag along for the next six months. But of course, I couldn't just pick up and leave my life.

Or could I? I mean, wasn't that what laptops were for?! I could line up some travel assignments—maybe something about the virtues of domestic road trips in vans, in the wake of 9/11...

But Zach clearly hadn't expected me to take him up on that "invitation." When I considered it out loud, he pulled away, clamming up, taking impromptu day trips without me. He started calling me "Dude," (there was no colder shower for me) and ending our phone conversations with "Take care," as if I were someone he spoke to occasionally, not a partner with whom he was essentially cohabitating. We started talking about ending things, both of us unsure. Our differences were glaring. But we liked each other. Zach was wrong for me in every way but an important one: he was the kindest, warmest person I'd ever dated.

"What do I do here?" I begged my shrink. "Do I try to make this work with Zach? *Could* I make this work?" I even brought Zach in for a session with me, and then he went for a separate session, on his own. After that, I posed the question to my therapist once more.

"Please, tell me what to do…"

"Sari," he answered, throwing up his hands, "if the guy was wearing a sandwich board that read, 'I'M UNAVAILABLE,' in all caps, it couldn't be more obvious. This is not about you. Give it up. This was supposed to be a fling, remember?"

∝

Zach and I broke up that June.

But then the first anniversary of 9/11 rolled around. Terrified and mournful again, I was happy when Zach reached out. We got together. And then, in a matter of days, we were cemented to each other once again. True to form, instead of just getting the little consoling I needed at a difficult moment and moving on, I held on for dear life, trying once again to make a complete meal out of what was merely meant to be a side-dish

It wasn't terribly satisfying. When Zach and I had gotten together the year before, our connection had benefited from newness and ignorance—from not yet really knowing each other, or how poorly matched we were. Now we knew we didn't have much of a foundation to build on. We knew we were doomed as a couple. We were bored with each other, but comfortable and cowardly.

We trudged on together like that for five months until one afternoon, Zach blankly asked, "Do you think my playing spin-the-bottle last night constitutes cheating on you?" Instantly my mind flashed to Elizabeth Perkins in the final scene of *Big*, when she turns around to glance one last time at full-grown Tom Hanks, only to see a little boy in a man's suit. I now knew without question that I had to move on. We had a long, weird debate again about whether we should break up, even though we both knew we should. As part of his argument for letting go, Zach said, "You know, I'm kind of tired of being the better athlete in the relationship," at which point I burst out laughing. Everything that was wrong with our now almost two-year relationship suddenly came rushing forward, and was impossible to unsee. It was time to say goodbye, for real.

∝

A few months later, in October, 2003, I met my husband, Brian, through an online dating site. We married a little less than two years later. So, I never did learn to have a fling. It's okay. I'll be perfectly fine going through the rest of life without knowing how to do that. It's fine for other people, but I'm pretty sure it's not for me. There are other more worthwhile learning curves for me to tackle.

I long ago gained enough distance from my relationship with Zach to look back with fondness, and also to laugh at how cluelessly I operated. These days I feel nothing but gratitude toward him. Each year around the anniversary of 9/11, I recall the hope and comfort he surprised me with when it felt like the world was ending, and I silently thank him.

Fred Talks

On my first date with Fred in the spring of 2003, he gets the impression that I don't like him very much. What gives him that impression is that I'm suffering from excruciating menstrual cramps, and rather than cancel, or end our lunch date early like a woman with healthy boundaries and a modicum of self-esteem, I decide to buck up and do my best impression of a person who does *not* have severe endometriosis, who is not silently calculating which Manhattan emergency room might be nearest.

It's all I can do to remain upright rather than curl into the fetal position on the floor of Mayrose, a diner in Manhattan's Flatiron District near enough to my corporate copywriting gig that I meet many of my internet dates there for lunch or dinner. I can't quite smile because I'm performing Lamaze under my breath, exhaling between tiny bites of my Niçoise salad and making whatever modicum of polite chitchat I can manage. I'm doing my best, but I'm a long way off from being good lunch company.

Fred is the only guy I've clicked with, even vaguely, on the five online dating sites I've been subscribed to for a few months, per the orders of my male therapist. He believes selecting potential suitors based on the information in their dating profiles—including their stated actual interest in finding a partner—will help me break my pattern of gravitating toward, and attaching myself desperately to, one unavailable man-child with an addiction after another.

Fred doesn't appear to have any addictions, so that's something. He's a responsible adult with a *job*-job in marketing; also good. Bonus: he makes sculptures in his spare time, which means he's also creative. He is smart, funny, quirky, and cute—tall, dark, and arguably handsome, but with enough "flaws" to seem attainable. He's nice, but not aggressively so, which is helpful, since I'm working on overcoming my apparent allergy to kindness in men.

Before Fred, in recent months I've been out with nearly 60 other men, rarely passing a day without an unremarkable internet date for breakfast, lunch, coffee, or dinner—sometimes filling more than one of these calendar slots on a given day, to up my odds. Online dating is a numbers game and *I am in it to win it* (along with my therapist's approval). Speaking of numbers, an important one in this equation is my advanced age, 37. With the clock ticking, I've been led to believe, I can't afford to miss just one opportunity to meet a marriageable man—even on a day when my reproductive organs appear to be violently self-ejecting.

∾

I might never have gone out with Fred a second time, except that very early on in our terrible first date—before he noticed my lack of enthusiasm—he invited me to join him at a baseball game he had tickets for the following week. I accepted without a second thought, even though I know little about baseball other than that I find it incredibly boring.

A week later, we're in the subway on the way to Yankee Stadium, making amiable small talk, when Fred begins rattling off references to bands and singer-songwriters he likes. I recognize a couple, and have maybe heard the names of another one or two. It makes for okay patter. *For a while.* Then it becomes tiresome, and I'm happy to arrive at the noisy stadium so we can shift our attention to a sport, which is saying something.

The game is…*fine*. Fred narrates most of it in a funny, engaging way that makes it slightly less boring. I pretend to be more interested than I am because I haven't yet learned not to pretend with men, to try to be different than I am so as to keep them interested in me, even when I don't yet know if *I'm* interested in *them*. He flirts with me, and I flirt back, and it's enjoyable enough that I can see going out with him again.

On the subway home, Fred switches from merely mentioning artists, to quizzing me on my level of familiarity with them.

"Do you know the song, XYZ?"

"Hmm. I don't think so."

"Of course you do. It's by the band ABC. You know them, right?"

"No, I…don't think I do…"

"What about Blah Blah Blah, by Yada Yada Yada?"

"Um…no…?"

This particular line of questioning hits a nerve. All my life I've been self-conscious about not being familiar enough with whatever music was deemed cool at the time. I was raised in greater Nerdville, in a house filled with opera and classical and standards and show music. In my twenties and early thirties, I managed to get a fair amount of work writing about popular music—admittedly in part to impress at least one other man—but most of the time I had no idea who or what I was writing about. I had to do extensive research every time I was given an assignment. I lived in a constant state of embarrassed anxiety. Early on in our courtship, I made the mistake of telling Fred about how I freelanced as a music writer, and left out the part about how much of a learning curve I had.

Fred and I continue to go out, once or twice a week. Increasingly, I'm stumped by his questions. Eventually, a switch flips; instead of feeling bored or annoyed, suddenly I'm anxious. I realize I'm failing at my audition for the role of Fred's girlfriend. What if I don't get the part? What if he loses interest in me because I don't get enough of his references?

So, after a while, when Fred mentions this musician or that, and asks, "Hey, do you know…" I just flat-out lie.

"Yeah, sure," I say. "Really, really great band."

We go on like this for a while.

"You know so-and-so's first record?"

"Yes, of course."

"Isn't it amazing how it's, like, so different from the direction she went in after that?"

"Oh, totally," I say. "I'd never really thought about it that way, but now that you mention it, *that is exactly right.*"

When he asks me for my own opinions about some of the artists he mentions, I try to come up with adjectives that can cover many bases: "mellifluous," "tuneful," "accessible." I monitor the changes in his expression after I speak and wonder: Has any of the shit I've thrown at this wall stuck? Or can he tell I'm completely full of it?

∞

Fred keeps asking me out, and I keep saying yes. We have chemistry, and he makes me laugh, and we have a nice enough time when we're together, if you subtract his frequently quizzing me. I keep hoping one day he'll stop, but the line of questioning continues. It begins to feel like a job interview, or game show. The grand prize? The approval and acceptance…of a guy I'm not even sure how much I like, and, to be perfectly honest, seems only moderately enthusiastic about me.

To wit: between dates Fred prefers to email infrequently, as opposed to ever talking on the phone. Also, he was never more interested and attentive than when he was worried I didn't like him, after our first couple of dates. I'm trying to believe my therapist when he says that not all men only want what they can't have, but I'm not there yet, and Fred isn't helping. Worst of all, whenever I go to his place, I'm struck by the photos of his ex that still litter his shelves and the mantel over his non-functional fireplace. One photo in particular gnaws at me, because I've seen some variation of it in the New York City apartments of so many of the other men I've dated: the ex-girlfriend emerging like a goddess from some beautiful, turquoise body of water they swam in together, on vacation somewhere. I've encountered enough of these to wonder, *Is this a thing?* So many men, so many ex-girlfriends on display emerging regally from the water like a goddess, half-in, half-out, serene, not looking directly at the camera, or the person holding it. At some point it occurs to me that each time I spot one of these photos, I should probably run for the hills. They are placed strategically *to warn me to run*, to tell me what a man who is not ready to move on to a new relationship will never actually verbalize: "You will never be *her*."

But I don't run. Again and again, I do everything I can to try and unsee this clue, even though I've come upon it before, even though it always points to the same thing. I realize that what I want is to *be* those women, to be self-possessed in the way they seem to be, and to be adored in that particular way that they are. If only I weren't such a bad swimmer that the lifeguard at Asser Levy Pool on East 23rd Street keeps begging me to take swimming lessons, so I don't drown on his watch. More to the point, if only I realized that the difference between those women and me is that they likely have the self-regard to remove themselves from situations where they are not appreciated for who they are, as they are. As opposed to constantly adjusting themselves, reinventing themselves, to keep a man's attention.

∝৯

For a while, a good couple of months, I get away with bullshitting Fred about knowing the music and bands he mentions. But the more time we spend together, the more dicey of a gamble it becomes. I'm getting in a little deep for this. I mean, I've now got a toothbrush at Fred's place. I've got to somehow start injecting basic honesty into our conversations if I'm going to keep seeing him.

Do I even want to keep seeing Fred? Or do I just want to make sure Fred wants to keep seeing me? I've invested a lot of time in my life trying to keep men interested in me whether or not I was sure I was interested in them. Attracting and holding the male gaze—whether or not I wanted the particular male doing the gazing—was the object of a game I learned unconsciously at a very young age, as if by way of osmosis. It was hard to know what I wanted and needed, other than *being* wanted and needed, to be chosen by those with the power and prerogative to choose. I was trying to unlearn this self-denying orientation in therapy, and it was incredibly difficult.

∝৯

One evening Fred starts talking about some cult favorite album, and as he's speaking I decide: *Okay. It'll be more believable if once in a while I acknowledge that I have no fucking idea what he's talking about.*

"So, you know Such and Such, that album by Whosey Whatsis?" he asks.

"Hmm," I say, really performing the business of scanning my brain for possible matches. "Nope. I don't think I do."

"Really?" he asks. "I thought you said you were really into that record."

Uh-oh.

"Oh, right. You're right! I got confused."

"Well, which *is* your favorite of their albums?"

"I really just know, like, individual songs," I blurt. I can see the next question coming at me and I head it off at the pass. "Oh, but I don't really know the *names* of any of the songs."

I am so busted. Mercifully, Fred doesn't linger on it. He moves onto another subject.

I'll never know whether he was just letting me off the hook, or felt like talking about something else. Because we don't last much longer. While it hurts when he breaks up with me in an email—on the very night that Berger dumps Carrie Bradshaw in a Post-It on *Sex and the City*—I'm relieved that, at least with this one man, I can finally stop pretending.

Inadvertent Matchmaker
Seeks a Love of Her Own

Once upon a time, in a gritty, rent-stabilized land called the East Village of the late '90s and early aughts, I introduced all my smart, interesting, kind, funny, straight guy friends to all my smart, interesting, kind, funny, straight girl friends, and they all got married and lived happily ever after.

This is the story of how I came to be known, far and wide, as the "East Village Yenta."

Introducing couples "IRL"—in real life, old school—was considered to be something of a major mitzvah in those days. One of the harsher ironies of living in New York City has always been that despite the crushing multitudes of people, it can be incredibly lonely. Finding a mate can be damn near impossible. If you think meeting someone in New York City is hard now, I promise you, it was infinitely harder in the days before online dating became not only acceptable but ubiquitous, and social media made it standard to know pretty much everything about a person before ever actually meeting them.

So many single people, but so little context for knowing who was, in fact, single, or for simply introducing yourself and striking up a conversation. How would you know whether the cute guy on the other side of the horseshoe bar at Vazac's on 7th and B, who sort of smiled at you, or the one playing pool at Sophie's on 5th Street, had a girlfriend? Or a boyfriend? Or if his relationship status might fall into the category of "It's complicated?" In those days, it was particularly helpful to have an informed human vector pointing you in the direction of that special someone.

For a handful of couples in the East Village, where I lived from 1993 to 2005, I was that vector. I tried to be subtle about it, creating low-stakes alternatives to that invariably awkward, arguably inhumane fix-up standby, the blind date. I'd throw big parties, cramming forty or more guests into my un-renovated, run-down East 13th Street tenement, sometimes for the express purpose of introducing just two of them in a low-key, dignified manner. I'd sneak a surprise guest into the exclusive weekly poker game I was part of at a friend's place, or into casual dinners at the restaurant 7A, with the group I came to think of as my East Village family, or at one of the inexpensive sushi places in the neighborhood, like Sandobe on 11th Street near 1st Avenue.

Sometimes I acted on my instincts almost unconsciously, making a last-minute phone call to invite someone along to a bar where I was meeting others, and it would invariably lead to a love connection—then marriage, then kids. But in all situations, whether I was acting deliberately or inadvertently, there was one constant: I was always the one person in the room who knew both parties.

∽

Mine was a full-service matchmaking enterprise. Not only would I introduce my friends, but in some cases, early in their courtships, before both parties were ready to consider themselves part of an "item," I'd even chaperone them. *Sure, I'll be a third wheel on your road trip to a community theater production of* The Cherry Orchard *in Bristol, Pennsylvania, so that you don't have to call it a "date."* Also included in the package was relationship advice for the unattached and lovelorn, which I'd provide for free. Ironic, considering that I myself was pretty consistently unattached and lovelorn, living as I did on a perpetual emotional roller-coaster ride, courtesy of a coterie of ambivalent man-children, most of whom behaved as complete jerks toward me.

Occasionally my friends would try to return the favor. But while I loved introducing couples, I, myself, hated being fixed up. First of all, none of my friends were insecure or co-dependent enough to go to the ridiculous lengths I had for them, so setting me up on awkward blind dates seemed to be the only option for them.

Second of all, in most cases, they wanted to introduce me exclusively to short dudes they had no one else to set up with. I'm a hair under five feet myself, so I'm not in any position to rule anyone out based on their height. But that's not what my issue was. I never had a problem with short guys. I dated men who were 5'2" and 5'3". I also dated guys who were over six feet. The problem wasn't the men's lack of stature. The problem was, more often than not, our being tiny was the only thing we had in common. Having already logged more than my share of meals with short men I was set up with who had no sense of humor, or had never read a book, and knowing that our mutual diminutiveness had been my friends' main criteria for introducing us, I just wasn't interested.

Third of all, in the cases where my friends did have great guys of any height that they wanted me to meet, I was forced to confront my aversion to…*great guys of any height*. No, not for me, the smart, interesting, kind, funny type! Let the other girls have them! I was in the market for a different breed of suitor: the rakishly cute/scruffily handsome, brooding, unreliable, intermittently mean, almost always broke, and decidedly broken species known as The Beautiful Mess, native to regions like the '90s East Village. The anti-suitor. As if it isn't already difficult enough in New York City to find someone to settle down with, try limiting yourself to the ones who are *just not that into settling down*. Or you. Or both. Stubbornly, I clung to this ridiculous preference way past the age when most women outgrow it.

I've invested more than my share of shrink hours trying to understand what kept me stuck in that unsatisfying, self-destructive groove. Low self-esteem? An envy-inspired attraction to aloof men's implicit power, and a desire to eventually flip the power dynamic? My own ambivalence about settling down—getting stuck with some normie who'd want to whisk me back to the suburbs to domesticate me, once again, in a homogenous, retrograde world where I didn't fit in, and also didn't *want* to fit in? How much of my issue was not knowing any other way to maintain my independence and personal space in a relationship other than to be with someone who was more commitment phobic than I was?

Those could all be valid explanations, but I also hold New York City somewhat accountable. It provided me with too many compelling distractions from my misery and loneliness to commit to dealing with those matters in a constructive way. New York is often anthropomorphized as a bad boyfriend who's both hard to keep and hard to leave. But for me New York was more like my gay boyfriend, a guy who wasn't going to give me certain key things you'd want in a relationship, but who would comfort me and cheer me up with shiny diversions when I most needed it. So much to see! Art, music, street fashion, architecture, crazy tourists. After a bad date Saturday night, I'd spend Sunday afternoon walking around the lower tip of Manhattan, intrigued at every turn—interesting buildings, shops, a veritable UN of cuisines, people, people, and more people. The blessed profusion of variety tranquilized me. Afterward, my mind could remain occupied and my spirits high, at least until the man-child du jour would do or say something just subtly rejecting enough to throw me off balance. Where another woman might recognize this as a good stop to get off that train, I'd instead expend tremendous energy trying to decipher the mixed messages, and contorting myself into someone I imagined they'd find more alluring—someone interested in punk rock, or sports, or outdoor adventures.

∽

Before I got tired of my tedious suffering, the people around me did. The last straw was a 34th birthday dinner gathering friends put together for me in October, 1999 at Jules on St. Mark's Place. I invited along Tim—the cute but perennially angry on-again-off-again boyfriend I'd never been happy with, but was, for some reason, staying with while I sublet my apartment for cash. He flat-out said no. My friends wouldn't take no for an answer, though. They took matters into their own hands, calling Tim and persuading him to surprise me at the restaurant in time for birthday cake.

When we were done eating dinner, a friend got up "to go to the bathroom," but on the way stopped to talk to our waiter, clearly ordering dessert with a candle in it. Then we waited. And waited. We sat and sat. The waiter kept eyeing my friend for the go-ahead, and my friend kept giving him the "one minute" sign with his pointer finger. I wondered why my friends all kept looking at the door. Finally, another friend, Donna, grabbed her Nokia cell phone and stepped outside. No one spoke. When she came back in, she couldn't hide her anger.

"Tim is blowing us off," she said. "He agreed to surprise you and come for dessert. I'm so sorry, Sari."

When I got back to Tim's place afterward—my temporary home until my subletters would depart the following month—I found him sitting on the futon, drinking beer. I couldn't even form the words necessary to ask why he hadn't shown up for birthday cake. I looked at him, and he looked at me, holding my gaze for mere seconds before just shrugging, and averting his eyes.

I don't know how, but I hung in with Tim for another seven or eight months. It was the worst of our time together. Tim was depressed, and wouldn't talk. He would often go to sleep at 8:30 or 9:00 without saying a word to me, shutting off the lights in the main part of his studio apartment. When we did speak, Tim was curt. Now and then he'd warm up and say something nice, and I'd find myself pleasantly confused. It gave me a shred of hope to hang onto, although each time the shred was smaller and smaller.

I avoided my friends completely. I didn't want to be lectured. I was crumbling inside, and I didn't want them to see. I couldn't even write in my journal about what was happening—couldn't admit it to myself, because for some reason, I wasn't ready to walk away.

It hadn't occurred to me that my friends might have been avoiding me, too.

"Buttons," my friend Kevin said to me when I called him one afternoon—using one of his many affectionate nicknames for me—"I don't know if you've noticed that I haven't been spending so much time with you these days. It's just that I can't watch anymore as you put yourself through the ringer with guys like Tim. I can't watch you as you keep staying."

After a moment, I said, "I'm working on it, Kevin." It came out more defensive than I wanted, but I didn't know how to fix that, and I couldn't utter any more words without crying. As soon as we hung up, the tears came rushing out of me.

What Kevin had said hurt so much, but it was what I needed to hear. It was one of the bravest, most important things anyone has ever said to me. It got me to dump Tim for good a few days later, and to then find myself a good New York shrink. And while I was busy getting my shit together, the East Village Yenta made her next match, almost inadvertently.

I got a call from a guy I knew who'd moved from New York to Montréal with his girlfriend the year before. His girlfriend, a lovely young woman I'd met at their going-away party across town at the Ear Inn, was now moving back to New York City. *Without him.* They'd broken up. Her name was Emily, and she was this pixie-ish, bookish dancer who also liked to write. She said she had just begun her first novel.

Emily was looking for a room to rent, and it so happened my friend Dave was looking for a roommate. I invited Emily and Dave to meet me for dinner at Jeoaldo, the cheap sushi place on East 4th. When I hung up, the gears in my brain started turning. Something told me to call Kevin, who was single. I made a third phone call, to him.

Kevin and Emily married two years later.

As someone who is religion-averse, I probably have no business invoking a Jewish adage about matchmakers. But it's said that if you introduce three couples who go on to marry, a place is reserved for you at the highest level of Heaven. (*Of course* Jewish Heaven has different levels that you have to strive toward!) Kevin and Emily were couple number three for me.

Was it just a coincidence that after I introduced them—and, granted, after $20,000 worth of shrink sessions—that I then found my own mate? That job I had to contract out; *Nerve* Personals served as my yenta—with the help of my gay boyfriend, New York City.

After communicating with a guy named Brian intermittently on *Nerve* Personals for about six months, but never meeting, I spotted him on East 7th Street, between Avenues C and D one morning when I was out jogging. He was standing behind his car, making sure it was parked beyond the no-parking zone in front of a church entrance. I recognized him from his dating profile photo, and had enough context, obviously, to know he was single and in the market for a girlfriend. So, I said hello.

As of this writing, we have been together 19 years, married for 17 of them. I'll be forever grateful to New York City and its Alternate Side Parking Rules, and to *Nerve* Personals, and my shrink. And even more grateful to Kevin, for a gift even greater than the mitzvah of matchmaking.

The Re-Education of the
Needless Wonder

From my early twenties through my early thirties, I would go about choosing a therapist in the same way one might go about choosing a primary care physician.

Step 1: Open the booklet listing providers who accepted my insurance.

Step 2: Pick the one whose office was nearest to my East Village apartment.

My selection process typically yielded results that were just okay. The therapists from that period of my life are a blur of nurturing, kind, middle-aged women who handed me many tissues and spoke softly, especially at the end of a session when they said, "I'm afraid we have to stop now…" That's pretty much all I can tell you about most of them. I rarely hung around for more than the precise number of sessions covered by whatever vaguely affordable health care plan I was on at the time. By that point, the most recent crisis would have been extinguished, or at least sufficiently quieted for me to be able to launch myself out of bed most mornings.

Step 3: Quit therapy. Do not go anywhere near it again until the next emotional crisis, at which point, repeat steps 1 and 2.

∝

My crises were mostly sparked by the same thing: a breakup with some aloof, difficult, emotionally withholding boyfriend I'd been trying, in retrospect, *god only knows why*, to hold onto. Ironically, each time I would find the courage to liberate myself from a man who treated me carelessly or badly, I would soon after move on to someone who treated me worse. I was one of those young women—you know the kind—who seemed to have a fair amount going for her—smart, hard-working, engaging, a thinking-man's idea of attractive—who inexplicably wasted her time dating jerks who didn't have half as much on the ball.

Two different boyfriends' *mothers* separately took me aside to ask why I was wasting my precious time on their messed up sons. I have felt similarly puzzled watching other women do what I did, sometimes even as I myself was doing it, but couldn't see the parallels. Or maybe I could see the parallels, but I rationalized that my situation was somehow different. Or I had gotten in so deep that I'd lost all perspective. The longer you stay, the more you endure small instances of unkindness with the hope that they'll be counterbalanced with (ever diminishing) gestures of kindness, the more normalized it all becomes. You get used to it.

When you finally find the courage to move away from one bad relationship, you think you won't ever get into another. But then you meet another appealing rake, and you're thrown off balance by pheromones and a charm offensive. Once the seduction phase is over, and he begins retreating, you're thrown off balance again, this time by whatever hormonal activity is incited by the fear of abandonment.

In my case, once I would start to see what was happening, I would convince myself I wasn't seeing it, or I'd try to unsee it; I couldn't bear to know that a man I'd become emotionally attached to was pulling away or being unkind to me, even though that was the exact information I needed. I seemed hardwired to remain hopeful, no matter what. The men were complicit in obscuring my view. Just as they could only sustain their charming behavior for so long, they could similarly only be distant or hurtful for short stretches. They'd alternate between the two, in shorter and shorter intervals, so that I couldn't easily hold onto one or the other long enough to be certain which message they were sending. It was perfectly inscrutable: *Now he's charming; now he's mean. Now he's charming; now he's mean.* The confusion was convenient for me, helping me to avoid facing harsh reality for as long as possible.

Eventually either I would tire of the rollercoaster ride and put my attention toward someone else. Or the man *du jour* would tire of keeping me on that rollercoaster ride, and strike out in some way that was worse than ever before, some overt act of destruction that was impossible not to see for what it was. This supreme betrayal, whether it was cheating or something else, would only ever occur after I'd wasted entirely too much time in the relationship.

The bottom line is that I lost a decade to those guys, and for the life of me, I couldn't see a way out of that rut. I don't know how I wound up so desperate, with such low self-esteem, nor why I seemed incapable of investing the same sort of time and energy into men who were thoughtful and kind, and who were actually interested in me.

∽

There were work crises, too. I struggled to land the kinds of journalism jobs I wanted—more interesting beats, more opportunities to shine than I was offered at the obscure trade publications I tended to work at in those days, covering various boring industries. Once I did break in at consumer publications, I was marginalized, harassed, and held back by men I worked with. The more I struggled to get ahead, the more depressed I became.

According to the career coach I briefly sought help from in my late twenties, my dissatisfactions at work and in relationships were related. I had to look at my life more holistically; if one of three areas (career, personal, financial) was not going well, it would naturally throw the other two out of whack.

For better or worse (mostly worse) the area I was most worried about, and put the most attention toward, was personal. And within the personal bucket, cliché as it sounds, the area I cared about more than anything was intimate relationships. I'm ashamed of how heavily I prioritized difficult men over my friends and family. I don't know whether it was a function of being a Libra, or Gen X, or just another woman raised in a relationship-centric patriarchy with an awfully large population of unavailable men, I was consumed by matters of the heart, and was always either starting, ending, or struggling through a bad romantic relationship.

A serial monogamist, I became a serial therapy patient, too, going from shrink to shrink to shrink. In those days I wasn't really interested in looking at that pattern—or any of my patterns—in treatment. I didn't give my health plan-designated shrinks much of a chance to push me in that direction, either. I was pretty sure that's what was supposed to come next, after the twenty-or-so insurance-subsidized sessions were up, but I was always too broke to pay a full or even partial fee out-of-pocket (another recurring pattern I avoided looking at), so continuing was rarely a viable option, assuming I was even willing. I honestly didn't want to be challenged. I was too afraid. Mostly what I wanted from therapy was to be comforted through a period of deep emotional turmoil, and that's what I got.

That is until the Swashbuckling Shrink appeared, like a comet, and knocked my dysfunctional existence off its axis.

∽

Some might find it disappointing that the person who had possibly the greatest effect on changing my life was a cis-hetero white man, a somewhat macho one at that. But it's the truth. Let's call him "Kieran" (not his real name). From the time I was 34 until I was 38, Kieran helped me jump-start a return to myself in a way that only a brash, rule-breaking, mountain-climbing dude could have.

I met Kieran by accident at the moment I needed him most, in the late spring of 2000. I was just a couple of days out of a very bad relationship, the only kind I had in those days. It figures our meeting occurred at one of my crisis breeding grounds: Angelica Kitchen, a vegan, macrobiotic restaurant around the corner from my apartment. I met him there on the second of two nights in a row that I ate dinner there.

Anjelica was where I'd regularly go to flirt with one sub-species of the withholding man-children I collected: those of the scruffily attractive, arrogant, progressive, health food-proselytizing variety. I could always count on there being at least one of their kind sitting at the restaurant's large "community table." The late May evening after I'd been dumped by Tim (my on-and-off boyfriend of three years) was no exception.

That probably would have been a pretty good moment to take a break from relationships, but if 34-year-old me knew that (*I totally knew that*), I didn't want to see it. No, I was back out on the prowl in fewer than 24 hours, just as clueless then about how to have a satisfying relationship as I'd been three years before.

I had no idea what constituted a good romantic union. There weren't many contented couples in my orbit. The one husband and wife I'd thought had it all figured out, a slightly older couple from whom I enjoyed a parental vibe, had each separately hit on me the last time I paid them a visit—unwelcome offers that made it hard for me to be around them afterward. A few years later, they split up. Without role models, or any insight into my own relationship tendencies, I kept looking for all the wrong things, most of all the hard-won attention, approval, and validation of guys who'd rather not have been bothered.

That first night after the breakup with Tim, with my ego badly bruised, instead of allowing myself any time to heal or gain perspective, automatically I began searching for a new potential source of hard-won validation. I made a beeline for Angelica Kitchen.

The community table there was always a hotbed of posturing, mostly among orthorexics with superiority complexes. Just about every restrictive approach to eating was represented: raw veggies only, steamed veggies only, macro, ovo-lacto vegetarian, vegan, kosher, no nightshades, yes nightshades. Day after day, the people seated at that table expressed Very Strong Opinions.

Not surprisingly, that night, an argument broke out at the table. The evening's edition of the "Dragon Bowl"—an ever-changing seasonal assortment of steamed veggies and sprouts over brown rice, with a choice of three aggressively healthful-tasting sauces—had some whitish chunks of something starchy in it.

"What *is* this?" wondered a petite woman, seemingly of college age, with a pixie cut and blemish-free porcelain complexion. "Is this *white potato*?!" She wasn't disgusted so much as offended.

"No way," insisted a thirtyish, goateed, anemic looking guy with bulging brown eyes behind wiry glasses. "That's probably a turnip. They'd *never* serve white potatoes here. White potatoes have *absolutely no nutritional value*."

"*Bullshit*," shot back a fortysomething woman with a sinewy yoga body and glints of gray in her long, long brown hair. "Potatoes, at the very least, have *carbohydrate* and *fiber*, and if you're starving, and that's all there is to eat, it is *sustenance*. It will keep you *alive*—even if you're a macrobiotic nutrition *snob.*"

Across from me, a tall, skinny guy with curly hair and a beard was rolling his crystal blue eyes. I flashed him a smile and made a nodding micro-movement with my head, enough motion to indicate to my new friend that I was in agreement that these people were nuts, but not so much that I'd offend those who were arguing.

Target identified. Tall Blue-Eyes was a potential candidate for the task of shoring up my fragile ego. We began talking, and continued until he walked me home and asked me out.

The next night, Danny and I went back to Angelica for our first of three dates in total (it turned out to be the only place he'd eat out; he was macro *and* kosher, and possibly suffering from OCD—insisting on chewing each bite of food 50 to 100 times, and only moving his food clockwise on his plate). This time we sat at a two-top in the dining room's center. As we waited for our meals, I told Danny about my plans to sublet my apartment for the summer and possibly move upstate. I wanted to get out of Dodge after my breakup with Tim. And since it was the height of the dot com boom, I could get a lot of money for my decrepit shoe box. "The only problem," I explained, "is that the room for rent I had lined up in Rhinebeck might not be available anymore."

Before Danny could comment, the man at the next table cut in. He was handsome, athletic, somewhere in his forties, and bald—*good* bald.

"I'm sorry, I couldn't help but overhear that you're looking for a room to rent in Rhinebeck," he said. "I happen to have a friend who might have one available. Can I give you her number?" He wrote the number on the back of his business card and handed it to me, and then I turned my attention back to my date.

The next day, I resumed my post-breakup breakdown—crying, wallowing, staring into space. It wasn't so much that I missed Tim; it had been a really unsatisfying three years, on and off, with him. It was that I felt rejected, like a failure, and hopeless that I'd ever meet someone with whom I could pair off happily. I lay in bed until I was too hungry not to get up and eat something.

When I arose, I began poring over the booklet of Aetna mental health providers, making my way down the list of practitioners below 14th Street. One by one, I'd call them and cry, "I'm going through a *breeaaaak uuuuup…*" They were all very kind and compassionate, but none had any openings. I extended my search to 23rd Street, then 34th, 42nd, and finally 72nd.

The whole time I was cold-calling Aetna-affiliated shrinks, in one hand I held the cordless phone receiver, and in the other, I had the business card from the man at the next table the night before. I was mindlessly flipping his card over and over as I made my calls. After the last therapist on the Aetna list offered no hope, I put the phone down and let the card drop. It landed *not* revealing the back side of the card, where the man had written the phone number of his friend in Rhinebeck with a room for rent, but instead revealing the front: "Kieran Somethingsomething, CSW." I dialed him immediately.

"Hi...I met you last night at Angelica Kitchen," I said when he picked up. "Do you take Aetna? I'm going through a *breeeaaaak uuuuuuuup....*"

He didn't take Aetna. "Give me your number in case any of my colleagues in my practice do," he said.

Ten minutes later, he called me back.

"Are you willing to really do the work?" he asked. "Because if you are, I'll cut you a deal." He offered to charge me $25 per session—only $5 more than my $20 co-pay with plan-sanctioned therapists—until I was able to get myself on my feet financially, which, he added, was one of the goals that therapy with him would likely help me achieve.

Really do the work, huh? I knew right away that this guy wasn't going to just comfort and coddle me the way prior therapists had. He was going to push me to examine the stuff I'd routinely avoided. He was going to make it impossible for me to rely on my well-worn exit strategy: "Oh, will you look at that—no more insurance-subsidized sessions...bye!"

What exactly did *really doing the work* in therapy look like? What would I be signing up for? I was just desperate enough to find out.

∽

A few days later, I entered "the laboratory," as Kieran referred to his practice. His office was, he explained, a place in which to examine my heart and brain, to hold them up to the light so I could take note of how they operated. The idea was to have me become aware of my patterns and assumptions, challenge every one of them, and then establish new patterns based on better assumptions.

I was terrified going in. Could I handle being exposed under the laboratory lights? How about having a dude for a shrink? This guy wasn't the central-casting version of a male therapist either—the paunchy, bearded, paternal Judd Hirsch. No, he was ruggedly athletic. Could I be candid with someone of the opposite sex? An *attractive* person of the opposite sex? This was going to be a challenge.

∽

While therapy with Kieran was indeed challenging in ways, it also turned out to be *fun*. I was surprised to discover I looked forward to it. He made it seem as if we were co-researchers examining a specimen together—the specimen being *me* and all my damage, but this gave me useful distance from myself. It probably helped that he got me to take a step back, see the absurdity of some of our specimen's ill-considered choices, and laugh.

He worked fast and didn't mince words. He dubbed me the Needless Wonder because of my doormat ways. At the end of a session, he would open his office door and bellow into the empty waiting room, "There she goes, ladies and gentleman, the Needless Wonder, able to exist on air alone." What a perfect way to disarm me, so I could really see myself.

Once inside the lab, as if on cue, I began making some *new* ridiculous choices, creating lab-fodder in real-time. Just a couple of months into treatment, I reunited with an active alcoholic who resisted recovery, a cheating (and ironically, insanely jealous), rageful ex—for a long-distance relationship between Rhinebeck and Manhattan. "I'm a little ashamed to tell you this…" I informed Kieran in one of our phone sessions while I was upstate. But he took an attitude of *Oh, good—something to put under our microscope.*

"Don't feel bad," he said. "This is *good*. For the first time, you'll be doing what you do with me helping you look at it and make sense of it. How else are we going to study this?"

And so began my time as both scientist and lab rat. I could fail miserably at relationships and it was okay; it was my *job*.

Kieran was right; his approach allowed me to witness my mode of operating with men in a way I'd never before been able to. It turned out I had been taking just about the most ineffective, passive-aggressive approach possible toward getting my needs met. I did it again and again, choosing guys who were cute and rakishly charming, but who treated me carelessly, and in some cases, outright badly. Eventually, when they least expected it, I would reach my limit and then pull the rug out from under them.

I couldn't have made worse choices in men over the course of my dating career. There had been the alcoholic artist—handsome, talented and seductive, but given to fits of rage and jealousy even though most of the time, he was the one who didn't want to be exclusive. There was the alcoholic/weed-addicted videographer whose birthday present to me was the opportunity to help him paint his apartment. Then there was the curmudgeonly, frequently drunk elementary school teacher. (Notice a pattern here? It was as if I was addicted to alcohol not by mouth, but on the breath of a man.) Professing an admiration for the Unabomer and his minimalist aesthetic, the teacher owned only one plate, which we had to share when we ate at his place.

I was complicit in my misery. No matter how badly men treated me, I hung around for more. I remained the best, most low-maintenance girlfriend in the world, requiring next to nothing. I would get out of a boyfriend's way whenever I sensed he needed space—anticipating it so he wouldn't even have to ask. I would never ask for a thing, fighting back tears when he flirted with other women or forgot my birthday.

I would tolerate my men's negligence, racking up resentments as ammunition until I couldn't take it anymore. Then I'd walk, and my favorite part would begin: I would get flowers and love letters and promises of better behavior. To a one, they would plead for a second chance, but by the time we had reached this stage, I was already out the door. Often at this stage I had my eye on someone else, who would no doubt turn out to be even worse, and the cycle would repeat. Eventually, though, I could no longer endure all the suffering required for that sick little thrill, an increasingly unsatisfying payoff.

In our sessions, Kieran helped me see the ridiculousness of—and the tinge of narcissism behind—The Needless Wonder routine (*I'm above needs...*), and to let go of it. He was determined to help me shift everything about my entire view. "Stop living in a women's magazine version of the world," he would plead, trying to prod me into action. "Start being real—and having needs. You won't have a satisfying relationship until you do."

We went around and around this. He would explain that he actually liked women who knew what they needed and weren't afraid to ask for it, who had a gusto for life that inspired them to reach for whatever it was they desired. He said he most appreciated those women who didn't crumble or turn cold when their men failed to meet, or psychically anticipate, their every need—women who didn't experience such a failure as rejection. This all blew my mind.

∝ఌ

I was learning so much from Kieran, The Swashbuckling Shrink. But I was learning too slowly. Yes, over time I was moving in the direction of nicer men—and becoming a whole person, with or without a man. But I'd started treatment at 34 and before I knew it, I was 37 and concerned about finding a life partner while there was still time to allow the possibility of having kids. (I hadn't yet come to realize that I didn't want them.) Kieran prescribed something he thought might help me advance more quickly toward better relationships with better men: online dating.

I was actually the one who brought it up, but not in reference to myself. I'd been working on an article about Match.com and other dating sites for *The Daily News*'s terribly named "T-hers-day" section for women. When I mentioned in one of our sessions how ingenious it seemed to be able to know right up front who had the qualities you were looking for, who was single, who was interested, who was *available*, Kieran asked, "So...why aren't you doing it?"

Uhhhh...

That was it. He made it our next lab experiment. My homework: sign up for at least one dating site. I complied—with a vengeance. In a matter of days, I had profiles on five of them: Match, Matchmaker, Nerve Personals, Yahoo Singles, and E-Harmony. As soon as the profiles went live, men started contacting me. It was thrilling! I'm ashamed to admit how much of a buzz I got off of all that male attention. That is, until I started corresponding with some of the men, and meeting a few, for coffee, or drinks, or dinner. Nope, nope, nope...

Most of the men reaching out to me were exactly who I was trying to train myself away from liking—shallow, unavailable men interested only in casual dating, many of whom seemed to be drawn in by my new blondeness. There was a notable uptick in responses a couple of weeks into my online dating experiment, beginning the day after I bleached my hair for the first time.

After I colored my hair that first time, on cue, one guy from Match—who'd ghosted me two weeks earlier, after meeting me as a brunette—suddenly reappeared in my inbox. He wrote, "My mother always told my sister, 'If you want to see how stupid men are, dye your hair blonde.' Want to go out again? " I met him for lunch, and then he ghosted me again.

∽

There were other men on the dating sites who caught my eye, men who seemed more thoughtful, at least according to their profiles.

"So, what happens when you reach out to them?" Kieran asked.

"Oh, no," I insisted, "I don't reach out to men."

"Why not?" he asked.

"Because men don't like women who make the first move."

"They don't? That's news to me."

I told him about *The Rules*, a retrograde dating guide I had hate-read out of curiosity, which advised women never to call a man and rarely return his calls, to always be the first to hang up, and to quickly drop guys who tried to split the bill on dates, or who didn't adhere to other strict criteria for princely behavior.

I didn't like the ideas behind *The Rules*. I resented—still resent—the capitalist notion that scarcity makes something, or someone, seem more attractive, or valuable. (Never mind that I was inclined to give more attention to less available men; that tendency, though, struck me as unhealthy, and I wanted to change it.) *The Rules* seemed to leave women little choice other than to be passive and manipulative. I figured there had to be a better, more direct way. Then again, my own weird approach to relationships didn't seem to be much more empowering: somewhere along the line I'd gotten the idea that the object of the game was to waste a lot of time appeasing the least interested and least attentive man (who'd made the first move, but then retreated) then reduce him to groveling by turning the tables. It was *The Rules* in reverse.

While I never fully got on board with the philosophy, I found myself intrigued by *The Rules*. I kept coming back to it, every time my own approach failed. I polled friend after friend, one of whom claimed to not even know her boyfriend's phone number six months into their relationship. "I don't call men," she huffed.

Half of me longed to try the hard-to-get approach, the other half thought it was unnatural and counterintuitive. I mean, how long could you keep that up, anyway? According to the original book (and the subsequent *Rules for Marriage*), it was never safe to drop your mask of indifference.

After I explained it to him, Kieran dismissed *The Rules* as pure, unadulterated bullshit. He insisted, once again, again that women who asked for what they wanted were *more* attractive to him and other men he knew, not less. I so wanted to believe him, to become one of those kinds of women, but I was having a hard time taking that leap of faith. So Kieran made it my next homework assignment. "You need to reach out to five men before your next appointment," he said. "No excuses. Just do it."

So, I did. I reached out to exactly five men. This was in direct defiance, by the way, of Rule 1 in the latest edition, *The Rules for Online Dating*. A few of the men wrote back and asked me out. I started getting involved with one, but I remained mostly passive with him. I would inch myself right up to the ledge, preparing to initiate a call to him, or to speak up about something I wanted instead of being meek and racking up resentments. Then I would dial Kieran. "Are you *sure* it's O.K. for me to call this guy?" I'd ask.

"What do you have to lose?" he'd say.

A couple of months later, on *Nerve* Personals, I spotted "bri_spy," a nice-looking guy with a boyish smile and twinkling Irish eyes who, according to his profile, liked to write poetry and music, but also couldn't live without his power tools. And he was searching, according to his profile, for a woman who didn't play games.

I was dying to reach out to him. Even if this wasn't my guy, I wanted my therapist to be right and "The Rules" authors to be wrong. I mustered the courage to drop bri_spy a line. My heart pounding, I read his immediate response, and for a couple of days we went back and forth, our "conversation" easygoing yet flirty. I knew it would be only a matter of time before we met.

Then he dropped off the face of the earth.

I was stunned. My faith in my therapist evaporated. Then, two months later, bri_spy showed up again in my inbox, apologizing for his disappearance: his mother, he explained, had had a heart attack. I'm ashamed to say I was relieved. We resumed our email relationship. Then he disappeared again.

Twice burned, I decided to give up online dating altogether and announced to friends the official death of "rubybaby," my online dating alter ego. Not long after that, I went on a run through the East Village, and ... wait, wasn't that bri_spy? Standing next to that car? Yes, that was the face from his profile picture. My mind churned through the options: Do I say hello, ignoring the original Rule 2? Or run right by, self-respect in tow?

He started to walk away. If I didn't act soon, I would lose my chance.

"Are you Brian?" I heard myself say. "I don't know if you remember me, but we e-mailed a few months ago. How's your mom?"

In his version of our story, this is where the heavens parted and the angels sang. "We should talk," he said, beaming.

❧

It was incredibly helpful having Kieran on board as I navigated my new relationship with Brian, the man who would become my husband. (We've now been married for 17 years. It has been a great relief to realize that Kieran was right—it *was* possible to find and have a lasting relationship with a partner who wasn't interested in games, who wasn't turned on by withholding behavior, someone with whom I could be fully myself, with regular human needs and desires and everything. I never have to play games with Brian. *Never.*)

I continued therapy for another year-and-a-half, during which time Brian and I moved in together and got engaged. But then we found out we were getting kicked out of our affordable apartment. We needed money to move. We had to lower our expenses. Therapy, now at $120 per hour (indeed, as promised, Kieran had helped me get on my feet financially), was a big one. It seemed like time to wrap things up.

❧

I've had more than my share of therapists in my life, and only one has made it easy to terminate—she closed her practice to become an academic. All the others presented a struggle, and sometimes it was valid. As I mentioned earlier, in several cases, I never stayed long enough to make any progress. But there were a few therapists with whom I spent a few years, and each time I felt ready to say goodbye, or take a break, they made it hard for me to leave. (I blame the application of capitalism to health care.)

Kieran was no exception. He didn't make it easy to say goodbye. He tried to convince me that I should stay, that I *needed* to. I went back and forth in my mind over a couple of months before making the ultimate decision.

"You know," I finally told him, "my ending therapy the way I am, having a discussion about it, staying on for another month or two, seems like progress to me." He nodded, considering what I was saying. "And having the courage to stand my ground even though you've made some good arguments seems like even *more* progress."

I'm not sure whether he agreed with me, or realized I had made up my mind and he couldn't change it. But finally, he gave me his blessing. I thanked him for changing my life. He wished me well, and told me the door was always open, any time I wanted to return. I've since referred eight or nine friends to him, some of whom in turn referred their friends. I'm of a mind that the world would be a better place if more people spent a few years as co-researcher/specimens in Kieran's lab.

It's Not Over Until the Bride's Father Sings

I couldn't have found a more effective way to break my father's heart. I eloped to City Hall—a dingy room in the Manhattan Municipal Building, to be specific.

Other parents grieve when their children run off, even when it's their daughter's second time down the aisle and she's 39, as I was. But my father is Mr. Wedding, a well-known cantor who just about every Reform Jewish girl in New York was eager to hire to sing at her nuptials. Twisting the knife, my fiancé, Brian, was Catholic.

My father gives good wedding, complete with soulful chanting in his Metropolitan Opera award-winning baritone and thoughtful comments about each couple. I can hardly say my last name anywhere in Manhattan without hearing someone gush about the wonderful wedding he performed for a daughter.

I grew up going to weddings. After my parents divorced, when I was 10, my father used to pick up my sister and me for visitation after Sunday school. Often, our first stop before the movies would be a wedding ceremony he was performing. These events always gave me a little thrill. I, a child whose father had just moved out, was fixated on matrimony. I'd already wed my gay neighbor twice, when we were 3 and then 6 (we both wore gowns). I couldn't wait to do the real thing.

In too big a hurry, I married my college sweetheart, in a ceremony performed by my father in a temple, when I was a clueless twenty-three. We split when I was twenty-six. After the divorce, I took my time—thirteen years—getting to my second wedding, the one that tore my father apart.

Upsetting him was never the point. My fiancé and I had a practical reason for going to City Hall on a blustery February afternoon in 2005. We were getting kicked out of our East Village apartment and needed to earmark our wedding money for a down payment on a new place. I had also harbored a secret desire to elope. Since I'd already had the Big Jewish Wedding the first time around and had attended so many similar affairs in the city, that custom had come to feel hollow. I wanted to live out a different New York fantasy.

The biggest factor in our decision, though, was religion, or our common lack thereof. Brian was nonpracticing, and I hadn't been to temple in years. The divisiveness organized religion could cause had troubled me for years, ever since 1976, when I was eleven and landed my first boyfriend, a non-Jew. We were "going out" in the sixth-grade sense of the term, which meant that we never really went out except to walk together to a pizza place near school at lunchtime on Fridays. If the relationship could have led to something more, I'll never know, because at my father's urging I broke up with him after two weeks.

"You must end this!" my father pleaded. "I counsel couples all the time, so I know it rarely works with two religions."

"I'm eleven," I reminded him.

"But dating is premarital behavior!"

That was the end of that.

When I was fifteen, on the way home from confirmation class at my father's Manhattan synagogue, I casually informed him, "By the way, I'm not Jewish anymore." I'd learned that afternoon that David Ben-Gurion, the first Israeli prime minister, once said that to become a Jew, all you had to do was decide you were one. I figured it worked in reverse, too.

This was not random rebellion. My declaration was coming from a much deeper place: the boy my father had made me break up with in sixth grade had now made the high school football team. He was suddenly very popular, and he hadn't spoken to me in the four years since I'd broken up with him.

My father was relieved when, in my junior year in high school, I picked a boyfriend who was a member of the tribe. My next boyfriend, in college, was also Jewish, and he became husband No. 1. But that was the end of Jewish boyfriends for a while.

Now and then my father would try to intervene. Once, he set me up with the fellow who stayed late after Friday night services to rearrange the prayer books. My father also campaigned endlessly for the television "gadget guru" I'd met at a trade show. When that guy got busted on a cocaine rap, I sent my dad the Associated Press article by email. Subject line: "Your son-in-law, the gadget guru."

When Brian and I announced our engagement, my father thankfully spared us the lecture about the challenges of a mixed marriage. He even offered to perform our wedding. But we wanted a ceremony that fit us uniquely—a "recovering Catholic" and a wayward Jew, both with Buddhist leanings. We wanted to make everyone happy, not just my parents, but also Brian's mother, an orphan who had been raised in convents. We decided to just go to City Hall and have a party later that year.

I loved our no-frills civil ceremony at the Municipal Building, in an institutional room with bad fluorescent lighting. It was intimate and private, and we got to focus on each other without worrying about whose heritage was better represented, or who would be seated on the dais. Afterward, we walked to the middle of the Brooklyn Bridge for a Champagne toast. I can't think of a happier moment. Before escaping to the mountains for a honeymoon weekend, we made a quick round of calls.

"Well, if there's anything I'm not," my father said slowly on the other end, "it's unhappy for you." His usually confident voice was unsteady, barely masking his disappointment. My throat grew a lump. A few months later, we argued over who was more neglectful of whom. My father won. "You ran off and got married without your parents present!" he yelled. "By a civil servant! A nobody!"

I thought I could make it up to him at the small celebration we'd planned for a few months later. Brian and I had discussed a "some from Column A, some from Column B ceremony," with a little Thich Nhat Han here, a little Rumi there. I could give my father something to do—a kiddush, maybe.

Then we went to a friend's Park Avenue wedding. Brian eyed the chuppah as we sat down. "It symbolizes the couple's first home," I whispered. "Oh," he whispered back. "Can we have that?" Next, he heard the cantor sing sheva bruchas, the seven blessings meant to send the couple off to a life of health and happiness. Brian leaned in again. "Can we have that, too?"

I couldn't very well have a chuppah and sheva bruchas without enlisting my dad to officiate. It felt surprisingly good to ask him. He didn't even try to hide his glee.

On a hot Sunday in June of 2005, under a homemade chuppah, my mother and Brian's mother lit a unity candle together. His brother and nephews took turns reciting lines from a traditional Irish blessing. Then my father did what the other New York Jewish girls were so eager to hire him for: he offered many kind words, and sang one blessing after another, magnificently.

PART 3

Blossoming

New York Cool

When I lived in the East Village from the mid-'90s to the mid-aughts, now and then my hip aunt and uncle from the West Coast would come to visit. Before they arrived they'd ask me to suggest things to do and see, and places to eat—the underground hot places not yet recommended in the *New York Times* and *New York* magazine. "Where do all the cool New Yorkers who dress in black go now?" they'd ask, half-kidding.

As if I knew! I'd only been trying for decades to become a cool New Yorker—a cool *anything*—and failing miserably at it. Growing up, I'd been sure that moving to the city from the suburbs was a significant step toward that coveted transformation. I figured once I got myself there, everything else would just fall into place. Ha!

I harbored that false impression from the first time I visited the city without my parents, as a young teenager.

—❧

In the fall of 1979, when I was 13-and-a-half, I was allowed for the first time to go unchaperoned to Manhattan with my stepsister, who was a year older. The plan was to get together with friends from summer camp, some of whom were a couple of years older. We assured our parents we were in good hands; our friends knew how to navigate the buses and subways. For the first time I felt like a real teenager and not a little kid, so grown up and sophisticated, even though before we boarded the Metro North from Westchester, where my dad now lived, my step-mother safety-pinned a five-dollar bill into each of our front pockets in case we were mugged.

We didn't do anything special with our friends that day, mostly just walked around the Village. There were six or seven of us casually bouncing from record store to pizza parlor to head shop to a boutique on MacDougal Street called Reminiscence, where some of the girls among us would spend our baby-sitting money on the store's famously inexpensive brightly colored carpenter pants. We hung out in Washington Square Park near the fountain, huddling around the guitar players strumming folk songs and singing along. We thought that was the coolest thing in the world. We were too young and un-initiated then to know how *uncool* and touristy a New York City cliché that was.

It was the first time I'd ever gone to the city to do *nothing in particular*, and that detail alone changed me. With my family, I'd gone to plays, concerts, the circus. This was different. It was actually more exciting, because you didn't know what you were going to see, or where you were going to land. I tried to seem blasé about it, though. There was something inherently blasé about coming to the city to do nothing in particular, wasn't there? *No big deal. I'm just walking around the city with my friends. I'm cool.*

As we traipsed around the park, an assortment of men passed us by, shifting their eyes, not turning their heads, asking each of us under their breath, "Want a lude?" I kept hearing it, over and over. *Want a lude? Want a lude? Want a lude?* By the fountain, by the playground, by the chess tables, by the arch. *Want a lude? Want a lude?*

I tried not to react. I didn't want to let on to my friends that I was so unhip as to have not even the vaguest idea what that was. I knew enough from the way the men asked that it was probably something drug-related. My friends probably knew what it was. Most of them were smoking pot already, or had at least tried it. I had not.

Or could it have been sex related? Were those men offering a *lewd*?

I waited until my step-sister and I were on the train back to Westchester to ask her plainly, "What's a lude?"

She thought for a second. "I'm pretty sure it's a thing you use to put the pot in the joint."

Hmm. I nodded but didn't say anything; I wasn't convinced.

When we got home, I asked, "Dad, what's a lude?" Needless to say, we were forbidden from visiting the city unchaperoned again.

That's when I started sneaking in on my own, walking around and doing nothing in particular, just absorbing the city's city-ness, letting it keep changing me. I often say that New York City is where I became *me*—I've heard many other people say the same—and it was in those days that it began.

I wanted desperately to be changed, to feel and be different. I was so unsure of myself—an awkward mix of extrovert and introvert, loner and social butterfly. I was a goody-two-shoes who felt out of step with my peers, who were less afraid to experiment with independence and rebellion—who were familiar with current music, while I mostly only knew show tunes, and pop standards. Like all teenagers, I wanted more than anything to be cool, and if the music you listened to determined whether you were, I was doomed.

Taste in music is how, from adolescence, we telegraph coolness and belonging to cultural tribes. I had no popular music literacy. An older friend—a surrogate brother, really—began making me mix tapes to bring me up to speed. To further fill in my huge gaps in knowledge, he suggested I listen to classic rock station WNEW. I started tuning in to 102.7 FM day and night, sometimes falling asleep to it, laboring earnestly to memorize the songs that were most frequently played, and all the trivia about each band that the deejays offered. Desperate to become conversant in popular-music-speak, I studied the subject of classic rock with greater diligence than I studied any subject at school. I ordered the WNEW calendar, with photos of the station's deejays, and hung it proudly on my bedroom wall, hoping its presence would lend me an air of coolness, of belonging, but it only took me so far. I was still an anxious dork. "Just be yourself," my mixtape making friend would advise me again and again when I confided about not knowing how to be at ease, socially. *Be myself?* I had no idea who that was.

In order to figure it out, ironically, I thought I needed to observe others. Where better to do that than the capital of cool? I'd ride the LIRR in and walk around the city studying people, searching for clues as to *how to be*—how to be anyone but dorky me, not to mention the kind of jaded New Yorker who knew what a "lude" was, and whether or not she wanted one.

—◦

A year later, when I was almost 15, I began traveling into the city one evening a week to attend Hebrew school. I miscalculated when I first met my classmates, a room full of prep school kids in school uniforms—crisply ironed Oxford shirts, wool skirts, trousers, monogrammed blazers—thinking they'd be a bunch of dorks. But I couldn't have been more wrong. Those kids were the hippest. They could go out to nightclubs and bars using obviously fake IDs. (This was 1980, and the drinking age in New York was 18.) They could go to the movies by themselves—someplace called Film Forum, which came up a lot among a certain subset when they gabbed before and after class and during break. I remember hearing some of them talk about someone named "Godard." I had no idea who Godard was—and because they kept dropping perfectly inflected French into the conversation, and not the *Voilà Madame et Monsieur Thibaud* kind of French I was learning on Long Island, I had no idea whether Godard was a he or a she or a musician or a poet, or their French teacher.

The kids from Hebrew school could go out *anywhere* in the city, and without having to ask their parents to drive them. They knew how to take the subway alone and weren't afraid of it. They listened to Lou Reed, Patti Smith, and John Coltrane. The girls smoked clove cigarettes. And they all knew that "lude" was short for Quaalude, the tranquilizer of choice among recreational users at clubs like Studio 54, which some of my classmates had been to. (A year later I'd try unsuccessfully to get in there with a couple of other kids from Long Island. The oldest of us would drive his family's paneled station wagon. We'd spend an hour trying to find a parking spot, only to be turned away at the velvet rope.)

I observed those city kids closely, listened to their conversations, envied their independence and sophistication. There was no way I was going to get in with them. I didn't even bother to try. I was too shy to even speak to them, most of the time.

Our teacher noticed and pulled me aside one day. "Don't let those kids intimidate you just because they're especially erudite."

"Okay," I said.

He paused a moment.

"Do you know what erudite means?"

"Of course," I lied.

I had never heard the word before, but I sensed it was another thing I envied about those kids, along with their cultural awareness, their worldliness, their self-assuredness—their cool New Yorkerness. I wanted to be like them. I figured it could happen, if I could someday move to the city.

—❦—

For the first fifteen years of my life, I grew up on Harbor Isle, a tiny island—just a quarter-mile square—within Long Island, just over the bridge from its main town, Island Park. As a weird, lonely teen, I'd take long walks around Harbor Isle's perimeter and stare off at the Manhattan skyline from its western edge. I'd tell myself, *Someday I'm going to live there.*

Eventually, beginning in my twenties, I did, in a variety of neighborhoods—the East Village, then Yorkville, then the Upper West Side, and finally back to the East Village, where I stayed for roughly a dozen years. I got a railroad apartment there, on East 13th Street, in the early 90s, and like so many who move to the East Village, I saw it as an opportunity to reinvent myself. Goodbye, bridge-and-tunnel goody-two-shoes! I was on my way to becoming...well, I didn't yet know what or who exactly. I looked to the East Village as my very own Dork Rehabilitation Program, designed to obliterate the social stigma of having grown up one of the teachers' kids in a rough suburban town—home of Henry Hill, of *Goodfellas* fame.

Growing up, I'd often overhear the tough, popular kids at school gauging their coolness relative to one another. "You go to the city? Yeah? Where you go?" CBGB's, Max's Kansas City, the Mud Club, even the folky bars on Bleecker Street were answers that would put you in pretty good standing. As opposed to: religious school.

A dozen or so years later, I *lived* in the city, while most of those kids, some of whom had bullied me, still lived in our hometown. Realizing that made me feel legitimized. Now in residence, once again I was studying people for clues as to *how to be*. This time I turned my attention to the outspoken, often pierced and tattooed, and Manic Panic-dyed women writers, artists, poets, and singers I came across. I saw them at downtown coffee shops and watering holes like the Nuyorican Poet's Café, Sidewalk, a grungy coffee house on Avenue A called Limbo, and Deanna's, a jazz club on East 7th Street where there were poetry readings on Sundays.

Deanna's was the first place I heard the late slam poet Maggie Estep, who passed away in February, 2014.

It wasn't the first time I caught sight of Maggie. I can't recall the specific moment when I first encountered her somewhere in the East Village. I'm not sure whether it was before or after I'd caught her hilarious spoken word MTV video for "Hey, Baby," a single off her "No More Mister Nice Girl" record. The one where she takes a lewd, crotch-grabbing cat-caller off guard with a brilliantly absurd response—basically, saying, "Sure, what you're proposing sounds fantastic, let's go back to my place..."

For some reason I have it in my mind that I hadn't yet known, the first time I spotted Maggie, that she was famous; that you didn't need to know that in order to get what a cool New Yorker she was, to be impressed by the confident way she stomped around the city in a fitted black dress, fishnets and combat boots, her full lips coated in that matte cinnabar red that was popular then, her expression equal parts "Look at me," and "Who the fuck are *you* looking at?"

I was in my mid-twenties then, just a couple of years younger than Maggie. I'm embarrassed to admit that before seeing the video for "Hey, Baby" on MTV, it hadn't occurred to me to feel anything but flattered and validated when men on the street cat-called. And that before hearing her perform her poem, "The Stupid Jerk I'm Obsessed With," it hadn't quite dawned on me that some of the men in my life qualified for that distinction, as well.

I didn't know Maggie yet, but I looked up to her. Knowing that she lived in the East Village like I did made me feel like a cool New Yorker by association. She seemed genuinely to not give a shit what you thought of her, and that, more than anything, made her cool—not just *tough* cool, but *smart* cool. *New York* cool.

I couldn't master that, though. For the longest time, I still gave too much of a shit about what people thought of me—kept earnestly, aggressively trying to up my coolness quotient. For example, I worked hard to pass myself off as a freelance music writer, eventually covering pop, rock, metal, hip-hop, and nightlife for *Billboard*, *Rolling Stone*, the *New York Times*, and *MTV News*. By day I wrote for trade magazines about the home furnishings and apparel businesses, but at night, I would go out to hear music mostly so that I could make connections. A lot of it was music I didn't like. I was, first and foremost, a musical theater geek, a lover of old standards and show tunes. I felt like a complete fraud in the worlds where I'd made my beat. Every time I was assigned another musician or band to write about, I had to do a Nexis search just to find out who they were.

This was me *trying* to be cool, which was, of course, the opposite of cool. Especially when not having enough of a background in what I was trying to write about led to full-on anxiety attacks and lack of sleep and imposter syndrome, which in this case was genuine. Ultimately, after too many instances where I had hardly any idea who and what I was writing about, I had to quit doing that work. It wasn't me. I switched to ghostwriting instead, which—well, obviously that really wasn't being me either, but in a different way.

—◌

I wish I could remember how or when, but at some point along the way, I stopped caring about being cool, or whether I was a real New Yorker rather than Long Island "bridge and tunnel." I somehow finally realized that being cool had nothing to do with being a music journalist or knowing about French film or wearing combat boots or getting piercings and tattoos—although I would get a navel ring in my thirties, and my first of three tattoos (so far) in my late forties.

I'll admit, though, that leaving New York City for upstate—as I did in 2005, after losing my apartment—elicited a certain anxiety about my ability to retain whatever coolness factor fifteen years there had bestowed upon me. I like to believe that once a New Yorker, always a New Yorker. That the city changes you, irreversibly.

There are moments, though, when I realize I'm completely out of the loop with things happening in the city. So many of my favorite places are gone. I don't know where to eat, or hang out—I have to figure it out each time I take the bus down. It's in those moments that I worry: am I clueless? Am I a hick now? Have I lost all my cred?

A few years ago, though, I was given a glimmer of hope that has mostly stuck with me. When a non-profit storytelling organization I was involved with held a story slam at a nightclub in my new home of Kingston, I was taken aback by one of the names on the sign-up list: Maggie Estep.

Could it be *that* Maggie Estep, I wondered. One of the people who first popularized and personified poetry slams? The performer who covered Lou Reed's "Vicious" in a music video directed by Steve Buscemi, in which Reed himself appears? The cool New Yorker I'd idolized?

Sure enough, it was *that* Maggie Estep. Although more demure in look and tone than I'd remembered her, her shiny black hair cropped short into a modern gamine cut. She read from "Diary of an Emotional Idiot," one of the seven critically acclaimed novels she'd written since her slam poetry days.

I learned that night that Maggie had left the city and moved upstate two years after I did, and never looked back. Knowing that, I thought, "Okay. Maybe I am still a little cool."

Unloading the Piano that Was Weighing Me Down

When you live in New York City, even the smallest objects in your apartment need to justify what scarce, high-priced real estate they occupy.

Every last jacket, book, serving bowl—*every single possession* must continually earn its keep. The meter is always running. Haven't used or worn it in a year? *Out.* Want new shoes? First evict an older pair. Signed up for Soul Cycle? Time to unload the exercise bike. No room for redundancy here, nor sentimentality for that matter.

Sentimentality, though, is no insignificant hurdle. It's an insidious force to be reckoned with, tripping up mechanisms in the brain otherwise reliable when it comes to making rational decisions.

This explains why I was living in small apartments in New York City for a dozen years before I put it together that a five-by-four-foot 400-pound object—one I'd paid various movers a small fortune to drag up and down creaky flights of stairs from one cramped dwelling to the next—was cluttering my 350-square-foot apartment. Also, my life.

I'm referring specifically to my upright piano, which became progressively more banged up each time it was manhandled by man-with-van types, who were less expensive to hire than professional piano movers. This was the instrument that had been in my family for multiple generations; the one I'd learned on (make that "learned"), and, mercifully for my neighbors, played infrequently.

This lightning bolt struck me in the summer of 2002. I was approaching 37 and going through the second break-up in as many years. After the last ex-boyfriend packed his stuff, I felt desperate for a fresh start in a new place. But as a perpetually broke freelance writer, I couldn't afford to ditch the $722/month rent-stabilized East Village walk-up I'd called home for nearly 10 years. I also couldn't afford to replace too many of my belongings. I'd have to find some cheap alternative for making my old place, filled with my worn-out furnishings, feel new again.

At the time, there was a good deal of buzz about space-clearing, and the Chinese art of Feng Shui. I was skeptical of its promise of better living through the very particular arrangement of apartment contents to encourage positive energy flow. But I was willing to give it a try. Most consultants charged high fees: $500 or more. So I did what I always have when I've wanted to sample something beyond my financial reach: I got a newspaper assignment to write about it, which would likely mean a free preliminary consultation, or a paycheck substantial enough to cover one.

Enter Carol, the sixtysomething Certified Apartment Organizer from the Upper East Side who boasted an additional certificate in Feng Shui. Carol was dressed in a Chanel tweed skirt suit, as if this were a lunch appointment at La Grenouille, and clearly wasn't used to visiting clients in run-down tenements in the East Village lacking elevators. I felt guilty for making her climb the three flights to my apartment. When she arrived, winded, she looked around and seemed utterly bewildered by the size and condition of the place—crooked, lopsided window sills and floors; peeling paint; too many books, too many layers of coats piled onto hooks affixed to lumpy plaster walls, too many threadbare flea market-purchased decorative appointments; not to mention a desk and chair I'd found on the street (read: in the garbage).

"Before I could even begin to tell you how to rearrange the place, you'd have to do some serious space clearing and get rid of *a lot*," Carol said. She echoed Maxwell, the guy from Apartment Therapy, whom I'd interviewed for the article the day before. He, in turn, echoed a palm reader who'd told me a few years back, "You hold onto things for too long."

"*Things* things," I'd asked the palm reader, "or, like, emotional baggage?"

"All of the above."

—◦

Carol instructed me to toss anything I didn't regularly use. "But what if it has sentimental value?" I begged.

"Take a picture of it. Then out it goes."

She saw a look of anguish cross my face and took a deep breath.

"Listen, if you're having a really hard time letting something go," she allowed, "put it aside in an *I'll Decide Later* box."

How do you put a piano in an *I'll Decide Later* box? It seemed like a Zen koan.

Carol eyed the mahogany upright. Out of tune and collecting dust, it had long ago become a catch-all surface for bills, greeting cards, free address labels from charitable organizations, packs of photographs, notebooks and other miscellanea.

"Do you play?" she asked.

"Sort of...?"

"How often?"

"Not often enough," I admitted, my eyes cast down.

Hmmm, I wondered, after the words left my lips. According to *whom?* To whom was I apologizing? Who in the world, in their right mind, cared whether or not *I*, a terrible pianist, played the piano more often? Certainly not the people living just beyond my paper-thin walls. I searched my mind. Was it Mr. Frank, my teacher until I quit, abruptly, *at 12?* My parents, who'd hounded me to practice more often as a kid? My dead grandparents, who'd paid for my lessons?

Talk about emotional baggage! I was staring at four hundred pounds of it, tapping its toe and judging me from across the room—a hulking *noodge* constantly reminding me of everything I ever thought I *should* do but either never got around to—or didn't really want to and felt afraid to admit it, or worse, doubted my own instincts. Everything from practicing musical instruments, to learning shorthand as a journalist, to calling back that nice but boring guy someone set me up with, to settling down and having kids. My sentimentality for the piano was inextricably bound up with guilt, and both emotions weighed heavily on me.

Suddenly I had a strong urge to get that monstrous thing out of my apartment. But was I ready to part with it *for good?* That seemed rash, and drastic. I wasn't sure.

—o

I got creative and devised my own *I'll Decide Later* box: I offered the piano for rent on Craigslist for just the cost of moving it, one way, to the renter's apartment. After the year was up, *I'd* have to pay to move it back. I deliberately made it expensive for myself to retrieve it; I had a strong inkling it would, in fact, be good, on many levels to clear the thing out of my space—that energy would flow better throughout my life without that clunky, imposing obstacle—but I was concerned sentimentality might get the better of me, once again, if the piano were too easily returned.

Shortly after I posted the ad, there were ten interested parties. I went with the Juilliard student living in South Slope.

I felt a twinge of sadness as his burly movers lugged the piano down three flights of stairs. But once they were gone, I was able to breathe more easily. It felt good, for the first time since I'd moved to the city after college, to reclaim the tiny strip of precious Manhattan square-footage the piano had occupied.

Months passed and I didn't miss the piano. I bought a guitar, took a few lessons from a friend, and suddenly I was doing something I didn't even know I could do, or wanted to: writing songs. Not terribly good ones, but I took it as a sign that some kind of creative energy was now flowing where it hadn't been. Soon, I'd meet my husband, and we'd play music together, too, sometimes recording the songs I wrote. That would happen a couple of months after I took my space-clearing initiative a step further and said goodbye to the piano for good.

—୨

The Juilliard student called one day to let me know he'd accepted a job with an orchestra in the Midwest. "You can come get your piano now," he said. But after trying out piano-less living for a year, I knew in my heart I didn't want it anymore.

Back it went on Craigslist, this time for sale. The Juilliard student let me show the piano out of his apartment one weekend. It wasn't long before I had a taker, a young guy who played in some kind of retro honky-tonk band.

I felt nothing as I watched him write the check for $350. But a second later, when he handed it to me, I was caught off guard by the return of my old friends, sentimentality and guilt, and I burst into tears. The Juilliard student grabbed a tissue for me.

"It's okay," the young buyer said consolingly, and then tentatively, "You know, I don't *have to* take it."

"No, no," I insisted, sniffling. "You do. You really do."

It was one thing to be sentimental. It was another to clog up your life with things—big things—you don't really want or need, and which long ago stopped warranting the valuable space they hogged, internally and externally.

I watched as the piano was hauled into yet another moving van. Then I wiped my tears, pulled myself together, and caught the subway back to my ever-so-slightly more spacious shoe box of an apartment.

Adventures in "Journalism;"
or
MFA vs. JOB

As an older writer, I'm often asked by aspiring younger writers for advice. How does one become a writer? How did *I* become one? I often pause before I answer, because a) there is no *one right way* to become a writer, and b) I'm pretty sure I went about it the wrong way. Or *a* wrong way. (Rest assured, there's no *one wrong way*, either.) Also, I feel very much like an under-achiever, and my career seems to me far from exemplary. Still, I get asked, so I answer.

(I'm also often asked whether I think it's worthwhile to pursue an MFA in creative writing, and despite being a two-time MFA dropout, and now an adjunct professor in two MFA programs, I don't have a clear-cut answer. More on that later...)

As with most creative professions, it helps to start out by being born rich, then going to all the best schools, where you make connections with people who can help usher you into the best jobs. Obviously, most people don't have that advantage. *I* did not have that advantage, and so perhaps it was foolish for me to aspire to career paths (plural) that favor the privileged. But I was (and kind of still am, against my better judgment) willing to be perennially broke and live lean, and juggle a million low-paying gigs, in order to stay true to myself and my dreams—or, at this point, keep doing the only work for which I'm actually qualified. It also helps to clarify your dreams early on, then commit to them doggedly—as opposed to, say, prioritizing useless, exhausting endeavors such as holding onto unavailable men. If only I hadn't gotten in my own way along those lines a million times. *If only, if only, if only...*

The younger writers who ask me for guidance see an older person whose name they've become familiar with, because they've read and heard it here and there. When they look at me, they don't see a person who has many regrets, who wishes she had more and greater successes under her belt. They don't see a person who has nothing resembling job security or financial stability, who, in her mid-fifties, has no idea what her future will look like, and whether she'll ever be hired for a job in her field again. (Or whether she will be competing for jobs with those very younger writers, themselves.)

I've had a weird, varied career—a function of both how misguided I've been in my pursuit of it, and how resilient I've managed to be when things have gone awry. I had an auspicious start when I was very young, then lost my way, putting me on a very circuitous career path, with assorted side-paths. As in most areas of my life, it's been a challenge within my career to truly...*find myself*.

Here, a little tour of the winding road I've been on—a bit more blooper reel than sizzle reel, I'm afraid.

—

I started writing at a young age, 7 or 8, but not with the intention of becoming a journalist or author. I was journaling because I felt unlike everyone else, and later writing plays, because I wanted to be an actress; I thought of it as, *ahem*, "writing my own material."

In college, although I was an English major and journalism minor, it hadn't occurred to me to pursue becoming a published author until the summer of 1986, between my junior and senior years, when I landed a much sought-after internship at *Newsday*. It wasn't even my idea to apply. I'd never written for a newspaper before, although in a prior college internship at the "I Love New York" campaign in Albany, I'd written travel articles that were picked up by local papers around the state. I didn't think I was really interested in writing for newspapers and magazines. But then both my father and my college boyfriend saw ads for the *Newsday* internship, and both pushed me to send in an application.

"I'm sorry," I insisted to each of them separately, "but I'm a *playwright*." Two plays I'd written at college had received staged readings, so I was feeling confident and mistook playwriting for an actual, viable profession you could just go into when you graduated. Also, the *Newsday* application was hard. You had to write three pieces: a 500-word news item, a 1000-word feature, and a 750-word mini-profile of yourself in the third person. I almost blew the assignment off entirely, but just under the wire, I finished the pieces and submitted them. I had no expectation of getting the internship. In the application they noted that they typically received three-thousand or more applications for thirty spots. I forgot about it and went about finishing up my junior year. That April I got a phone call offering me a spot. I was so shocked and thrilled and honored, I screamed.

—

In the '80s, *Newsday* was a very prestigious, Pulitzer Prize-winning newspaper, and I couldn't believe I would have a summer job there. But first I needed to locate a car, which was required for the internship. There was no extra car in my family, and I didn't have the money to buy even the world's ricketiest beater.

I reached out to my maternal grandfather. I was nervous about asking him for help, but I didn't know where else to turn. After we spoke, he rented me a car for the summer: a fancy Chrysler New Yorker. *From a mobster.*

My grandfather told me to meet a guy named Bob at a sketchy, nondescript building with no company name on it, in the center of Long Island. Tall and meaty, with an enormous neck, and dressed in a double-breasted suit, Bob looked like he'd just walked off the set of *Goodfellas*. In the back of the building, Bob showed me around my summer car. Inside it was newly detailed and plush, with velour seats, and a leather-covered steering wheel. The car talked at a time when that was unusual and fancy; if you started it before all the doors were closed, a clipped robotic woman's voice announced, "A door is ajar." Except there was a beat between "a" and "jar," so it sounded like she was saying, "A. Door. Is. A. Jar." I would often answer back, "No, a *door* is a *door*."

When Bob popped the trunk to show me the spare tire, I almost fainted. It reeked of vomit. There were dark stains on the felt lining. Bob was unfazed. When I got home and opened the trunk again to air it out, I found several crack vials, one of them with a few rocks in it.

I wasn't in any position to be choosy, though, or complain. It was a car for the summer, for free. And it was elevating the *Newsday* internship from possibility to reality.

—

I assumed that at *Newsday*, at least part of my work would be secretarial. But it wasn't. Not in the least. I was placed on the arts desk, and as soon as I arrived, my editor threw me in the deep end. She assigned me arts features and profiles, one or two a week. I interviewed actors, directors, filmmakers, writers, and artists. I was sent on assignment to Manhattan with my long, narrow reporters' notebook. On some of those days, I would work in the paper's Manhattan office in the Wang building on Third Avenue in Midtown, where the offshoot *New York Newsday* was headquartered. There I met legendary newspaper figures like Sidney Shanberg. It was all an incredible thrill, but none of it matched seeing my byline in the paper I'd grown up reading on Long Island.

Taking a little shine off the experience though, I was going through a breakup with my college boyfriend. As the summer went on, I got deeply into my work, and stopped worrying so much about that. I was meeting interesting people all the time, and flourishing, and enjoying my work, and starting to feel as if my future could possibly be bright. But then after my *Newsday* internship was over, and I returned to school, my ex- and I rekindled, and I resumed making our relationship the primary focus of my existence. Still, once back at school, I was able to get some freelance assignments writing arts pieces for the *Albany Times Union* and a now-defunct alt weekly magazine called *Metroland*, which I enjoyed, and which made me remember, in some small part of myself, that I was more than just some guy's girlfriend.

After interning at *Newsday* and then freelancing my senior year, I assumed I was set for a career as an arts journalist. Then I graduated and started looking for jobs, and boy did I get a reality check. *Newsday* made a point of telling interns that no matter how well you did while you were there, they wouldn't hire you right out of college; they wanted you to develop your chops at smaller papers, in smaller cities around the country. It's conceivable I might have been able to land a job at a small paper somewhere else in the U.S., or in another country, and eventually make my way back to New York, or to a bigger paper in another major city. But I didn't even apply to any.

If I had, I might have benefitted from the experience of living somewhere else and broadening my horizons. I might have followed a clearer career trajectory as a journalist and editor. If I'd taken just a little time away from constantly being in all-consuming, difficult relationships beginning at 15, I'd have also had the time and energy for the creative writing I wanted to pursue, separately, on the side. But I didn't do any of that. After graduation, I moved back home to my mother's house, and looked for jobs in the city, so that I could be near my boyfriend.

As I embarked on my post-college career, it never occurred to me that as a 22-year-old, I'd have to now take a step back and work up to the kind of jobs I'd already been doing as an undergrad. I sent my resume and clips everywhere, but got zero bites. To hold myself over, I took a retail job at the costume jewelry counter at Macy's, weekends and three weekdays, leaving two weekdays for job interviews.

I scoured the Help Wanted section of the *New York Times*. (There was no internet yet.) Each week under "Editorial" there were listings posted, mostly by the Helen Akullian agency, but they were typically $12,000-a-year "gal Friday" or secretarial jobs at book publishers and magazines, and they required typing tests. Basically you needed to be from a rich family, which I was not, and to be able to type sixty words per minute, which I could not (without several errors per try).

After not hearing back from a single publication on my own, I brushed up on my typing (I'd failed that class in high school) and went to see Helen.

Helen took one look at my resume and clips and told me I had to make a choice: I could become a secretary at the kind of publication where I wanted to write, and hope that eventually it would lead to something bigger, or I could write, right away, for a trade publication. I had never even heard of trade publications—newspapers and magazines that were targeted toward people who worked in particular industries. It sounded incredibly boring, but if it meant being a writer *now*, I was game.

I interviewed for both kinds of jobs. At the consumer magazines she sent me to, Helen instructed me to refrain from showing my clips, because she thought I'd seem too ambitious and unwilling to pay my dues. I was stunned by that advice. It wouldn't be the last time I was advised to shrink myself and seem less threatening. I refused to do that. But I've often wondered whether in refusing, I made the wrong choice, derailing myself early on: I was so impatient for a chance to be a writer *right away* that I got myself stuck, for a good eight years, in trade publications.

At least I didn't take the first job I was offered, at a trade magazine covering the pest control industry, with a readership of professional exterminators. (That's right, there is literally a trade magazine for *everything*.) I was drawn instead to *Body Fashions/Intimate Apparel (BF/IA)*, then published by Harcourt Brace Jovanovich, covering the women's underwear trade.

I have a protective little soft spot for 22-year-old me, the cub reporter who took her job as an assistant editor at *BF/IA* verrrry seriously. It might not have been the arts pages of the *New York Times*, or even my alma mater, *Newsday*, but I was going to act as if it were, goddamnit. I was not willing to be hidden like the underthings I was writing about! I was going to stand out in this job, and I was convinced that was going to eventually help me get my light out from under the trade magazine bushel. I took on extra assignments on my own time, and applied my arts writer flair to them. I wrote a long essay—my first longform— drawing connections between Madonna's penchant for wearing bustiers and bras publicly, and the Rococo period of art, when Jean-Honoré Fragonard painted "The (Happy Accidents of the) Swing," in which a woman's long bloomers peek out at the viewer. How important I felt visiting the Mid-Manhattan Library in pursuit of permission to reprint this masterpiece—*in an underwear trade rag*! I was so proud of the resulting piece, I stayed late on the night that month's issue came out so I could sneak ten copies home.

When *BF/IA* flew me out to a bra-fitting promotion at a Marshall Fields in Chicago sponsored by a company that manufactured underwire, I looked to it as an opportunity to build my chops as an *investigative journalist*. By gum, I was going to get the bottom of what percentage of women wore the wrong size bra, and why!

Aside from those two assignments, though, I found the job tedious and stifling. I wrote a column called "Behind the Seams," featuring round-up articles on trends in underwear design. Per the publisher's instructions, I interviewed only those manufacturers who'd bought ads that month, and allowed them to dictate and approve what was published. There was no proverbial "wall" between editorial and advertising there, as I'd been taught in my college journalism courses there should be.

Back I went to Helen Akullian, begging her to find me a job at a consumer magazine—preferably at Condé Nast or Hearst. While I waited for one of those jobs to materialize, I attended a press event for Givenchy Intimate Apparel and there met a reporter on the accessories beat for *Women's Wear Daily*. She told me she was about to shift into a new job, and she'd be happy to introduce me to her editors if I wanted to apply for hers.

—❧—

Women's Wear was different from other trade publications. I'd been peeking at it since I worked weekends and summers for my grandfather's women's sportswear firm on Seventh Avenue. Sure, *WWD* covered mainly industry news, but it was *real* news, not promotional advertorial that brands dictated, like at *BF/IA*. *Women's Wear* also had *attitude*, and it had a gossip column called the Eye, and occasional arts coverage, which made it less boring and trade-like. Plus, Fairchild Publications owned *W Magazine* and a new additional celebrity/gossip sister magazine called *Scene*.

If I could get the job at *WWD*, I thought, maybe in time I could move over to their arts and gossip departments, and get myself out of trade publishing before long. I'd been at *BF/IA* only nine months when I was hired as assistant accessories editor at *WWD*. My salary jumped from $17.5K to $23K. I felt like such hot shit.

I was also thrilled that I'd now be working in the Village, as opposed to midtown, where my job at *Body Fashions/Intimate Apparel* had been located. Fairchild Publications was headquartered at 7 East 12th Street in those days, between Fifth Avenue and University Place, across the street from Gotham Bar & Grill, which provided great socialite- and celebrity-watching.

I was given a desk in the front row of the third floor newsroom, right across from the receptionist, Jean, who chain-smoked cigarettes all the livelong day. Jean smoked so much her teeth were falling out; she looked like a public service ad for why you shouldn't smoke. Smoldering cigarette butts overflowed from the ashtray on her desk. I have never smoked a single cigarette in my life, but I worry all the time about the second-hand smoke I took in while working across from Jean.

Obviously, this was before smoking was banned inside office buildings and restaurants. It was 1988, and there were even still smoking cars on the LIRR, which I rode to work each day, from Long Island.

At *Women's Wear*, we had to share computers. There was one desktop PC for every two reporters, balanced on the edges of our adjacent desks, with a monitor on a sort of lazy Susan, so it could be easily swung to face whichever reporter was using it. I shared mine with a fashion editor, who did less writing and more styling of photo shoots, so it was rarely a problem. If your computer was occupied, you looked for another vacant one at someone else's desk. At super busy times, like Fashion Week, you just had to wait, or use one of the many IBM Selectric typewriters scattered around the newsroom, which we regularly used to write letters to people in the industries we covered.

After working at a monthly publication, it was exhilarating to get back to the pace of a daily. I took the subway out into "the market" a few days a week to visit accessories manufacturers and retailers in the fashion district, to get the scoop on the latest trends and happenings. (While there I'd hit up sample sales I'd read about in The S&B Report, where I'd regrettably purchase the least expensive, least ugly item I could find in the shortest amount of time.) I'd often return with samples that I then had to bring to the art department at the back of the newsroom so that one of the fashion illustrators, brilliant artists like Steven Stipelman and Robert Passantino, could draw renderings of them.

Then I'd write my articles and send them to my editor, who'd do a round of tightening and tweaking. From there my pieces were sent on to either the city editor or the managing editor, two older men, depending on who was free. This is where the hard lessons were learned.

Those men went through your work with a fine tooth comb. You had to sit beside them on the hot seat and answer questions about every aspect of your article, from angle to structure to word choice. They were not at all friendly about it, and sometimes when I was done getting the third degree, I'd run to the bathroom and cry. Many reporters did. Still, I learned so much from those editors. They made me a better writer, and also taught me how to be an editor myself—and just as importantly, how *not* to. I incorporate much of what I learned from them in my editing work, although with much more patience and kindness.

Every day, flowers arrived for *WWD* reporters, sent by the manufacturers and retailers who were covered in that day's paper—as long as they liked what was published. If you didn't get flowers, you knew your subjects were pissed.

When I received my first bouquet, the managing editor came over to my desk. "Don't ever think that has anything to do with you," he said, rather brusquely. "But also, don't take it personally when they don't send flowers. It has absolutely nothing to do with you, your work, or your worth."

—◦

I was good at my job at *WWD*, but I could have been better. Once again, my main focus was on the man in my life, instead of my work. I was busy pursuing the validation that came with being chosen by a man who was difficult to hold onto, seeking to fulfill my married, suburban destiny. I was 23, and obsessed with earning Elliott's commitment. In June of 1989, four months before my 24th birthday, we married. Marrying young might not be a wrong choice for everyone, but it very much was for me. The marriage would last three years, and in that time, I'd engineer all my other choices in support of it.

One of those choices was leaving *WWD* after eighteen months so that I didn't have to commute to and from my home town on Long Island, where we'd moved together. Okay, that wasn't the only reason I left. I had quickly become dissatisfied with my job on the accessories beat at *WWD*. Occasionally I got to report on stories that felt as if they held significance beyond the hollow world of manufacturing and retail—for instance, crackdowns on sweatshops and manufacturers of counterfeit goods. But most of what I covered seemed insignificant and boring to me. I longed to write for the Eye; for *WWD*'s sister publication, the consumer title, *W*; and for *Scene,* which Fairchild had recently launched to compete with the original, pre-Condé Nast *Details* and Forbes's short-lived *Egg*. It wasn't that I loved what they were publishing. I just saw it as a route out of trade journalism, which bored me, and did not allow me to shine.

Goddamnit, I wanted to *shine*. After my early career experiences, I was spoiled. I worried that the longer I wrote for the trades, the more entrenched I'd become, and the harder it would be to switch to consumer publications. I was too young and shallow to recognize the quiet respectability in well-executed trade journalism at an established paper.

But the reporters and editors who worked on the arts and gossip beats were part of a kind of exclusive club, and I couldn't find a way in. They were from moneyed families, and had gone to fancy colleges and prep schools. Many of the women were tall and modelesque, the men preppy and well-connected. Some were from families that had connections to the Park Avenue socialites *WWD* and *W* covered. I didn't stand a chance. That part of the newsroom was incredibly clique-y. Some of the top editors were notoriously bitchy. Just before I left *WWD*, *Spy* magazine ran a damning profile of one top editor, a cruel modelizer, alleging, among other sins, that he liked to punk guests to the office by offering them glasses full of "white wine," which was actually his urine.

WWD was also a hard place to maintain any kind of healthy body image. I'd struggled with an eating disorder as a teen (who in my age group didn't?), and was still progressing in my recovery. There were days I felt okay—better than okay—about how I looked. Then I'd go to the women's room, which doubled as a dressing room for the photo studio. There I'd find the likes of Christy Turlington, Linda Evangelista, and Naomi Campbell—or a gaggle of willowy teens newly arrived from the South, or the Midwest, or eastern Europe—dressing and undressing for a shoot, a foot taller than me, and flawless.

I might never fully recover from the embarrassment of needing to gargle after wisdom tooth extraction beside Cindy Crawford, as she fixed her makeup.

—◦

As I was approaching a year-and-a-half at *WWD*, a friend of the family got in touch to say he was launching a news weekly on Long Island. Did I want to be the "People Editor"? It entailed writing and editing human interest stories about Long Islanders—albeit for a pay cut. This job would solve multiple problems, though: I'd no longer have to commute to the city, which cost a lot of money, and I'd have a path out of trade journalism. I was ecstatic—so ecstatic that I didn't ask enough questions about what the publication would be like. I had no idea that I was leaving a coveted position at a respected news organization to work at a shitty *Penny Saver*, one that would fold six months later.

After that job ended, while on unemployment, I freelanced and applied for jobs. Again I sent my resume to Condé Nast and Hearst, landed a few interviews, and never got the jobs. I was only 24, but I was certain my career was over. I did *not* apply for jobs at trade publications—not until after my unemployment ran out. That's when I got hired as the editor-in-chief of a monthly trade called *Fashion Jewelry Plus!*

The magazine was published by a family-owned trade show company based in Newton, Mass. I was based in their New York office, on Seventh Avenue in Manhattan, but I had to fly to Newton each month for meetings and fashion shoots. At *Fashion Jewelry Plus!* the editor-in-chief did pretty much everything on the editorial front. I wrote all the articles (many of which were little more than coverage of the company's own trade shows, and the manufacturers who spent the most money on booths and ads), and styled the photo shoots.

The magazine was utterly hideous. It wasn't a real magazine—by and large it was a trade show directory. I was mortified by my association with it. The most humiliating thing was running into to my former colleagues from *WWD* out in "the market." I didn't want to tell them where I was working. I didn't want them to ever encounter that stupid rag with my photo and editor's letter in each issue. More than that, I didn't want them to know how much I regretted leaving *WWD*, how far I'd set myself back by trying to move forward too quickly, without thinking things through. Eventually, though, after about two years, I admitted these things to my former boss. I begged her to take me back. She said there weren't any jobs at *WWD*, but that there might be some at other Fairchild titles. She suggested I get in touch with HR, which I did.

—◦

Next stop on the trade magazine train: *Home Furnishings Network* (*HFN*), one of *WWD*'s sister publications. At *HFN*, I would cover the most unlikely combination of four beats: decorative pillows, luxury linens, air purifiers, and personal alarms. (There was a moment in the early '90s when women were carrying personal alarms. How that category wound up being covered by *a home furnishings publication* escapes me, other than to guess that one of the ad sales people randomly got some personal alarm manufacturers to advertise. The biggest news story while I worked there involved Tonya Harding scaring away an assailant in a parking lot after setting off a personal alarm of her own.)

My day-to-day job was the old trade publication standard: a slog of manufacturer and retailer round-ups about consumer trends, and trips to boring trade shows. Gosh, I hated trade shows. More generally, I hated my job. But at least *HFN* was situated in the Fairchild newsroom on 34th Street—a *real* newsroom, which it shared with *WWD* and *W*.

I had the idea that if I could aim myself back toward *WWD*, where I'd started four years earlier, I could regain the footing I'd had before I left hastily, at the end of 1989. Maybe I'd eventually be poised to wend my way out of trade publishing altogether.

—◡

But that wasn't all I wanted. Now I had additional difficult-to-attain goals. The year before, in 1991, I'd taken a personal essay writing workshop at NYU, and it reignited my passion for creative writing, making my arts-journalism dreams pale in comparison. I'd enjoyed studying both creative writing and journalism in college, and it seemed there were elements of both in personal essays. I'd written them before, starting all the way back in fourth grade. (I won the school-wide essay contest that year, and the next. Yay, grade-school me!)

I had also started writing fiction that year—out of nowhere, for fun, with no real goal. A story was born in my head about a character named Julia Rosenbloom, a woman similar to me but not exactly the same—a woman who found the courage *not* to marry her college sweetheart.

Julia Rosenbloom was both worse and better than me. Meeker at first, more courageous in the end, willing to do and say things I never would. When I tried to get it all down on the clunky Mac PowerBook I'd just bought second-hand, I felt as if I were just following a thread, rather than making it all up.

I knew that publishing any of my creative writing was going to be much harder than even breaking back into consumer journalism. Now I had two difficult ladders to climb. I needed to allow myself time, and also study more. Another reporter in the Fairchild newsroom attended Sarah Lawrence's MFA program. I started applying to programs, submitting chapters of my novel-in-progress. I was pleasantly surprised when I got into several, including Sarah Lawrence.

—9

I tried desperately to make a go of juggling an MFA program with a full-time job, first at Sarah Lawrence, which I couldn't afford, and then at City College. But I couldn't pull it off. There were only so many hours in the day, and I only had one brain. So I eventually gave up on my MFA dreams, and went back to trying to climb the Fairchild ladder, hoping that would eventually lead me out of Fairchild publications to better places.

Over time, I was able to hopscotch from the boring 35th Street end of the newsroom, where *HFN* was located, to the exciting 34th Street end of the newsroom, where *WWD* and *W* were headquartered, with a few stops in between, at other publications. Finally, I landed on the Eye desk.

Ironically, part of how I got myself there was through freelancing for other publications in the evenings while I worked at *HFN*. I'd work all day, then go out to events at night with a paparazzo I was dating. Our "dates" coincided with work. After a quick bite, Steve would take me along to nightclubs, or to stalk celebrities in places where he'd gotten tips they could be found. We once spent several hours sitting on a stoop across from Nell's on West 14th Street on a tip that a major celebrity might show up. We gave up around 3am and went back to Steve's place. Then his beeper went off. He jumped on his skateboard, cruising across 14th Street to get the shot.

When I married and moved to the suburbs in 1989, I could not have predicted that a few years later I'd find myself out at all hours many nights, observing famous people and their hangers-on partying to excess—drinking, dancing, snorting things, hooking up in the shadows. I was both repulsed and riveted. I've never truly felt I belonged anywhere, but in the nightlife scene, that was even more pronounced. Witnessing another world provided a kind of thrill I hadn't experienced before.

Early on, Steve suggested I bring along a reporter's notebook. "Take notes," he said. "Maybe get some quotes to go with my photos." This presented a new kind of challenge for me. I was awkward, shy, self-conscious. But I recognized this as an opportunity. I had to get over myself and take it. And I did.

Suddenly I was wearing yet another hat: In addition to being a trade reporter, arts journalist, and aspiring essayist, I was now also a gossip reporter—a job I'd long looked down upon. Steve and I packaged his photos and my reporting together and sold them to various outlets, including the Eye page at *WWD* and *W*, where I'd soon be hired.

But along the way to that, on the side, I'd turn nightlife into my beat for the *New York Times* City section.

—◎—

Ironically, it took freelancing for the *New York Times* to advance within Fairchild Publications, where I had my full-time job. They were impressed with my *Times* clips, and let me move up. At last, I had the job I wanted, or *thought* I wanted. As a reporter and editor on the Eye desk, I would be covering the arts, being a gossip reporter at night, and editing other writers, as well, including the veteran society reporter, Aileen Mehle, aka "Suzy." I was better at some parts of the job than others. I wrote strong profiles of people in the arts, and I came up with zingy copy and headlines for our gossip column. My biggest stumbling block was covering society events. An urchin in pilled office wear and tights, I stood out among the social X-rays dressed in couture. As an outsider in that world, I often made observations that were too sharp to publish, because the job of our society coverage was to *flatter* the subjects, even when we were playfully ribbing them, and feature flattering photos of them in the gowns that our biggest advertisers had made for them.

The job was incredibly demanding. I worked days and nights and some weekends—but that didn't stop me from continuing to build my freelance career on the side. Opportunities had come my way at *Billboard, MTV News* and other music outlets. While I was being an arts and gossip reporter in my full-time job, I was also trying to be a music writer outside of it. I'd become such a hustler over the years after languishing so long in trade publishing, that I never wanted to miss a single opportunity. I used vacation days to go and write news scripts for Kurt Loder, Tabitha Soren, and Serena Altschul.

—◎—

I lasted on the Eye desk for about a year. In 2020, after reading a colleague's book about the way in which they were fucking up back then, I have a new understanding of what happened, which led to my departure—an unfortunate pivot in my career at a critical juncture, when I was 31 and becoming established.

In 1996, there were some big errors on the Eye pages, and I got blamed for them. I was fairly certain the errors weren't my fault, although I was juggling a lot. Maybe I was off my game? Deep down, I knew that wasn't the case. Someone was fucking up, big time, but I didn't think it was me. Still, each time, I was the one called out on the carpet, not my colleague. Our boss, a notoriously brilliant but mean man, started bullying me in the newsroom, loudly, in front of everyone. He put me on probation because of the many errors I was certain I wasn't responsible for, and which—it would become clear to me after reading my former colleague's memoir—my opiate-addled former colleague likely was. But I wouldn't know that for another 24 years.

I became determined to leave my job. At an Author's Guild dinner I was covering that August, I was seated next to an agent who was looking for a ghostwriter for one of her clients. Was I interested? Was I ever.

And so began a new, weird chapter of my career.

—❧

I did not go toward ghostwriting because I thought I would like it, even though I adore memoirs. As with so many choices I've made over the years, I chose it because it was somewhat writing-career-adjacent, and a place to land after another career move wasn't working out for me.

Ghostwriting had its positive moments, when I got to help someone who wasn't a writer tell an important story. But over many years, I would come to have mostly negative experiences with entitled, spoiled, selfish rich people who were so used to having people do things for them, they didn't even realize they weren't doing those things for themselves. A celebrity wife for whomI wrote a book went on the radio and lied, insisting that her publisher had fired her ghostwriter after just one poorly-written chapter, and that she wrote the rest of the book herself in just five weeks, flat. It was mortifying.

One of the worst parts of ghostwriting for me was the self-abnegation involved. I had to use all my ability and creativity to write *someone else's story*, when I wanted to be writing my own. I would spend inordinate amounts of time in rich people's homes, interviewing them, coaxing their life experiences out of them, then trying to put it all together in a compelling way. Then I'd have to act as an intermediary between the editor and the ghostwriting client, and often they didn't agree on big aspects of the stories, or the framing of the books. There was almost always drama because of that, and extra work for me. If I weren't desperate for the money, I wouldn't have done any of it. Eventually, I swore off ghostwriting, and tried to find other means of gainful employment.

Sometimes I landed stints at newspapers and magazines—writing gossip for Rush & Molloy at the *Daily News*, or writing and editing at *Time Out New York*. Other times I scored short-lived high-paying copywriting gigs, writing the text for websites for brands like Maybelline and the United State Postal Service, or coming up with new names for standard pantyhose colors for New York & Company. (Black became "mascara," sheer off-white became "gossamer.") All of those gigs kept me temporarily afloat, but always took so much out of me, I never had enough brain juice left for my own writing. Maybe I needed a different kind of day job.

—❧

In 2011, while Brian and I were struggling through a major national recession, I decided to shake things up: to try to find work outside of publishing and media. I thought if I could find a job that had nothing to do with my creative ambitions, I could make a living, leave the job's concerns at the office at the end of the day, and then find time for my own writing, on the side. More than that, though, I was eager to find something resembling job stability after juggling so many different gigs for so long, and being perpetually broke despite working constantly. Things had gotten bad, financially—so bad that we'd briefly taken in a boarder. When it got too awkward sharing our house with a complete stranger, we decided to rent out the whole house and move to an inexpensive apartment nearby.

The first job I found at that time was as a biographer at a law firm about a half-hour from where I lived. I was tasked with meeting and profiling personal injury clients—writing stories about the very personal ways their lives had been impacted by the accidents they'd been through, to try to appeal to judges and juries that might award the clients settlements. I loved the work, loved that what I wrote could constructively improve people's lives, but hated the corporate culture at the firm. I had a bad feeling from the day of my orientation in a cramped conference room, which smelled overwhelmingly like the complimentary flavored coffee K-cups stocked in bins inside the adjacent break room, with top notes of Lipton Cup-a-Soup (also complimentary). I knew I'd have a hard time fitting into this corporate setting, and that I'd be miserable.

The head lawyer, the name partner, was a petty and mean man. He observed everyone who worked for him very closely, and nitpicked. *Did you look at your phone on company time?* (Some of the women tried to explain that they needed to keep an eye on texts regarding their children, but he didn't care.) *Did you go to the bathroom too many times a day? Were you wearing the wrong kind of clothes?* (Some of the women on staff seemed to confuse the type of clothes you'd wear to a discotheque with office-wear—they seemed to only know they were supposed to "dress up.") *Did you write only two client profiles this week? Couldn't you have written three? Couldn't you have just stayed later, and worked longer?*

I wasn't being paid enough for the job to take over my life. I resented how it impinged on my own writing time, so I started defiantly arising at 5:30 to write until 7:30, before heading into the office.

I stayed at the law firm just seven weeks. I jumped ship for a digital marketing job that came available, which I desperately hoped I'd hate less.

—◡

The rubber chicken employees tossed around to each other...the foosball table in the middle of the office...the circular business cards...the "name your own job title!"

policy—these details should have told me everything I needed to know about the digital marketing firm. I'd seen these gimmicks at other companies I'd had brief gigs at in the '90s—companies that wanted you to know that they were FUN, DAMMIT. You were going to LIKE YOUR JOB THERE, OR ELSE.

Rule of thumb: If they have to shove the idea of how FUN they are down your throat, they are likely overcompensating for how un-fun the job actually is. This rule held up at the digital marketing firm.

It turned out they were also overcompensating for not really knowing what the fuck they were doing. They never clearly identified most of what *I* was supposed to do. They wanted me to "figure out what I could offer," other than the one clear assignment they gave me: writing blog posts in the voice of a non-existent person, an avowed fan of one of the brands they represented. "Giselle" was a made-up enthusiast of the high-end silverware company that was their most prominent client. We would have meetings where we discussed such topics as, *What's Giselle's origin story? Where did she go to college? How would that impact what piece of silver she buys next, and wants to blog about?*

As if it wasn't hard enough to figure out what a non-existent person might have to say about forks and knives, I had to also make sure that my headlines and copy in her blog posts were perfectly search engine optimized. It became almost unimportant if they made sense; it mattered more that they lure in as many eyeballs as possible, even if those eyeballs landed on the blog post for the wrong reason.

Young writers: if you think you want a job where you just write inane bullshit all day, think again! It's actually very taxing. That and trying to keep a straight face when everyone else around you is taking that nonsense seriously.

I lasted just seven weeks at the digital marketing firm, too. There were many problems, the biggest of which was that I felt uncomfortable around my boss, a moody, pompous man who alternately brooded and flirted inappropriately with me and other women who worked for him. I was already contemplating quitting when the entire team got scolded one day for not putting in extra hours off the books. "This is your *career*," the office manager said. Nope! Writing blog posts for non-existent people was not my "career." It was just a job, a way to make a living using my one and only skill. The situation was untenable enough that even after having sworn off ghostwriting years before, I caved and I called my ghostwriting agent. Begrudgingly I took on a new client, and announced my departure from the digital marketing firm.

On my last day, a Friday, as I was walking out the door, my boss called me into his office. We were the only two remaining in the whole place. Brooding in the dark on a beanbag chair, he told me to sit down across from him. "You made me fall in love with you," he said, "and now you're breaking my heart." My pulse quickened with terror. I felt like hunted prey. Intellectually I didn't think he'd do anything to physically hurt me, but at a cellular level I had doubts, and I didn't want to stay long enough to find out.

Immediately, almost involuntarily, I started running my mouth: "Oh, don't take it personally—I just don't like office jobs, or fluorescent lighting…" I heard myself nervously laughing in between statements. "Don't feel bad! But I've gotta run." And with that, I took off, trembling.

My new ghostwriting gig was looking better and better. (Spoiler: It was a horrible experience, after which I swore off ghostwriting yet again.)

⎯⎯9

During the years from the mid-aughts to the mid-twenty-teens, in the background of all the work I was doing for a living, I *was* making time, wherever I could, to write personal essays. Helping me reconnect and recommit to my writing was work I did for a non-profit organization, TMI Project, where I co-led writing workshops that culminated in live storytelling performances, onstage. It began as a very part-time gig, but later grew into something almost full-time.

In the organization's early years, the founders and I would actually *take* the workshop as we gave it—writing and performing our own true stories alongside participants. Writing in a different medium for a non-publishing audience, then performing onstage, turned out to be an incredibly freeing combination of conditions for me. My writing flowed in a way it hadn't for a long time. Suddenly I wanted to write all the time, and so I did. I got up early before whatever gigs I was being paid for, and also wrote on weekends. I eked out some pieces I liked, and began publishing them here and there. It reaffirmed my passion for memoir and essays, and I became committed to building a career around writing and editing them.

In 2013—after being discouraged by everyone who's anyone in publishing *for years*—I found myself a book deal for the essay anthology, *Goodbye to All That: Writers on Loving and Leaving NY*, featuring 28 essays by women writers I admired, and it brought me to a new place, as both a writer and editor. That immediately opened new doors and led to other opportunities, including being brought on at a literary website called Longreads, first as a contributing editor, then as essays editor. I spent just over five years there editing longform personal essays, and it was a wonderful experience. But then, a few months into the coronavirus pandemic of 2020, that job came to an end.

⎯⎯9

And now, here we are in 2022, which finds me back in the position of juggling several low-paying gigs in order to survive. I'm a contributing editor in a few places; I teach creative writing in two MFA programs and at an MFA alternative; I publish a couple of paid newsletters… At 56, I worry intensely, often in the wee hours of the morning, about what the future holds for me, work-wise, and otherwise. The fields I've worked in have been decimated. The few places left standing are on life support. I'm left with more questions than answers. Such as…

Where do I turn next? How can I find a place for myself again? How many more times can I reinvent myself, I wonder, repackaging my experience and skills in an ever more competitive market, in a collection of dying fields? Who will hire a 56-year-old woman for a job that people in their forties and even thirties are competing for?

Do I switch tacks and go for some job unrelated to my skills—a civil service job, maybe—and write on the side, maybe even edit a little bit, and teach still? (Surprise! Teaching as an adjunct in two MFA programs hasn't turned out to be financially stable, either.) Or, in this age of creative individualism, do I keep building the paid subscription newsletters I write and edit, which so far have brought in just pocket change? At a moment when unfettered capitalism is destroying everything, is my only viable option *to become a better capitalist*?

I find myself dogged, once again, by the kind of self-doubt that has haunted me my whole life. Do I deserve to continue in my fields? As time goes on, and the cast of characters in those fields get winnowed down to only the best (and the best-connected), am I able to hold my place?

I've never been one of the stars in any of these fields. I've held my ground somehow, barely—mostly by adapting again and again, and trying not to let rejection deter me. Long ago I adopted the philosophy that "no" only means "not right now." But after years and years of that, at what point do you just accept that you'll never really make it? Or if you haven't failed exactly, at what point do you accept that you have had only limited success, and there won't likely be much more? When is it time to stop seeking "optimal" and start settling for the least bad scenario?

Maybe it's time for me to go the way of many of my other colleagues, and splinter off into side fields that tend to employ our skills, like corporate "comms," or public relations? Or to move into other fields altogether, like real estate.

When I peruse LinkedIn I feel depressed falling upon a former colleague's new job posting as a "digital storyteller" for a brand. Shades of my 2011 job, which to me seemed so pointless. I'm sad for my former colleague, and sad for the state of journalism and digital media—that it can no longer hold so many of us. On the flip side, I feel encouraged when I look more closely at the bios of some of the respected authors I follow on social media, and discover that they list their day job as some kind of "comms," or weekends working in a bookstore.

The one thing I'm sure of is that I need to plan for my future more intentionally, as opposed to the willy-nilly way I've ambled through my career, and my life. I can't afford to take chances the way I once could. But what does that really mean? Does it mean I need to seek out the work most aligned with my talents, no matter how hard it gets? Or does it mean I need to just seek the most assured means toward a stable and steady income, whether or not the work aligns with my talents and interests? Is "fulfilling work" just some outdated, bourgeois concept? Optimally there would be a way to achieve both on the same path, but journalism, publishing and digital media have never been more competitive or broken.

Is there still room for me in this landscape? Is there a role for me that might align with who I now know myself to be? Does that even matter, in these dark times?

Maybe it's time to try something new, entirely. And maybe that's what I should suggest to young writers when they ask for my advice, going forward. This might sound bleak, but right now I can't recommend pursuing writing as any kind of "career." That's not the same thing as discouraging people from writing, and even pursuing publication. That I'm all for. Write to your heart's content. Develop your craft, take courses, whether in an MFA program or elsewhere. Join a writers' group and/or become part of a larger community. Send your writing out.

But unless you're independently wealthy—or have a partner, parent, or patron who is—I can't encourage that you try to make a living the way I (barely) have for too long. At 56, it's probably too late for me to switch fields. My only real option right now is to take this "platform" I've been building since I first learned about writers' platform and its importance, and make being Me™ as profitable as I can for as long as I can—through my books, my newsletters, whatever articles and essays I can place.

Nothing anyone said to me during college or after could have dissuaded me from this difficult path. In hindsight, instead of trying to talk me out of my dreams, I wish someone had told me this: you can do something else for a living, and still become a writer.

If I were to find a new line of work to pay the bills right now, I'd still be a writer. But my chances of gaining new marketable skills are likely behind me. If it's not too late for you, do it. Then make time to follow your writing dreams after hours.

The Cadillac

In the early '90s, when I was in my late twenties, to my great surprise, I got into some MFA programs in creative writing, including at my top choice, Sarah Lawrence. I was thrilled, and accepted right away. Unfortunately I had no idea how I was going to pay for it—other than a small divorce settlement that wouldn't go far—nor how I'd fit graduate school into my schedule. I had a full-time reporting job at a trade publication called *Home Furnishings Network (HFN)* that involved covering industry events in four disparate industries after hours, and a fair amount of travel to trade shows around the country.

Still, I imagined I could somehow juggle it all, as I had in college. I had managed to put myself through undergrad at a state school by writing freelance articles for local publications, processing insurance claims at Blue Cross/Blue Shield, and teaching Sunday school at a nearby synagogue.

I mailed a check off to Bronxville—draining my bank account of something like $11K for just one semester—boarded Metro North, and signed up for some evening classes.

Very quickly I started panicking. With a full-time job, when would I write my assignments, and read my fellow students' pieces so that I could participate in workshopping them? Would I do it on the hour-plus commute, each way, between the East Village and campus, in lower Westchester? More pressingly, how was I going to afford tuition after that first semester?

Then my phone rang.

—◦

"Suh-REE Buh-TON? You've won a Cadillac Coupe de Ville!"

The call came from a number in Las Vegas. I mean, when the phone rang, I didn't *know* where it was coming from, because there was no such thing as Caller I.D. yet, or even *69. In the early '90s there were just plain old landlines without any fancy features. I wouldn't have my first cell phone for another seven or eight years.

I knew it was a Las Vegas number because it was the beginning of a volley of calls back and forth between the caller and me—initially in pursuit of verification of this grand prize, and later to arrange for delivery of "the car."

The number was similar to another Las Vegas number I'd recently called to ask how to mail back, at no charge to me, an enormous makeup kit I'd never ordered in the first place, put out by a flashy makeup artist who starred in late night infomercials. The makeup kit had been sent to me in error by the same direct marketing company through which I had, in fact, ordered a set of Tony Robbins *Personal Power!* tapes.

The tapes were meant to take the place of my, um, *life coach*, whom I realized I couldn't afford. I'd been referred to the life coach by the woman who taught a personal essay workshop I took at NYU in 1991. She had become something of a mentor to me, after she invited me to continue studying with her at a private workshop at her apartment in the West Village, which I paid for in trade, by babysitting for her kids.

I confessed to my mentor one day that I was feeling like a complete failure. At 27. I was having difficulty staying focused and juggling everything in my life—working my day job as a reporter, trying to freelance for consumer publications plus do my own creative writing on the side, all while going through a divorce and, oh, dating a few different men who acted like jerks toward me, to whom I devoted a ridiculous amount of mental energy. My mentor suggested I visit David, a former Marine drill sergeant-turned-actor-turned-life-coach.

Once each week I'd hop the subway to David's Theater District office. There, I'd confess I hadn't done most of my coaching homework—because I didn't have time, but also because the assignments were plain weird. They were based in Neuro-Linguistic Programming (NLP), through which, David explained, he was going to "re-language" me. For instance, I was only allowed to use the word "no" in limited contexts (I can't recall which). I was not allowed to *ever* use the word "but"; in its place, I had to use "and."

Each day, I had to call into a number David had set up with an answering machine, and declare my (positive!) word for the day, and recite a particular line declaring that I *was* my word: "This is Sari Botton, and *I am my word!* Today is October 26th, and my word for today is *focus*. Today I will be *focused!*"

All this for $100 per session, which in the early '90s was a lot of money, and frankly still is for me. After a handful of appointments, I quit. My writing teacher recommended Tony Robbins *Personal Power!* as a cheap substitute. Right after the tapes arrived, so did the coffee-table-sized makeup kit I'd never ordered, plus a heavy bill for it. Thus began my phone calls to the direct marketing company in Las Vegas, followed shortly after by the call from a similar number regarding the Cadillac I'd allegedly won.

—◎

Obviously, in my life as a struggling twentysomething writer in a crumbling East Village tenement, I did *not* need a Cadillac, nor any car for that matter. Neither did I possess any kind of desire for one. But I liked the idea of having one *to sell* to fund my grad school gambit. It was worth about $30K. I had a plan: once that massive boat of an automobile arrived, I'd drive it right over to the Potemkin Cadillac dealership on 11th Avenue, and cash it in. I'd use the winnings to pay for the rest of my MFA at Sarah Lawrence.

All I had to do was mail a cashier's check for $850 to Nevada for shipping. It was just that simple...

I had many, many, many—*too many*—conversations with the guy who'd originally called to tell me I'd won the car. Doubt had begun creeping in; I was struggling to determine whether the offer was legit. Every time I considered going to the bank and getting a cashier's check, I would call the guy again.

"You're sure this is real?" I'd ask. Because obviously if it was a scam, he'd tell me.

"I've already told you a million times," he'd say, at first chiding me in a friendly tone, but later becoming audibly annoyed. I did not like having men annoyed at me, so eventually I just got the check and sent it.

Then I waited.

And waited.

And waited.

I tried calling my pal in Vegas. *The number you have dialed is not in service*, said the robovoice. *Oh.*

Reader, there was no Cadillac. I was out $850, and my attempts to have the bank recoup it were in vain.

Before the semester was over, I dropped out of Sarah Lawrence. I mentioned my financial distress to one of my professors, and she shared a little money-saving secret with me: "Many of us also teach in the program at City College, which is a fraction of the cost." I enrolled there, and went part-time for two semesters. But although I could afford tuition, I couldn't afford to leave my job and attend full-time. And I found it nearly impossible to balance work with even part-time enrollment. And so, I dropped out of my second MFA program.

It was painful giving up on my dream. But when I realized that a number of the teachers I encountered at City College didn't have MFAs themselves, it hurt less. It was, instead, writing and publishing books that had qualified them to teach.

I hoped that someday, I might be able to parlay my writing into teaching, too. So many years later, I have. For better and worse.

Elegy for "the Non-Creepy Realtor"

In the summer of 2013, my Gmail was hacked. Every single person on my contacts list received a note from me announcing I'd become a ReMax real estate agent. It was a convincing facsimile, complete with the red, white and blue ReMax parachute logo. "Click here to view listings!" it lied, luring recipients instead to a link that ensured they themselves would contract the email virus, then unwittingly pass it on to others.

Cue the succession of annoying replies: random contacts admonishing me to change my password; otherwise intelligent people duped by the scheme, believing it was really me.

"Don't you think you should at least ask me how I've been before you start sending me real estate listings?" wrote someone I'd briefly flirted with more than a dozen years before.

"Wow, small world!" gushed a new acquaintance in earnest. "I just got my real estate license, too!"

Emails like those irked me most. They were cruel reminders that publishing and digital media were in such a state of free-fall (although not nearly to the degree they are now!), it seemed plausible that I might have given up on writing and started selling houses instead. Those notes also reignited an uncomfortable long-standing internal debate over whether the taxing, suboptimal, mercenary work I've juggled for decades under the banner of "freelance writing"—writing an article or essay here and there, but much more ghostwriting of other people's books, slinging ad copy, plus editing and teaching—has actually hindered my progress toward becoming a different kind of writer, the kind I've always wanted to be, of memoir and fiction. It's a question I still ask myself almost daily: Would I be more successful with my personal writing by now, at 56, if my day job were in a completely unrelated field?

Some of my colleagues seem to believe that's the way to go. In recent years I've been hearing about writers in my Gen X demographic taking jobs in real estate, one of the more flexible, potentially decently paying occupations that, say, a middle-aged writer can qualify for with relatively little prior training. First it was the former bureau chief of an NPR affiliate station. Next, a colleague from a magazine I once worked at. At the time my email was hacked in 2013, the most notable writer to add "realtor" to her resume was Maggie Estep—a slam poetry icon of the 1990s, and author of seven critically acclaimed novels, whom I admired.

Maggie wrote on her popular blog about having difficulty supporting herself in the crumbling publishing economy, where book advances and fees for writing assignments were steadily plummeting—where being a "freelance writer," as I've been for over two decades, had become a ridiculous proposition for everyone but the independently wealthy.

"The writing biz has changed and my income from it is modest," she wrote. "Being broke isn't very interesting anymore." Teaching yoga, her first sideline, hadn't turned out to be an effective means of financial support either. "So I'm going to real estate school."

I didn't know Maggie well at all, even though she contributed an essay to the first edition of *Goodbye to All That: Writers on Loving & Leaving NY*, an anthology I edited, in which she wrote about quitting New York City for Upstate, just as I had. I was just beginning to get to know her when, in February, 2014, she had a sudden heart attack and left this world too soon. In the '90s, I'd idolized her. She was this cool, sexy, punk rock feminist poet and spoken word star with an acid wit.

After her death, I started reading her blog. In the final months before her death, Maggie wrote there about her new profession. It was unnerving for me to learn that this accomplished writer and performer who'd once been able to earn at least a good portion of her living—sometimes all of it—from her creative output was no longer able to do so; that she was now becoming a real estate agent *for real*.

I mean no disrespect to real estate agents. They work hard in what is a demanding field. I've heard the few I'm acquainted with talk about having to frequently update their licenses with more classes and certification. I've also heard them gripe about squiring some of their clients around from home to home (to home to home) for months on end without it ever yielding a sale, all while working solely on commission.

But the field also has some notorious image problems. Like sales people in certain other fields, some realtors are perceived as hucksters—deceptively ameliorating less desirable listings with euphemisms like, "cozy" for small, and "convenient to everything" often meaning right on the highway; using bait-and-switch advertising; or luring unwitting investors into problematic (or non-existent) developments, Glengarry Glen Ross style.

Those image problems weren't lost on Maggie. At a memorial for her at Club Helsinki Hudson, Steve Buscemi read aloud an email she'd sent him letting him know about her new profession, and asking for buyer and seller referrals. "A lot of realtors are kind of creepy," she wrote, "so I guess my angle is that I'm the non-creepy realtor."

After she died, a close friend of Maggie's told me that in ways, real estate seemed like a perfect fit for her—that she had been given to regularly poring over listings and looking at properties just for fun, often trying to match friends with the perfect homes for them. But scrolling through her blog, it becomes evident that Maggie had pretty mixed feelings about real estate as a *job*. In a post entitled "Kill the Poor," she wrote that while she was happy she'd passed the first part of her real estate exam, "... my soul is a little sick. I met several interesting and lovely people who I know will be honorable in their future real estate dealings but, mostly, real estate school taught me a lot about capitalism, the killing of nature, and why most folks are suspicious of real estate agents." This was after one of the lecturers, whom she dubbed "Mr. Kill-the-poor," had talked blithely about such mercenary endeavors as evicting long-standing, low-paying tenants.

She lamented, too, no longer having the luxury of writing all day, at home: "I'm having to learn to do what thousands and thousands of people do in this world: Snatch tiny windows of writing time when I can and where I can."

Sometimes, it sounded as if she were trying to convince herself that taking a day job as a realtor was okay, a move that could possibly help her writing, maybe leading her to clients who'd inspire fictional characters.

"It's kind of fitting that, in my nascent realtor career, the sellers I'm representing have a house that belonged to a gangster..." she wrote after checking out a home that had once belonged to Legs Diamond. "I've had a fifteen-plus years love/hate relationship with *The Angelmakers*, the female gangster book I've written seven times and not yet gotten right...I am soaked in gangster lore and now I'm selling a gangster house...Never mind that it's on a busy-ish road and vaguely in the middle of nowhere, I instantly knew I was destined to sell this house."

She sounded resigned to making peace with her new circumstances: "For me, selling real estate in an honest way while writing books I care about is a good path. My next adventure."

And it seems as if, for the brief time she worked in the Halstead office in Hudson before passing away, Maggie did manage to also focus on her writing. Which is more than I can say for myself, with all the writing-related work I do for a living. Even at times when I've lucked into short-term, undemanding, higher-paying dream gigs I've found that working with words all day, whether at home or in a proper office, doesn't afford me the time or headspace for the writing I really want to do.

Despite this awareness, and publishing's steadily diminishing returns, I find myself obstinately resistant to the idea of giving up and finding a different kind of day job. For one thing, I am short on other marketable skills. But more than that, I'm too spoiled by years of making my own schedule and working from home to embrace showing up at an office, and at the times someone else tells me to be there—a *boss*. The irony is that I'm kind of lonely at home, and with no boundaries between my living and work spaces, I am never *not* working. What's more, as a freelancer, I answer to roughly *nine* bosses at any given time.

The biggest obstacle to other forms of gainful employment, though, is probably my misguided, stubborn pride in telling people I'm a writer, and that other than a three-month stint behind the costume jewelry counter at Macy's just after my graduation from college, I have supported myself solely with writing and writing-related jobs. Never mind that a good portion of the writing-related work assigned to me is work I probably wouldn't do if there weren't a paycheck at the end of it. The validation of my title still makes me feel accomplished. What's more, I've accrued seniority here, something I'm too old to accrue in any other field at this point. The ladder might be collapsing—some might argue it already has—but I'm still holding onto my rung for dear life.

Do not attempt to strip me of the false senses of success and security that I cling to. Because if I quit freelancing and become a real estate agent—or lab technician, waitperson, barista, cashier, nutritional counselor, whatever—and I *still* fail to produce and succeed with my "real" writing, then what (and whom) do I have left to blame?

I suppose then I'd find out just how much I want to write. Maybe I'd find that the psychically draining nature of my gainful employment as a writer/editor/teacher is merely an excuse; that what's largely stopping me from succeeding as a *writer*-writer are fear and procrastination.

Just two weeks before she died, Maggie wrote about her own tendency to procrastinate. As if there were time for that. I'm now quite certain there isn't.

The Girl with the Nerd Tattoos

I had something of a mental breakdown in the hours before getting my first tattoo. According to everything I learned growing up, nice Jewish girls aren't supposed to get them. And according to everything I learned about women and aging, we're not supposed to get inked when we're much too old to be considered "girls," or even young women. These "rules" overtook my mind October 1, 2012, the day before my 47th birthday, as I prepared to walk into East Side Ink on Avenue B in Manhattan—but I didn't let them stop me from sitting down in the chair, extending my arm, and getting my first of what has now grown in number, at this writing, to three tattoos.

I *almost* let them stop me. Those deeply ingrained dictates, plus my aversion to pain, nearly put the kibosh on my plan. There was also my concern for how my parents might feel.

—◯

That fall afternoon in 2012, my husband, Brian, sat with me on the lawn in Tompkins Square Park and listened to me spin out, tearfully debating with myself whether I was prepared to permanently alter my right forearm. Deep down I knew I'd go through with the appointment that I'd set up weeks in advance. But as with many experiences I didn't feel I had permission to try, I seemed to believe I'd only be justified in enjoying it if I first put myself through a fair amount of suffering.

Mind you, I was carrying on about this and crying *out loud*. In the middle of a public park. God bless Brian. As we sat on the lawn, he entertained all my rhetorical questions from every side of the argument. Brian is kind and incredibly patient with me when I get caught up in this kind of endless, circuitous back-and-forth of *should-I-shouldn't-I?*.

I wasn't just debating with myself, but with my parents and other relatives, dead and alive, too—all in my head. This entailed a fair amount of projection, but as an empath, I was already a pro at taking on other people's emotions and points of view, or what I imagined them to be. One therapist described me as "a radio receiver for other people's feelings," with a woeful inability to determine whose emotions I was experiencing when other people's wants and needs got thrown into the mix. My parents are pre-boomer Jews. In the hours before my tattoo appointment, I couldn't stop putting myself in their (theoretical) shoes. (You might consider playing "Sunrise, Sunset" from *Fiddler on the Roof* on the turntable in your mind through this part of the story.)

I'm not a parent. I do not have first-hand knowledge of what it's like to have your baby, your first baby, alter one of her limbs irreversibly with a variety of body art your age group still associates with tough guys and outlaws, and which is forbidden by your religion. But my non-mom status didn't deter me from the mental gymnastics involved in taking on my parents' presumed viewpoints.

(It's true, by the way—the Torah forbids tattoos. In Leviticus 19:28 it is written: "You shall not make gashes in your flesh for the dead, or incise any marks on yourselves." What's *not* true is the notion that you can't be buried in a Jewish cemetery with them. Misconception or not, it happens to be the premise of "The Special Section," my all-time favorite episode of *Curb Your Enthusiasm* [Season 3, Episode 6]: Larry learns that his newly deceased mother can't be buried in a regular plot in the Jewish cemetery because she had a tattoo on her butt.)

I made a major production out of my internal debate. Back and forth I went—first imagining my parents feeling wounded, upset and angry with me, then countering those thoughts by reminding myself I was 47, very much past an age at which I'd need their permission or approval, or to consider anyone else's feelings about what I do with my own body. Ironically, this tendency to be overly concerned with other people's opinions and feelings—allowing them to keep me from being fully myself—was *part of the point* in a) getting a tattoo in the first place, and b) getting the specific one I'd chosen, the following quotation, in the American Typewriter font: "And the day came when the risk to remain tight in a bud was more painful than the risk it took to blossom."

I kept perseverating until five minutes before my appointment. I needed to pull myself together, not just for me, but for my "tattooula," as well.

—❧

My friend Emily—a much-tattooed writer I admire who is sixteen years younger than me—had offered to come and support me through the experience, as she'd done with other friends. She joked that she was a "tattooula," like a doula for people getting tattoos for the first time. She began her work the night before, talking me down from my fears over dinner and karaoke in Chinatown. The next afternoon she was waiting for me in front of East Side Ink armed with a box of gluten-free cookies. "You want to make sure you have energy and that you keep your blood sugar balanced," she said.

She had already assured me several times that the application of the tattoo wouldn't hurt, at least not too badly. "Do you swear?" I'd asked each time. I had almost been scared off entirely by Brian's story of getting tattooed on his left shoulder blade in his thirties—a hippie tattoo, "Mother Earth," in the form of a pregnant tree. It had hurt so much, he wrote a song about the pain. But Emily insisted the degree of pain was different depending on the part of your body, and the inside of the forearm was one of the areas where it tended to hurt the least.

Emily and Brian sat on either side of me as the tattoo artist, Minka, applied a "transfer," a temporary tattoo of the quotation, to my forearm, and then began tracing it with her pen. One letter at a time, I was surprised by how little it hurt. Minka had suggested it would have the sensation of a series of mosquito bites, but it was even less annoying than that. Maybe it was the attendant endorphin rush, but I found the experience bordering on enjoyable. (The night before, Emily had said getting tattoos was addictive, and I'd insisted I'd be getting only this one tattoo for the entirety of my life. Well, famous last words.) As Minka applied ink to my skin with her buzzing pen, I began to understand what Emily had meant. I felt perfectly elated.

When it was over, Minka applied Aquaphor to my arm and covered the tattoo with plastic wrap. It was oozing ink, which she said was normal. I looked down at the words on my arm, and felt a rush of satisfaction. I had not one regret. All my fears, all the drama from before vanished. I wasn't ready to tell my family about it quite yet. But it was enough for the moment to enjoy it as my little secret.

—∘

I awoke the next morning in the East Village Airbnb where we'd stayed, and admired my arm. I was still elated, and self-satisfied for having gone through with my appointment.

The apartment we were staying in was directly across from the spot on East 7th Street between Avenues C and D, where Brian and I had met nine years prior. Meeting Brian had been both a function of, and a furthering of, becoming truer to myself in relationships. Before meeting him, my dating pattern had been to tune my antenna to the most ambivalent, or difficult, or damaged, or self-absorbed man in the room—or some cursed combination of those qualities—and then twist myself into a pretzel to become whatever version of me I thought might earn and keep that man's hard won attention. That had often meant keeping my true thoughts to myself, and making myself small and needless, so that I didn't ruffle feathers, or reveal parts of myself that might offend, or scare a man away.

In the years leading up to meeting Brian, I had been in treatment with a male therapist I often referred to as The Swashbuckling Shrink, who was helping me break that cycle and find satisfaction in every aspect of my life by getting comfortable being myself, and expressing myself. Brian had also been "working on himself" in therapy. He and I have often said that if we'd met even just a couple of weeks before we did, in the fall of 2003, neither one of us would have been quite ready for the other. We each had final hurdles to get over before we were ready to "tolerate" a relationship with a kind, available person, someone who knew that for a relationship to be mutually satisfying, each person had to consistently consider the other's needs. It seemed like such a simple, intuitive concept, but in a patriarchal capitalist culture, where value is based on austerity and scarcity and we've all been taught to be withholding, accordingly, it can be hard to feel secure enough to just let our guards down and be generous with one another.

The next hurdle toward becoming more fully myself was finding the courage to put myself out there more as a writer. I'd been hiding myself for years, chickening out when opportunities to publish personal essays came my way. For years—decades, even—I felt as if I were standing on a ledge, but too scared to jump. It was as if I were waiting for some "right time" that never arrived. In the meantime, I floated aimlessly from one writing or writing-adjacent gig to another, including ghostwriting assignments. (Could there be a better metaphor for hiding as a writer?)

Then, in 2012, after a ghostwriting assignment with a particularly difficult author had gone south, I felt desperate to commit to my own work. That was what made me choose the quotation I did for my tattoo. Every single word of it rang true: *And the day came when the risk to remain tight in a bud was more painful than the risk it took to blossom.*

I'd come across that quotation so many times in my life—on mugs and candles and journals and yoga mats. There was a corniness to it and its proliferation. It was also phrased awkwardly. Still, those words had always spoken to me. I had often felt exactly what they meant to convey—the sense of reaching a point where staying stuck, staying small so you don't offend anyone, becomes more impossible than finally speaking out. Now I felt it more strongly than ever.

I assumed they were the words of Anais Nin, because I'd frequently seen the quotation attributed to her. After I had the tattoo inked on my forearm, I began to feel bad that I hadn't included her name. It seemed appropriate to attribute it.

It turned out to be a good thing I didn't add attribution.

—⌇

In March of 2017, an upstate arts magazine assigned me a profile of legendary magazine editor Joan Juliet Buck, who'd just published her memoir, *The Price of Illusion*. In the course of the interview, Joan noticed my tattoo. She asked to read it, and I held up my arm before her eyes. When she was done, she looked up and said, "I knew Anais Nin." Then she asked, "Which of her books is that quotation from?"

Uhhh…

I had no idea. I felt like such an idiot. I'd read a little bit of Nin over the years, but I wasn't any kind of avid fan. I'd chosen the quotation for my tattoo because the sentiment resonated so strongly, not because I was any kind of Nin aficionado.

"I'm embarrassed to say I'm not sure," I admitted to Joan. And then we moved on to the next part of the interview.

The first thing I did when I got home was google the quotation, to see if I could determine which book it came from. That's when I stumbled upon a blog post by the Anais Nin Foundation explaining that the quote hadn't come from Nin at all.

Six months prior, in the fall of 2016, a woman named Elizabeth Appell spoke out publicly about her poem, "Risk," being misattributed. In the '70s, at the time she wrote it, she was known as "Lacey Bennett," and she was a publicist for an adult education college in California. She'd included that portion of "Risk" in a press release encouraging people to go back to school. She reached out to the Anaïs Nin Foundation, explaining the situation, sharing with them a copy of the original press release.

I got in touch with Appell to ask her about the story behind the quote that was now emblazoned on my arm, for life.

"I was Public Relations Director for a university that operated just for adults," Appell explained. "I put out a quarterly bulletin about the school, and classes we had available. I always tried to find interesting themes. I remember the moment I wrote it. I was on the telephone talking to somebody and I said, 'Excuse me, I have an idea, hold on.' I sat down and wrote those lines, and then I wrote another four lines. I have no idea what happened to the other four lines, they're gone. I just wrote them down. Then I took them to the fellow who was the Director of Development. I said, 'This might be a good kind of inspiring thought for the next bulletin, and we could create an image of roses opening around it to convey the idea that adults are going back to school and opening their lives to all new things.' He liked it very much. We put it out. It went out in Contra Costa County, here on the west coast. A lot of people saw it."

Appell hadn't thought to give herself credit for the poem when she put it on the press release. "I didn't put my name on it," she recalled. "I didn't even think about it. Then I started seeing it in weaving shows—people would weave it into tapestry. Then I went to a calligraphy show and saw it. Then, in 1979, I was in a little card store, and I saw it attributed to Anaïs Nin. I bought the card and I wrote to the company. I said, 'I'm not going to sue or anything, but this is not Anaïs Nin's; I wrote this.' They wouldn't even speak to me, because I think they were afraid."

She gave up the fight—until a few years ago, when the quotation was absolutely everywhere, including her own small corner of the literary world.

"I was giving a reading of my work, and a woman who had read just before me opened her reading with that poem and attributed it to Anaïs Nin," Appell recalled. "My husband was there and he raised his hand. He said, 'I just want you all to know that that poem was not by Anaïs Nin, it's Elizabeth's poem,' he said, 'and I can prove it.'"

Her husband speaking up made Appell uncomfortable. "At that point, not a lot of people believed me," she said. "I was kind of upset with him. I said, 'Don't do that. Who cares who wrote it?' He said, 'No, *you* wrote it. Lots of people like it, they should know you wrote it.'" Wow, I thought: Even the woman who had written those very words was susceptible to remaining tight in a bud!

In the end, though, Appell was glad her husband spoke up. It inspired her to get a hold of the Anaïs Nin foundation. "I told them the whole thing about how I wrote it, when I wrote it. The fellow who was the Director of Development for the university wrote them a letter saying, 'Yes, I corroborate this, she did write it.' Finally, they believed me, and then they put a notice out."

—◦

Before getting tattooed, I'd already done something like it once before—altered my body in a way that was more in keeping with people younger than me. At 33 I got a navel ring. It made me feel sexy and bold, and it also helped camouflage a scar I'd long hated, a keloidal slash across the middle of my belly button, the result of laparoscopic surgery I'd undergone at 18, to diagnose endometriosis. (In getting the incision for my navel ring, I risked developing another keloid—I've had three keloids surgically removed in the course of my life.)

I couldn't wait to show the simple stainless steel hoop with a little, round, jade stone as its closure to Tim, the guy I was seeing at the time. I didn't do it to please him, but I thought that might be an advantageous by-product. I imagined he'd find me irresistible. When I lifted my shirt to show him, he gave it one look, then lifted his eyes to mine. "How antithetical," he said, in a sarcastic tone. "Good for you." It did not have the desired effect.

But it didn't matter what Tim thought. Getting the navel ring made me feel in control of my body, which I'd felt out of control of since it began growing curves during puberty, and then developed an eating disorder, and later endometriosis. The tattoo had a similarly salutary effect. I felt in control of my body—in charge of it— and empowered. There have been so many times and places in my life when I was pretending to be someone else, trying too hard to fit in, and getting a tattoo later in life could have easily been one of them. *But it wasn't.* With my new ink on my arm, I felt more like myself, more committed to being who I was, and more committed to my writing.

Incidentally, I took my navel ring out after a few years. A psychic I was ghostwriting a book for told me it was messing with my third chakra, the one responsible for my self-esteem. So I took it out. I wish now that I hadn't. (Of course, *after removing it*, I developed a tiny keloid there.)

—◡

Even though I'd had such a positive experience with my first tattoo, it hadn't initially occurred to me to get more of them. I figured I was done after just the one. But then, as my 50th birthday rolled around in 2015, I felt the urge to get another. I wanted to mark my half-century, but there was more to it. In the three years since I got the quotation on my arm, I'd taken some risks with my writing. But I was still holding myself back. I wanted to embolden myself to take things to a new level.

A friend had gotten a tattoo of a flock of birds flying across her shoulder, and just seeing it on her gave me feelings of flight—of freedom and liberation. I wanted to get something on my own body that would inspire similar feelings. Looking online at images of birds led me to images of them seated on cherry blossom branches. I've always loved cherry blossoms, and have a weeping cherry tree in my front yard. Next I started going around to tattoo parlors in Kingston, where I live, with printouts of cherry blossoms I'd found online. Most artists said they were too delicate, and passed. Then I found Pat Sinatra, an older artist who was getting ready to retire in a few years. She said she could do it, and so, once again, the day before my birthday, I sat in a chair and had ink applied, this time to my upper left arm.

Shockingly, it would not occur to me that there was a correlation between my text tattoo about blossoming and my new tattoo with blossoms until I woke the next morning and took stock of both. *Duh.*

Okay, now I'm really done, I thought. Apparently I wasn't.

—◡

There are few things I dread writing more than book proposals. What could be more anxiety-provoking than writing what is essentially a lengthy book report on something you haven't written yet?

In 2019, as I was slogging through a proposal for this very memoir-in-confessions, I made a bargain with myself: get yourself a book deal, and you can mark the occasion with a new tattoo.

In June of 2020, during the coronavirus pandemic, I got the good news: Heliotrope wanted to publish me. I was thrilled—and I was itching to celebrate by getting inked again. But at that time, tattoo parlors in New York were still closed, due to Covid-19 restrictions.

It was just another of so many letdowns in a hellish year. I yearned for the ritual of getting a tattoo, and I had the perfect design in mind: a rudimentary typewriter that I've been doodling in crayon for years. I've used the image before as a logo—for a writers' group I ran in the early aughts; on the first iteration of my website; on stationery. Now I wanted to get it imprinted on my left forearm to commemorate signing, at the ripe old age of 55, the first contract for a book filled exclusively with my own writing (I'd published anthologies before, but they were mostly filled with essays by others), and to help me commit to getting it done.

I'd already learned that there's something galvanizing about having images and words permanently scrawled into your flesh. It sends your mind the message, "I mean business." After signing my book contract, I was ready to send my brain that message with the typewriter tattoo. New York tattoo parlors were allowed to reopen in July. But the continued spread of the virus gave me pause.

I got to work on this book, but struggled. Once again, I'd taken on too much editing of other people's stories to write my own. Finally, in November, 2020, I cleared my decks to commit more deeply to my writing. The urge to visit a tattoo parlor grew stronger. One afternoon, on a whim, I called Metamorphosis Tattoos. Initially, the woman who answered said there were no open appointments until mid-January, but then she paused. "Actually, we have a cancellation this afternoon," she said. "How soon can you come in?" I asked about their adherence to Covid-19 protocols, and the woman assured me that they took the greatest precautions. Fifteen minutes later I was sitting in Tania the tattoo artist's chair.

At the sound of Tania's tattoo pen buzzing away, I grew elated. It gave me a thrill, and it gave me the sense of self-determination and self-assurance that I needed.

After that day, I became emboldened, writing more committedly and bravely than ever before. Yes, it was still hard staying focused when there'd been so much illness and fear and bad news—including three Covid deaths within my extended family. But I made progress every day. When I wasn't writing, I couldn't stop staring at my lovely new ink.

My Hysterectomy, a Love Story

It's not an all-out lie when I tell my first husband I'm leaving largely because he's ready for a family and I'm just not there yet. What we have here is a *scheduling* problem, I tell myself. It's 1992, and I'm a few months shy of 27. There's still plenty of time for me to come around to feeling the urge to have kids. People assure me, "You'll know when the time is right." I believe them.

—

Fourteen years later—2006—I'm a weeping mess on the drive across the river to Rhinebeck from my home in Rosendale, NY, the one I moved into with my new husband, Brian, the year before, after we lost our New York City apartment. The occasion should be cause for celebration: Brian has just become a grand uncle! We're on our way to the birthing center at Northern Dutchess Hospital to meet the baby. But little Henry's timing sucks. He enters the picture when Brian and I are trying— well, "trying"—to become parents ourselves, even though the standard issue built-in maternal alarm I've been told about still hasn't gone off.

I'm now 41, Brian is 44, and we've hit a surprisingly heartbreaking juncture in what had begun as a willy-nilly, passive approach to family planning, originally meant to entail nothing more than ditching birth control and "letting the Universe decide" whether or not we should have kids. Fourteen or so months into newly-wed-frequency fortysomething-on-fortysomething action, there's no baby. It looks as if the Universe has decided.

We aren't supposed to question this. On the dating site where we met in 2003, Brian and I both used the word "ambivalent" when describing our interest in having kids. Since then, when friends and relatives have inevitably asked, our official stance has been a shrugging, "If it happens, it happens." But when the Universe hands down a decisive, "No," it's as if everything gets turned upside-down and we enter Bizarro World.

Cut to scene of us taking out a calendar to schedule sex around my ovulation cycle...to me hanging upside-down in *sarvangasana* for 10 minutes after each go at it...

to Brian racing a plastic cup to a lab in the next town before the crucial thirty-minute time limit is up...

We figure he's got this. He's one of six kids, and he'd been party to two accidental pregnancies (followed by abortions) in the years before I met him. But, as my gynecologist explains, it's easier and less invasive to rule out men's fertility issues, so they're always tested first. Once we're done going through the motions with him, we can get down to the business of figuring out what exactly is wrong on my end, beyond a painful pelvic auto-immune condition called endometriosis, which I was diagnosed with at 18.

...Cut to scene of my boyish, usually upbeat husband looking stunned and crestfallen when his test results come back. Sperm count: negligible. Motility level among what few sperm he has: next to none. Brian surprises us both by going wobbly and collapsing into the nearest chair. He's not at all macho, and yet, he is devastated by the news of his questionable virility. I've never seen such sadness in those hooded blue eyes. It destroys me. It also scares me. I wonder: does this mean he *isn't* truly ambivalent? Does he actually *want* children? Are we going to have to do something about it?

Now comes the most unlikely scene of all in this Bizarro World montage: a visit to a fertility specialist. Yes, that's us there in the antiseptic waiting room—the couple who'd been content to casually outsource this major life decision to Whoever Is In Charge Of The Universe. The free spirits who resent anyone who dares to impose on the precious time reserved for our assorted creative pursuits. *Me*—the person to whom goldfish seem an imposition, who can't keep a houseplant alive.

And you may find yourself...at a fertility clinic. And you may ask yourself... Well... How did I get here?

—~

The doctor is tall and fit, and he smiles too much. When he enters the consultation room, he wastes no time before launching into an upbeat infomercial about the miracles of In Vitro Fertilization (IVF) and Intrauterine Insemination (IUI). The man goes *on and on*. I'm rarely granted a full five minutes with my primary care physician or my regular gyno, but this guy seems to have all the time in the world to try and close the deal.

"What about the cancer risks associated with fertility drugs?" I ask. My maternal grandmother's death from breast cancer puts me at high risk.

The doctor's smile tightens. "You've been reading too much WebMD." That's all he has to say about that. He admits our chances of conceiving are relatively slim, even with his aid. That information hardly has a chance to sink in before he's off on another tangent, regaling us with happy stories of patients who ended up reproducing after all, even though all hope had seemed lost.

I keep waiting for him to indicate that we're categorically different from those couples, that we're in some way disqualified as candidates. That we should just give up. But he doesn't. He just keeps talking. As he continues, a foreign, greedy feeling suddenly arises, and I think, *Let's grab this slippery possibility before it's whisked away again…*

With his sales pitch over, the doctor escorts us to a beige room in the back devoted entirely to calling insurance providers about qualification for coverage. He introduces us to the woman who is going to help us, and she is very friendly and kind. She makes a call to our insurance company, and isn't on the phone long before she dully says, "Thank you," to the person on the other end and hangs up. She places a box of tissues in front of me before speaking, and I know.

"I'm sorry," she says. We're not covered. Not for *anything*, not even this appointment. We'll have to pay for it out of pocket.

My tears surprise me. It's as if a rug has been pulled out from under me, yet I barely have any recollection of ever stepping onto one in the first place. The woman fetches the doctor and he comes back to talk to us some more. He suggests we try one round of IVF if we can afford it. We can't. "Some couples use their home equity lines of credit," he says. That's what people are doing in 2006, two years before the housing bubble bursts. For a few days, we consider it.

Back at home, I read the fine print on the paperwork we've been given to fill out. There's a disclaimer I must sign, stating I'm aware that in some studies, fertility drugs have been associated with an elevated risk of reproductive cancers.

That fucker. Too much WebMD, my ass.

—◦

We're still navigating this alien vortex the day we go to meet little Henry—newborn son of Matthew, Brian's then 29-year-old nephew.

I wipe my eyes before leaving the car. Brian gives me a squeeze, and then holds my hand through the parking lot as I fight back more tears. Suddenly the prospect of meeting a brand new baby is heartbreaking. This is unusual, because newborns have never held much appeal for me. I see a newborn, I see a bottomless well of urgent, indiscriminate need, and it freaks me out. I fear not knowing exactly what's needed. I fear feeling put-upon and unable to escape.

I tentatively enter the birthing room, afraid that merely laying eyes on Henry will crush me. His mother—Matthew's girlfriend, Lori—is propped up slightly in bed, holding him.

"Here," she says, lifting the baby, gesturing to Matthew, wincing with every micro-movement. "Can you take him for a little while?"

Matthew reaches over and grabs his six-pound son, who is not much bigger than one of his father's huge hands. This is the tiniest baby I've ever seen, wearing the world's most miniscule diaper. Although, come to think of it, is that how tiny all newborns are? I wouldn't know. I'm not much in the practice of meeting children on their first day of life.

Matthew scoops the baby up to his chest and proceeds to lose himself in what I imagine to be the powerful, all-consuming new-parent love I've always heard about. He notices me staring. "You want to hold him?" he asks, extending his arms. I'm terrified. I haven't held many newborns. Henry looks so unbelievably fragile.

"I'm not sure I know how to hold him the right way," I say.

"It's not that complicated," Matthew snaps. All-consuming love or no, Matthew's been up 36 hours and would probably like me to give him a break.

I take a deep breath and step forward. I lift my hands.

Then—*PFFFFFFFT. PFFFFFFT-PFFFFFFFT.*

"Was that a fart?" I blurt, retreating almost involuntarily.

"Probably more than a fart," Matthew says.

"Do we need to change him *again*?" Lori asks. "*We just changed him.*"

"No," Matthew replies. "I don't think it was *that* much."

I'm viscerally repelled—and at the same time, mortally self-conscious about it. I don't know which is worse, how disgusted I am by the mess in Henry's diaper, or how disgusted I am with myself for feeling disgusted. Regardless, I can't ignore my overwhelming aversion to holding that writhing, pink creature.

"I'm so sorry," I say. "I can't do this."

On the ride home I cry some more. I've been crying a lot these days. Heading to the hospital, the triggering thought had been, "I'll never have this..." Heading home, it's, "I'll never truly *want* this," and the sense that it means something is fundamentally wrong with me.

— 〇 —

In the weeks following, the Universe seems to taunt me with the notion that in fact there *is* something fundamentally wrong with me.

First, Brian and I receive an interesting visit at the family-ready, three-bedroom Victorian house with a yard we bought in Rosendale two weeks after marrying, just as we were losing our apartment in the East Village. We answer a knock at the door to find a cluster of people, several of whom have slightly different variations of the same face. They're members of a family who'd lived in our house from the late 1940s to the early 1970s, all of them visiting from out-of-town to inter their late mother's ashes. "We were a Brady Bunch family," one of them says as they take us on a nostalgic tour of our own home. "There were ten of us." At one point, all ten children lived there, together. *Ten* kids lived in our house. And there I was, dreading the thought of giving up my vintage floral wallpapered "office" (which doubled as our guest room) to just one child.

Next, a few days later, we're out in the backyard having lunch when through the lilac hedge at the edge of our property we spot a set of tiny eyes peering at us.

"Who are you?" says the voice of a five-year-old boy, dispensing with pleasantries.

"I'm Brian, and she's Sari. Who are you?"

"I'm Nicholas," he says. "But who *are* you?"

Who *are* we? "What do you mean?" I ask.

"Whose mommy and daddy are you?" he says. There's an implied "duh" in his tone. "*Who are your children?*"

Oh. Thanks a lot, kid. I work hard not to take on a five-year-old's judgment, rendering me strange and irrelevant for my lack of offspring. After I break the news that we haven't got any children, Nicholas pauses for a moment to think.

"Well...then who's gonna play with the toys?"

I'm stumped by this one—an existential question, a Zen koan—not least because *there are no toys in our yard*. Not a one.

—๑

There are two incorrect assumptions people make upon meeting me in my fifties. The first is that I have kids. When I make it clear I don't, new acquaintances often redden with embarrassment and trip all over themselves trying to find the right words. "Don't worry," I always assure them. "I'm okay with it."

That happens to be both an understatement and a lie—an understatement because I fucking *love* not having kids; a lie because I often judge myself harshly for that, which leaves me anything but okay.

My harshest self-judgements arrive when I'm in the company of people who have kids. I compound my self-criticisms with projections of how I imagine they see me, telling myself I'm a sad specimen of an adult woman—lazy, coldhearted, cynical, misanthropic. *Damaged.* None of this is out of left field. It's related to things people around me say. "Life is a conveyor belt," muses an older acquaintance, "it delivers all of us to the same points, one by one. And then it's over." Some of the "points" mentioned are parenthood, then grandparenthood. It makes me realize that instead of the conveyor belt everyone else is on, I'm off to the side, on a hamster wheel, revisiting the same life challenges over and over before I finally master them. In another conversation about a woman roundly considered a "train wreck," an acquaintance defends the woman by saying she has "done normal-people things" like raising children and holding the same job for decades. I realize that by this definition, I do not qualify as "normal people."

The second mistaken assumption people make about me: once they learn how happy I am to not have kids, they assume I'm "childless by choice." They ask, "When did you decide you didn't want kids?" But the thing is, I didn't decide. I didn't have the nerve to—not even to let myself in on the secret that I didn't want kids. I hid it from myself. I turned my mind away from the topic altogether. I blanked out on it, went completely numb.

In the decade-plus following my divorce from my first husband, I never so much as entertained the topic of whether I wanted children—even though I had two accidental (and unviable) pregnancies and abortions. Each time, I had strong feelings of *get this out of me*, which I attributed to getting pregnant at the wrong time, by the wrong men. But then I didn't look any more deeply into it than that.

This is the crazy thing I'm saying: throughout most of my twenties and thirties, I avoided gauging my own level of interest in making babies, in any kind of conscious way. I suppose that in and of itself, that should have said something about my level of interest. It didn't matter that I was surrounded by the predictable chatter about ticking clocks. Friends obsessed over theirs. Family members treaded lightly but still inquired about mine—or half-joked that I should reproduce at least for the sake of having someone to care for me when I grew old. The neighbor upstairs, a slightly older gay man who'd come to my parties, felt compelled to stop me in the hallway one day when I was 35 or 36.

"If you want to have kids," he said urgently, and completely unsolicited, "you should probably do something about it soon." He added a cautionary tale about his sister waiting too long before she figured it out. She was now in her late forties, childless and regretful.

Even amid all that talk, in the thirteen years between ending my first marriage at 26 and embarking on my current marriage at 39-and-change, as I flitted around the East Village with a string of Peter Pans, I firmly resisted considering whether I was interested in motherhood—in truly knowing my own heart. "Ambivalent" seemed like a sufficient descriptor, a safe place to land that didn't require me to really think, because I was too afraid to really think—to confront the gap between what I might really want, and what I thought I was supposed to want. Wasn't having kids something I was *built* to want? I didn't feel permitted to question that. Nothing and no one around me suggested I was. The few other childless women in my world growing up were demeaned, treated as less-than.

Looking back now, I think I was also afraid to know that I wanted to be an "art monster," unencumbered by motherhood in my creative pursuits, because I believed such a desire was selfish and shameful; afraid to realize that my struggle with depression and my pessimism about the state of the world made it seem unfair to bring kids into the world—more specifically *my* world, the one in which I, a frequently depressed person, might give a kid a shitty life.

On the flip side, I was also afraid to poke around the tender region of the heart where maternal longings lie, for fear of discovering *I might actually possess some*. What if I found I wanted kids, only to learn I'd never be able to carry them to term because of my endometriosis? What if I wanted them, but couldn't find a partner in parenting because of my penchant for choosing non-committal men?

I was afraid to know my own heart and mind—afraid to *make up my mind* and choose wrong. So I didn't choose. I just sat on the fence and waited for some wise outside force to push me over into what I hoped would be the right direction.

—⟋

How appealing to turn your fate over to…*something*, to believe there's some greater power you can defer to in the face of life's most frightening decisions. I have a complicated relationship to faith. With my clergy-kid baggage, I'm inclined to reject formal religious practice, but I'm also tempted to believe in *something*, or an assortment of somethings from column A and column B. I'm always aware of when, astrologically speaking, "Mercury is in retrograde," and when it is, I'm inclined to blame everything from car problems to tense human interactions on it. I have in my possession not one but *two* copies of Shakti Gawain's *Creative Visualization: Use the Power of Your Imagination to Create What You Want in Your Life* and a copy of *The Secret* video. I've also been to more than my share of psychics. When I was younger, I'd ask them to predict whether and how many kids I'd have, as if I were trying to get a sneak peek at the answers to an upcoming quiz at school.

For someone who can be rather skeptical, I can also be rather suggestible. This becomes glaringly obvious when, in 2007, a homebirth midwife hires me as a ghostwriter for her memoir and predicts that just by working with her on her many birthing stories, I'll miraculously conceive.

—⟋

Cara's eyes light up as I fill her in on our bad luck at the fertility clinic, and subsequently with acupuncture, herbal cleanses, dry skin brushing, castor oil packs, plus a litany of other holistic infertility antidotes. How with each unlucky gamble, the emotional stakes have risen—how I've gone from sensing no maternal instinct, to feeling desperate.

"I have a good feeling about this," Cara says. "You're going to get pregnant writing this book." She believes that is partly why I was "brought" to her. She's very persuasive, and I want to be persuaded. I begin to believe something greater than me has brought me to Cara, that I am somehow *meant* to write her book. Maybe working closely with her, constantly discussing pregnancy and childbirth, I'll be like those women who seem to only be able to conceive after they've adopted and been immersed in baby life.

After Cara's book is finished, another year and change goes by, and no pregnancy. I'm now approaching 42. *Tick, tock.* As time runs out, I become increasingly anguished. I feel powerless, confused.

It's in this state of turmoil that I attend the annual holiday party for a Manhattan law firm, one of Brian's I.T. clients. It's my third or fourth year attending this party, so I'm acquainted with the cast of characters: the attorneys, their spouses, and their ever-growing ranks of offspring, who clamor noisily about. With many of the attorneys in their thirties, conversations tend toward the "I can't believe how much she's grown!" and "When did he start walking?" variety.

This year I'm not in any emotional condition for forcedly cooing at babies and asking toddlers to hold up however many fingers represent their present age. Fortunately I'm rescued by Ginny, a pixie-ish lawyer, and her husband, who don't seem too terribly interested in the kids, either. They must have noticed I was keeping my distance from the veritable nursery at the center of the holiday tableau. I've had two glasses of wine—my limit—which probably explains how Ginny and I quickly get onto the topic of infertility, right down to the anatomical nitty-gritty of Brian's and mine.

After Ginny nods to her husband to suggest he move away so we can talk alone, I unload on her—all of it: my trajectory from detached ambivalence to "letting the Universe decide" to actually considering paying for IVF with our home equity line of credit. My lingering doubts about whether Brian and I are cut out for parenthood. The sense that my sorrow over being unable to reproduce isn't necessarily an indication of a desire to have kids.

Following my flood of emotion, Ginny opens up. "We tried, too," she says quietly, "a long time ago. We thought we wanted kids. We were very sad when we failed. But we've actually come to be very glad about it."

I let that sink in for a moment.

"You know what the Dalai Lama says about those who can't have children?" she asks.

"No," I say. "What?"

"He says they're off the hook, for this lifetime."

I tuck it in my back pocket.

—⟲

When I get home—and for years to come—I search the Internet for that quote, or anything resembling it. Into the search field I type "Dalai Lama on those who can't have kids," and "Dalai Lama on infertility," "Dalai Lama quotes on being childless," to name a few variations. None of the results come even close. But fuck it. I decide to believe what Ginny has said is true. There's no way I'm letting go of a hall pass like that, from so high an authority.

And then I'm let off the hook in a different way: I learn that I'm certifiably ill equipped for having kids—like, *equipment*-wise. I have such painful menstrual cramps so often, and for so long—fifteen days a month, most months—that my gynecologist thinks it's more than just endometriosis. She sends me to a uterine specialist.

After he examines me, the doctor determines I have adenomyosis, a condition related to endometriosis, in which the uterine lining corrupts other layers of the uterus, including the muscular walls.

"You need to have a hysterectomy," he says matter-of-factly.

Some part of me expects to fall apart when I hear these words, but instead, I feel myself suddenly relax. What the doctor has said rings true on a cellular level. My body knows it to be irrefutable. How could I have not thought of that before? I mean, I *had* thought of it before, but as a remote fantasy on the most unbearable days of my cycle. Like, "How great would it be if I could just have this fucking thing yanked?"

Once I've had a couple of days to try on the knowledge that, no, really, I will never have another human emerge from my loins, I think: *YES. I am officially off the hook.* My doctor and the Dalai Lama said so.

—◦

I undergo a Davinci Robotic Hysterectomy and experience tremendous relief immediately, and not just physically. It's as if I've been granted a reprieve from some looming, difficult test, like the SAT. I take additional comfort in the surgeon's report on the wretched condition of my uterus.

"There's no way you'd have ever been able to carry a baby to term," he assures me. Knowing this makes me feel confident that those two pregnancies years ago—one of which was ectopic, the other of which I began to miscarry before my scheduled abortion—would never have resulted in my becoming a mother. But even more than that, it makes me feel as if I have permission to consider that *maybe... I... just... didn't... want... kids.* It's as if I've been given a doctor's note: "Please excuse Sari from procreating in this lifetime, as she is not in any way built for it."

—◦

As liberating as it is to be given an out, it's disappointing that I still feel as if I need someone other than me, someone with greater authority—some *dude*—to give it to me. Why can't I give myself the out? Why do I need the Dalai Lama and the surgeon to all rubber-stamp my choice, or what would have been my choice if I'd ever thought I were allowed to choose?

I'm not alone. At a party a few years ago, I came upon a group of women around my age huddled in a corner. They shushed each other as I approached. "We're talking about not having kids," one said after an uncomfortable pause. "About *choosing* not to." The group looked at me for an awkward moment, waiting to see whether I'd identify myself as one of them before saying more.

This sort of thing keeps happening—I find myself in the company of women, old and young, who are "coming out" about not wanting kids. It's 2022, and women are still speaking in hushed tones about deciding not to be mothers. The conversation is only just beginning. Although we're finally talking, some of us still have a long way to go—toward knowing and owning what we want, and feeling entitled to it, when it's different from the norm. I hope it won't always be this way.

Losing the Plot

When I graduate from college in May of 1987, I receive a call from the Sephardic Brotherhood. After congratulating me on this auspicious milestone, the man on the phone suggests I begin planning for another bigger one down the road: When I die, would I like to be buried in their section of a Jewish cemetery in New Jersey? If I sign up now, I can lock into their special rate of just $90 per year.

I'm only 22 at the time, but damn if I don't recognize a bargain when I hear it. I mail off a check and then go about the business of hunting for my first real job in journalism; beginning my adult life while responsibly covering my bases for the end of it.

—⁀৹

Two years later I marry for the first time, and the Sephardic Brotherhood calls again. Would I like to have my husband—he's 25—buried beside me?

"Hang on," I say to the man on the other end. "Honey?? Do you want to be buried with me in the Sephardic part of a Jewish cemetery in New Jersey? It's $90 a year."

"I don't know," my husband shouts from another room in our small apartment. "Can we think about it?"

"I'll get back to you," I tell the man.

That weekend, at dinner with my in-laws, we inform them of the wonderful opportunity before us. "What?!" my mother-in-law shrieks. "But we're already paying for plots for you—*and your children*—with the Shpitzernitzer* Society!"

(*In America from the late 19th to the early 20th Century, European Jewish immigrants formed hundreds of groups like the Shpitzernitzer Society and the Sephardic Brotherhood. Originally these societies served multiple purposes—helping members find jobs, learn English, and navigate immigration issues and assorted other legal matters. Many also became discount burial plot brokers.)

It's news to us that our corpses and those of our theoretical future children

188

are already spoken for, but we aren't about to argue over it. On Monday I call the Brotherhood and cancel my burial plan. They issue a refund.

—◎—

My first husband travels for business, and I live in constant fear he'll die in a plane crash. It's an anxiety exacerbated by my mother's habit of phoning every single time she's about to board a flight and reciting the same litany of worst-case information: her bank account numbers, who to call to cash out her life insurance policy, which jewelry I can expect to find in her safety-deposit box.

Around the time of our wedding there's a news story about a flight attendant on Aloha Air getting sucked out of a plane when the roof was randomly blown off. From then on, every time my husband flies, I obsess about this happening to him. Each time he exits the apartment with his suitcase, I compulsively half-joke: "Don't get sucked out of the plane!" and then nervously laugh. Sometimes I say it twice, or three times.

—◎—

The instinct to ward off death with OCD-like rituals is not a new one. I'd first resorted to this type of irrational behavior when I was 6 and learned my beloved maternal grandmother, "Nanny Clarisse," was dying of breast cancer.

"Nanny is very sick," my mother explained. "She has been sick for a long time. She will probably die very soon."

Six months earlier we'd had nearly the same conversation about our miniature poodle, Figaro, after he'd had an epileptic seizure and my parents rushed him to the vet. The dog never came back home—he died that night. At 5-and-a-half, that had been my first and only exposure to death. It had scared me and made me feel helpless, and also somehow responsible, as if despite having been warned Figaro's life was in jeopardy, I'd failed to save him.

Now, less than a year later, death was back, and it was gunning for one of my favorite people, my grandmother, with whom I had a special bond. We were kindred creative spirits and I could not imagine life without her. I felt charged to take some kind of action—to act out in some way.

"No!" I protested when my mother was done explaining. "No! No! No! No! No!..." I kept going, imagining that if I said No enough times, I could reverse the likelihood of Nanny dying.

When my voice got tired (and I got tired of hearing my voice), I was struck with a new compulsion: to clench my fists hard and hold them indefinitely. In that moment I convinced myself that if I didn't let go, I could vanquish whatever evil force threatened to remove my grandmother from my life. I squeezed and squeezed, hard, until I had cramps in my hands, and couldn't hold my grip any longer. When I finally let go, I saw that my fingernails had dug half-moons into the flesh of my palms. The next morning I was back at it, squeezing my hands into fists for as long as I could before it hurt too much and I had to stop. Later that day my mom broke the news that Nanny had died. I was wrecked. I cried and cried—tears of sadness, but also of bewilderment and frustration. How could I have failed to save her, too?

—❡

Three years after my first wedding, it's my marriage that dies. (We hadn't considered the possibility that we might both outlive our union.) You-know-who gives me a jingle and offers me the chance to reclaim my solitary grave for the same $90 per year, plus the $180 they'd returned to me. But I'm struggling financially—working full time while also starting an MFA program I'll soon have to drop out of, and spending too much on New York City rent and takeout. "No, thank you," I say.

Each year the Sephardic Brotherhood reaches out again. When Caller I.D. is invented, I screen their calls, all the while promising myself that someday I'll do the adult thing and start investing in my burial.

—❡

"Someday" turns out to be an amorphous, highly postpone-able target date. As of this writing, I am 56, my second husband, Brian, is 60, and we have exactly zero end-of-life plans. We possess nothing even vaguely resembling living wills. We don't know each other's bank account numbers or passwords. Back in 2005, around the time of our elopement, I did sign up for cheap life insurance from the Freelancer's Union—for about $75 a month, when the first one of us dies, the other gets $25,000. But that won't go far.

What happened to the super-responsible young woman who made the first payment on her burial plot at 22? When I got divorced at 26, I retired the role of Prematurely Adult Sari , a girl so eager to seem grown up that she married before her frontal lobe had finished developing. When I moved out, I swung the other way and started living a bit more on the edge, swearing off full-time jobs for less stable freelancing, leaving the staid Upper West Side for the rough and tumble East Village of the early '90s, traipsing around it with a string of Peter Pans in threadbare concert tee shirts, 501s and Chuck Taylors—a grunge-era Tinker Bell in Never Never Land. It would be another thirteen years before I'd settle down again, with Brian.

Until recently the matter of our deaths hadn't seemed too pressing, probably because we have no children to leave anything to (which of course also means that in our old age there will be no one to care for us, or to bury or cremate us), and also because we're both generally healthy, and have each always seemed kind of young for our age. But a few years ago I stopped coloring my hair, and boy is there a lot of gray. And the other day a 30-ish woman from the local power company came to my house and I overheard her describe me on the phone to her supervisor as "an older woman" even though my hair was in pigtails. It's getting harder for me to deny that I'm middle aged, which is in turn making it harder for me to ignore the encroachment of death.

Maybe "middle aged" is generous. Maybe I'm way past the middle, and closer to the end. Both of my grandmothers died around my age—Clarisse at 55; Sally at 51, a few years before I was born. A writer I admired essentially dropped dead in the middle of a conversation when she was 51, despite being a vegan with a dewy complexion, who did yoga every day. Recently I attended a memorial for a friend two years younger than me who died of breast cancer.

I wonder, how do I know where I currently stand along the timeline of my life? How does anyone? We're all living stories whose twists and turns—and conclusions—we know nothing of until we reach them. The science of genetics allows us to predict only so much about which illnesses we might contract when, and whether they might kill us. We live in more advanced times than our ancestors, so maybe the cancers and other diseases that took their lives are curable now. Maybe you'll survive them, but then hang on indefinitely with lifelong debilitating side effects from the treatments. Or maybe you'll get hit by a car before the cancer ever has a chance to establish itself. (That said, I have already survived being hit by a massive S.U.V. in SoHo, as I was crossing Spring Street.)

What determines when and how you die, anyway? Is it a simple function of genetics and chance? Is it predestined the day you're born? Is it a constant negotiation with some fickle, all-powerful being (whose sense of irony I am possibly testing by daring to write this)?

These questions and a million others have been consuming me lately, keeping me awake at night while Brian sleeps soundly beside me. He and I have reached a phase of life where death is naturally occurring more often among our family, friends, and acquaintances. Social media keeps us instantly informed every time someone in our circle has passed on, or is about to. With each new posting, I find myself more unsettled, and troubled by our lack of plans. What's more, living across the street from a senior housing development—where the sirens and flashing lights of ambulances frequently interrupt the quiet of my life—is a constant reminder of the end of life.

—◦

Lately, we can't seem to escape the specter of death. Even in the years before Covid-19 took three members of our extended family, so many friends (and "friends") have died, or announced they were about to: The husband of a friend, who one day couldn't pee, and a year later was dead from prostate cancer, leaving her a widow. The friend who died of stage IV breast cancer who blithely live-blogged her demise, posting frequently about how she had one foot in living and the other in dying. She introduced me to concepts like death doulas, and green burials, and "living funerals," where those with terminal illnesses get to hear their loved ones eulogize them before they actually pass. There's the 15-year-old who lost her four-year battle with a rare pediatric blood disease. The 50-something guy who went to bed one night and didn't wake up the next day…the family friend in his forties who did the same thing…the 49-year-old guy we only knew a little (and, to be honest, didn't like), who did that, too. So many wives have woken up in the morning to find their husbands dead beside them.

The quickening stream of obituaries in my Facebook feed—along with crowd-funding campaigns to pay for burials—makes me hyper aware that someday Brian or I might suddenly drop dead, or fall ill and die slowly, painfully, and expensively. That unless we're killed together in a car accident, or in some major catastrophe like a plane crash, a nuclear attack, another pandemic, or, ever more likely in these dark times, a mass shooting, Brian and I will likely *not* die simultaneously. One of us will be left alone, bereaved, heartbroken, forced to go on without the other. And unless we make some end-of-life decisions soon, the one left standing will have a lot of heavy bills and difficult shit to figure out, while also grieving.

—໑

Somehow, Brian is not worrying like I am. He's not walking around like a sleep-deprived zombie after hours-long bouts of death-related anxiety overnight—not even after suddenly losing a childhood friend a couple of years ago, who had a heart attack behind the wheel of his car while driving home from a gig with his band. I bring up the idea of living wills and Brian seems to think I'm being alarmist, as if death is an unfortunate thing that only happens to unfortunate people, not a regular feature of life that occurs for everyone. I've tried framing the topic neutrally and speaking calmly, but repressing my emotions in this way has backfired, leading me to become somewhat hysterical, periodically blurting out our doom. Last winter, for instance, after he says he's found a dead mouse at his office, I hear myself saying, in all seriousness, "One day, one of us is going to wake up and find the other lifeless and rotten-smelling, like a dead rodent." On another occasion, when I notice he is procrastinating on finishing the collection of songs he's been working on for at least as long as I've known him, I say, "Life is short, and if you don't do it soon, you may die without ever having finished."

Don't worry—he can take it. In fact, when I say these things, it barely makes a dent. Brian maintains a certain sangfroid about death. He waxes TED Talk about what a privilege it was to be at his father's hospice bedside when he died at 85, to witness the look of awe that came over his dad's face as he took his last breath: "It's as if he saw something assuring, and thought, *this* is what I have been afraid of?" Brian is able to focus on why *not* to be scared of death, and I can't stop thinking of reasons to be petrified.

I resort once again to my own weird rituals. Many nights, as we're about to turn out the lights, I'll find myself compulsively issuing the same desperate plea: "Just don't ever die, okay?" I say it, half-jokingly, again and again, like a mantra, as if those words alone could make him immortal.

"You know I can't promise that," Brian will say, then pull me in for a hug meant to suggest the assurances that his words, and reality, can't.

"Well, maybe don't always eat only corn chips for every meal when I'm not around," I'll burst out.

When I travel without Brian, I make sure the refrigerator is stocked with ample alternatives to his default staple, Tostitos. I'll buy an organic rotisserie chicken, broccoli, salad, fresh, local corn on the cob. I leave him post-it notes reminding him to eat it all, and every time I call, I remind him to read the notes. As I'm putting myself to bed wherever I've traveled to, I worry about whether he'll drop dead before I return home. I try to soothe myself and ward off death with the ritual of imagining the healthy food traveling around his body, depositing into his flesh and bones the specific units of protein, good fat, and fiber necessary to buy him many more days on this earth.

People turn to rituals as a source of comfort, but mine don't seem to work that way. They don't stop me from frequently trying to predict which one of us will die first. If I die first, I wonder, will Brian remarry? Will it be to someone younger? If he dies first, will I remarry? Or will I learn to be single and content with it—not see it as a condition that needs to be remedied as the culture does, as I once did, before we met? If I remain single, who will find the body when it's my turn to die?

Sometimes my fears are most pronounced when Brian and I are just hanging out, having a sweet old time together. I'll think, *What if this all suddenly ends?* I know coupledom is hardly the only way to live, and that *happy* coupledom is a rare privilege I enjoy. But it's the life setup I have, and love. He is the person I have, and love, and would be devastated to lose. What if the rug is pulled out from under me as it was when I was six and Nanny Clarisse died? More than once I've interrupted our good time to say, "If we have to die, I hope we can go together, at the exact same minute, so neither of us ever has to grieve or bury the other," and I mean it. We know a couple who have stockpiled Halcyon, enough to end both of them, in case of a nuclear war, or other apocalyptic conditions. Occasionally I've suggested we devise a similar pact. "Sure, why not," Brian says each time with a laugh, humoring me.

—◦

A few years ago, death crept in way closer than just our social media circle, ratcheting up my anxiety even higher. In late 2015, Brian's mother died at 94. She'd been spry and impish until 92, but a few weeks after that birthday, she fell and broke her hip. She spent the next two years miserable, eager for her life to end. She was aged and infirm, but not unwell enough to *just fucking die*. She asked over and over, "How much longer? When will it be over? I want it to be over," giving me something new to worry about: how hard it can be, how long it can take, to actually exit this plane when you no longer have the will to live.

Next came Stanley, my stepfather of thirty years, in May of 2018, at 89. Stanley was the youngest, most boyish 89-year-old you ever met. He enjoyed life more than anyone I've ever known. He was strong and hearty, and seemed indestructible. *Seemed*.

—◦

The night before I travel to a journalism conference in Chicago, Stanley is taken to the hospital in Florida, where he and my mother live half the year. He's had a bad reaction to a medication prescribed by his cardiologist to lower his triglycerides. He tells me on the phone from his hospital bed that he thinks he's actually okay, but at a deep level of my consciousness, I'm not convinced.

He winds up in the ICU, clinging tenuously to life. I fly from the journalism conference to Florida for ten days, to keep my mother company and help out at Stanley's bedside. Day after day, we trade shifts. For the next two weeks, Stanley's numbers are up and down. It's hard to have any sense of which overall direction things are moving in, although I'm hyper-aware that ultimately they're pointing toward death—not just for Stanley, but for all of us. Everything points toward death. We're all dying as we're living, hurtling ultimately toward some kind of shitty exit. No one gets out alive.

In this hospital, every time a baby is born, a few bars of Brahms's "Lullaby" are piped in over the loudspeaker system, throughout the building. It's particularly surreal to have this hit your ears every few hours when you're sitting at the bedside of an old person who is becoming ever more baby-like. It makes me wonder whether Boca General isn't running some kind of soul-exchange operation.

After ten days at his bedside, I'm encouraged that Stanley's at least hanging on, and I fly back to New York. There's talk the next day of sending him home and hiring a visiting nurse. Maybe being in familiar surroundings will help. But the next morning, everything goes haywire. By the afternoon, he's gone.

My mother calls with the news, and I'm wrecked. And once again I'm overcome with the feeling that somehow I've failed to save someone.

At 89, Stanley's passing shouldn't be surprising—to us or to him, really—but somehow it is. More surprising: how many loose ends he and my mother had to go over in the days before he died—like teaching my mom his analog system for paying and keeping track of monthly bills, involving pencils and legal pads. Even at his advanced age, it hadn't occurred to him that he might need to prepare for death in certain ways. Realizing that made me feel both better and worse about my own lack of plans.

—◦

It's too bad that instead of a "living funeral," Stanley of all people had to have the regular kind, where the guest of honor misses everything. Over five-hundred people attended. Many of his friends and family expressed how shocked they were, how hard it was to imagine that a man so full of life could be gone.

After the ceremony at Gutterman's, a police escort led a long procession of mourners to the cemetery. We arrived as the Blue Angels were rehearsing their flight demonstrations overhead for their coming Memorial Day show. It was a coincidence, but it felt as if they'd come just for my stepfather.

Stanley got the burial he wanted, a send-off fit for him—for which he'd saved for many years. In that way, I suppose it was money well spent. But it's certainly not the kind of thing Brian and I can afford for ourselves, nor would we want to. In the days after we bury Stanley, I begin to think about how I might leave this realm as inexpensively as possible, taking up the least space, with little impact to the earth. In death, how can I be the least burden possible to Brian, and to my family? I don't want anyone to have to start a GoFundMe so they can afford to dispose of my corpse.

—◦

"Can you donate your whole body to science?" I ask Brian at breakfast recently. "Like, not just your organs on your driver's license. *The whole enchilada?*"

This, of all things, catches his attention. He looks up from his iPad and tells me he's heard of these farms where they study how bodies decompose. "It's kind of cool," he says.

We agree to look into it. But then weeks go by, and nothing. I realize we're both avoiding this. Maybe we're afraid that addressing our mortality will make it real. In my moments of greatest terror, I remind myself of something my friend with terminal breast cancer posted on her blog, about how planning for her burial was one of the most empowering things she'd ever done in her life. I could take this on myself, I think. But I don't want to do it all alone. Besides, I'm already in charge of handling too many of our practical decisions, about things like health insurance. I want Brian to get on board with planning for death with me, but this is where we come upon another fundamental difference between us: I am a planner, and he is not. I find it freeing to take out a calendar and schedule my busy time so that I can see where my free time lies, and make the most of it. He thinks just the act of scheduling things impinges on his free time. But I don't know how much longer I can obsess about this and not take action, because it's taking a toll on my quality of life—and Brian's too.

The morning after we learn the owner of a local restaurant has died suddenly in his forties, as Brian leaves for work I blurt, "Drive safely...so that you don't DIE..." and burst into tears. He consoles me, but then an hour later texts, "Lovey, I love you so, but your anxiety about my health and potential demise are stressing the hell out of me." We talk later and he suggests therapy, which I've been out of for a while. I agree it's not a bad idea, but also hold my ground on our need to awaken from our Gen-X protracted adolescence and get living wills.

—૭

A few more years pass, and somehow we *still* haven't made any kind of end-of-life plans. Not even after Covid-19 takes my death obsession and ratchets it up a few notches. There is so much loss everywhere, among friends and family and acquaintances. I live in a constant state of terror, worrying that I might be next. Then Brian's oldest sister gets the virus and dies from a combination of it and cancer. Next, my cousin, a year older than me, decides not to get the vaccine and shortly thereafter contracts the virus and dies, leaving behind her 10-year-old daughter. Then my cousin's mother dies from it.

Every few months during quarantine, I remind Brian that we still need to find an estate lawyer, or download some free living will from the internet, or *something*. When he closes the storefront for his Apple Authorized repair shop and brings his business into our basement, cluttering it with broken Macs and computer parts, I hear myself say, "If you drop dead and I have to figure out how to sift through all this stuff on my own, I will dig you up and kill you again." I'm only half-kidding. We get the name of an estate lawyer from one friend, and another from another friend. I realize Brian is never going to take the lead on this. It's going to be up to me. I promise myself I'll act soon. Then I do nothing, except obsess some more.

—૭

The Buddhists say you should think about death every day, but I'm pretty sure I'm not thinking about it in any kind of healthy way. In my most rational moments I realize you can't ward off death, but you can perhaps quell your anxiety about it with a little forethought. I want to plan for death so I can free myself up to stop thinking about it so damn much. Abraham Lincoln said, "And in the end it's not the years in your life that count, it's the life in your years." I'd like to find some peace with all of this so that I can enjoy the life in my years—however many I have left. Because *not* planning for death is killing me.

Gray Hair Don't Care

Just before my birthday in October 2020, my husband introduced me to a new acquaintance of his, a man in his early forties whom he'd met through work. "We're going away for Sari's birthday this weekend," Brian said.

The man asked how old I'd be. "I'm turning 55!" I exclaimed, like the 5-year-old I turn into on my birthday each year.

"Wow," he replied, "if only you colored your hair, you could pass for 35!"

I knew he meant it as a compliment, so I simply said, "Thank you." I spared him the lecture about how much I love my gray hair; how I have a weird relationship to time and aging that makes it difficult for me to grasp how old I really am; how I (mostly) do not mind the numbers climbing higher; and how regardless of the increasing ways in which my external meat suit reflects the ravages of time, internally I still feel like a young girl.

Not taking offense to his comment felt like something of a victory, especially since it was exactly the kind of gendered ageist expression of the straight male gaze that I'd feared before I found the nerve, at 51, to lop off my signature long, brown hair striped with obvious, wide, blond highlights.

—◎

After I threatened for literally ten years to shave my head and go "gracefully gray," Brian stopped believing I would ever do it. It became a running joke between us. I'd say, "I'm so tired of my hair and the time it takes every couple of months to get it done. I'm thinking of cutting it all off and going natural. But will you still find me attractive with gray hair?" He'd always insist that he would, adding, "You'll never do it, though."

Part of the problem was that my half-bleached hair was nice, and pretty cool, frankly. I'd strived my whole life to feel cool in any way, and I finally hit on something when I arrived at my signature look. I was also, ironically, concerned that if I stopped coloring my hair too young, there wouldn't be *enough* gray that it would look good. I wanted plenty of silver in my hair, so that it could resemble Emmylou Harris's when she was in middle age, rather than be mostly boring brown with a few straggly, wiry, gray pieces mixed in.

I started coloring my hair in the spring of 2003, when I was approaching 38, and in the throes of my big online dating project—signed up on five different sites per an assignment from my therapist, and going out on several dates a week. I'd been toying with changing up *something* about my look. I was tired of my plain, long, brunette locks, and had been fascinated by women who were brave enough to make big statements with hair dye. This wasn't, by the way, about coloring over gray. Forever the late bloomer, in my late thirties, I had a total of about five gray hairs. No, this was about freeing myself from staid, boring convention, with a look that was radical.

With that in mind, I skipped over my usual hairdresser, because he was only interested in giving me natural-looking "nice Jewish girl" highlights, meant to give the impression that I'd just been hanging in the sun for a really long time. I couldn't have been less interested in that kind of stealth artifice, which also required frequent upkeep, once your roots started coming in. I wanted obvious artifice that made a statement, and something a little less high-maintenance on a regular basis.

So I made an appointment at Kropps & Bobbers, a salon on the Lower East Side that I passed by often, and where I often admired the radically-dyed hair of clients as they walked out. Right after I scheduled it, I called a friend. "Can you meet me at the salon?" I asked. "I'm afraid that otherwise I'll chicken out. I need someone to help me go through with this." Sure enough, she met me there on the day of my appointment for moral support.

Tony, my new hairstylist, didn't flinch when I told him what I wanted: glaringly obvious wide, platinum stripes alternating with my own brown color. I, a lover of show tunes, wanted to look vaguely "punk," and even after I explained this to Tony, he didn't for one second judge my choice. He simply honored my wishes, and went to work mixing up some bleach.

When the whole three-hour process was finished—it took a looooooong time for my dark hair to lift to blond—I looked at myself in the mirror. Surprisingly, I didn't have the kind of identity crisis I'd worried I might, in the days leading up to this. Instead of seeing reflected back at me someone who wasn't me, I saw a new dimension of myself, and I loved it.

It was an interesting experiment. How often had I wondered, *What would life be like if I were tall? Blue-eyed? Blond? A shikse goddess?* Of course, I was still short and brown-eyed, and thinking-man's attractive, as opposed to a raving beauty. But I felt like a new me, in a new world, and it was awesome.

Men responded favorably to the change, too. It was this specific kind of preferred treatment I was afraid to give up before, at nearly 51, I finally committed to saying goodbye to the highlights, and hello to a head full of gray. (I desperately want not to care what men think of my looks…but I also want to look beautiful to them as I'm doing that.)

—૭

I had a respectably long run as a semi-blond with short bangs—thirteen years! People complimented me on my hair all the time. I caught men checking me out frequently, which I hate to say I quite liked. Chic women asked me for the name of my hairdresser. Someone who saw me at a reading I took part in posted glowingly on social media about my "Sontag hairdo realness," and I felt like some kind of legend.

But I also felt stuck. For a long portion of those thirteen years that I colored my hair, I was tired of it. I felt confined and defined by it, and resented that. I wanted to be done with that. The blond stripes also felt like a cosmetic lie I was no longer willing to live with; in the weeks after each application, I had the feeling I was wearing a hat, or a wig, that slid slowly off my head. Once I started thinking of it this way, I could no longer really enjoy my hair.

There was a new wrinkle, too: my gray was starting to come in more seriously so that now, instead of alternating stripes of blond and pure brown, it was alternating stripes of blond and salt-and-pepper, which was much less striking. I wasn't willing to additionally dye the brown/salt-and-pepper hair. I was already spending too much time, every few months, just sitting through the bleaching process.

Then I started seeing images of women in their twenties dying their hair gray, and I thought, *Okay, if they can do this, I can.*

Still, it took me a long time to work up the chutzpah to make a move. It was one thing for a twentysomething with supple skin and no wrinkles to play with gray color, and another for a woman who was old enough to allow herself to *go* gray. I was worried that unlike those younger women, I might become "invisible," especially to men, in the way older women have often described feeling. I was loath to give up the ego boost I got each time some random straight man checked me out.

I wrote all these concerns down one morning in August, 2016, when I was leading a first-person storytelling workshop for a non-profit organization at an adult education center in upstate New York. It was customary, during free-writing sessions, for me and Eva, the organization's Executive Director, to work on our own stories too, then share them with only each other. Just before our lunch break, I read to her what I'd written about my resistance to cutting off all my hair and starting over with a gray buzz cut. (There was no way I was going to let the gray gradually grow into my existing long hair, leaving me with two different hair colors, one on top, and another on the bottom!) Mostly I wrote about my fear of no longer drawing the male gaze during the two or so years it would likely take me to grow my hair long again—as stupid and retrograde as that sounded. I'd tried short hair before, and I was decidedly *not* a short hair person. (You know when people feel compelled to pay you dubious compliments like, "You have a nice shaped head," that they can't find ways to genuinely flatter you.) I had no plans to make a pixie or short bob my permanent look. Cutting my hair off would be only ever a temporary move.

After I was done reading to Eva, we broke for lunch. I was washing my hands in the cafeteria bathroom when, like an apparition, behind me appeared a striking older woman with a perfect silver bob, dressed head-to-toe in Eileen Fisher linen.

"So, what are you going to do with your hair?" the woman asked.

I looked around to make sure she was talking to me. "Are you in my writing workshop?" I asked. "I don't recognize you, but I think maybe you overheard me talking about this there?"

"No," she said. "I'm here for a Qi Gong workshop, not a writing workshop, and I have no idea who you are. But I see blond...and brown...and a little silver. There's a lot going on in there!" She pointed to my head. "So, I just wanted to know what you're going to do about it."

Well!

I could have taken offense. Instead, I took the woman's appearance out of nowhere, at the particular moment she appeared, as a sign: it was time for me to do this.

—◌

As soon as the weekend writing workshop was over, I drove straight to my hairdresser—my *upstate* hairdresser, the one I'd been going to most of the time since I'd moved up from the city in 2005. I walked in the door and said, "Do you have enough time to cut all my hair off before I lose my nerve?"

She looked at her watch. "I have twenty minutes before my next appointment," she said. "Have a seat."

And so I parked my butt in her chair and let her shear off all my locks until I had the equivalent of a buzz cut, with not one single remaining dot of blond. Looking at myself in the mirror afterward I felt shocked, mostly in a good way. It felt as if I had a new slate, a fresh start. After I paid my hairdresser, I headed to my husband's office. When I walked in, his jaw dropped.

"Oh, my god," he said. "I really thought you'd never do it!"

He swore he loved it. I wasn't sure I believed him, but somehow I didn't feel anxious about it. It was temporary, anyway; I was committed to growing my hair long again. I was not looking forward to the eighteen months ahead, with one awkward growing-out phase after another. But with a slew of barrettes and headbands, I got through it. And now I love my hair.

Surprisingly, it grew in with natural wide highlights, similar to the fake ones I'd had applied to my hair for years—some stripes are much more bright and silvery than others. People often ask me whether it's a dye job, or whether I got silver highlights added to my natural gray. Nope. It's just my natural hair, doing its thing.

—⁓

Here's the part where I put the obligatory disclaimer about how there's nothing wrong with coloring over your gray if that's what you prefer. *Seriously.* Just as I don't want to feel pressured to color my hair, I don't think anyone else should feel pressured to leave their gray untouched. I'm for more options, more acceptance, more freedom for everyone to do as they wish. Sometimes, when friends change their mind about their gray and return to coloring it, they feel the need to justify it to me, and this is not necessary!

This is also where I must acknowledge that I know not all women can afford to "transgress" against the societal dictum to color over their gray. I am fortunate not to work in a field where I'd be discriminated against because I don't adhere to this kind of "grooming," fortunate to have a husband who loves and accepts me with gray hair, fortunate to live in a country and a state and a culture and a liberal community where it's acceptable for me to be a fashion rebel.

It also doesn't hurt that I have pretty good genes, when it comes to aging. Everyone in my family looks young for their age. Unlike my husband's new work friend, many people still guess I'm younger than I am, head-full-of-silver notwithstanding. Maybe it's because I wear it in the same style I've mostly worn since I was five—straight, long, with little-girl bangs. Or maybe they're just being polite. Who knows?

But I've arrived at a place where I don't care what anyone else thinks. I love my gray hair, and I can't wait until it's even whiter. Just like Emmylou's is now.

Epilogue: Found (-*ish*?)

When I finished writing the proposal for this book toward the end of 2019, my life was quite different from how it is at this writing, more than two years into the Covid-19 pandemic. The changes that have come to pass have been surprisingly instructive, reminding me of things I'd almost forgotten, like how uncertain life can be.

This time in the world has also had an impact on the perspective I set out to share when I conceived of this book, and it put an end to some fixtures in my life that had come to seem permanent before everything in the world came to a halt and radically changed. And so, as we come to the end of this book—the part where my "character" was supposed to be fulfilled and moving forward, graced by New Wisdom—it bears noting some ways in which my life and outlook have changed.

———

I won't say that before Covid appeared in the scene I thought I finally had it *all figured out* but at the risk of embarrassing myself here, I'll admit it was something approaching that. In 2019, my life was working for me on a number of fronts all at once in a way it never quite had before. I saw it as confirmation of what I'd long hoped to be true: that if you dare to tune out everyone else's voices, then make choices in keeping with who you truly know yourself to be, it's possible to make a life that's genuinely fulfilling. I mean, I had done those things. Clearly the Universe was rewarding me for excelling at being myself. Right?

Oops.

Kidding aside, I still believe in all of that—within reason, given how many conditions in life I now realize are beyond one's control. But there have been a few humbling blows since the advent of the virus that have tested my faith in that hypothesis, shown me the world is scarier than I knew, and left me feeling even more uncertain about my future. It's been a painful reminder of how unpredictable life can be, and that there's no single static version of your existence, good or bad, that can reliably, indefinitely persist.

Just as something was going to eventually disrupt the worst conditions in my world, something else could be counted on to disrupt more favorable ones, too. Of course, I should have known that because, well, I am kind of old to be surprised by this kind of thing. Certainly, this has happened to me many times before: everything seemed like it was moving in one direction, and then suddenly, out of nowhere, it was moving in another. Note to self: change really *is* the only constant.. I'm kind of embarrassed by my shock (shock!) at landing at another new, uncertain juncture.

—◌

At the end of 2019, I was riding high—or high-*ish*, anyway, as good as it gets for a perennially struggling writer/editor/teacher. After long stretches of my adulthood where several things went wrong and life seemed pretty challenging, at last, a lot of things simultaneously were going right. I was a full-time contractor at an online magazine I loved, editing personal essays and publishing some of my own. I'd begun teaching in an MFA program—a long-held goal of mine. I was also regularly spending weekends in my favorite city, New York, while teaching courses at Catapult. I enjoyed working each day at Kingston Writers' Studio, a co-working space for writers that I operated, and which helped me foster the very writers' community I needed for myself. It contributed to my happy existence in Kingston, where I love living with my husband, Brian.

Then Covid forced me to close the co-working space. It contributed to the unraveling of the online magazine, and my departure from it. And it made it impossible for me to travel to the city to teach. My life shrunk significantly, and so did my opportunities.

Relatively speaking, I was (am!) luckier than many. I was fortunate to be sheltering in place with my favorite person, to be housed and fed, able to afford heat, and to work from home. But through the difficulty of 2020, 2021, and much of 2022, I found myself once again questioning so many of my life choices and wondering how to construct a new, more steady pathway ahead for myself.

In Pandemic World, feeling more isolated and lonely than ever before, I found myself wondering: as a person who hates the cold and is prone to feelings of isolation, what was I doing in a small upstate city like Kingston? What had I been thinking my whole life, choosing to be a freelance writer and editor? What ever gave me the idea that writing about myself and my life was a worthwhile endeavor? Before these times it was a questionable choice; in the midst of a global pandemic—at a moment in American history when authoritarianism and climate change are growing threats, and myriad forms of oppression have led to warranted social unrest—it seems to make almost zero sense.

But was I ready to turn my back on my memoir, or my work as an editor and teacher in that genre? So much of my identity has been bound up in it, because I love it. Did this work still resonate with *who I was*? (Oh, no, not *another* identity crisis!) Did I still believe in memoir and essays as worthwhile endeavors? I had to remind myself how much identification I've experienced while reading other people's personal writing, and how many readers had reached out to me each time I published personal writing to say that what I'd written had resonated for them, or validated their feelings about something, or emboldened them to make a change. So, while being a memoirist is not even vaguely in the same stratosphere of helpfulness as many other professions, it does have its purpose and value.

Suffice it to say that in the throes of anxiety and depression and loneliness and debilitating self-doubt, each day I gave up, then re-sold myself on my career, as well as this very book.

—⁀

Obviously I decided to go through with the book, or you wouldn't be reading this. I recognized that after decades of wishing for this opportunity, it would be foolhardy to squander it—that I might never get another chance, and regret it for the rest of my life.

The writing was a struggle at every turn. A world that was already fairly dark and scary became only more so just as I set out to work. Nonstop traumatizing news kept my nervous system in a state of high alert, making it difficult to relax or concentrate.

Amidst all the anxiety, though, something incredibly reassuring emerged: I realized that despite all that, I finally feel solid in my knowledge of myself. That I no longer wonder who I *really* am. Mystery solved! There are enough "right" aspects of my life for me to feel as if I am firmly *me* now in a way I once wasn't. I know I can carry that with me wherever I might need to travel—whether Brian and I find we need to relocate (we're applying for Portuguese citizenship because of the growing threat of anti-Semitism in the U.S.), or I discover I need to quickly take a job that doesn't align with my interests but pays the bills. I will always be *me*. And I will always be *a writer*, even if I go through periods where I need to take on other kinds of work to survive.

After throwing off a lot of false notions about who I thought I was supposed to be, and reaching an age at which I care less about other people's opinions of me, it is a relief to feel firmly grounded in who I am. That doesn't mean I won't grow and change as I learn and discover new ideas. It doesn't mean there won't be challenges to what I've come to hold true, or triggering events that temporarily make me confuse the present with the past. I mean, can you ever permanently let go of old programming? *Eternal Sunshine* it out of your brain? Maybe not. But whatever surprises the future holds, I feel secure enough in my sense of who I am that I believe I can remain true to myself.

—◦

I suppose what I'm saying is that you may indeed *find yourself*…but then lose access to what seemed like a clear path ahead of you. You may think you have your life figured out…and then discover you're once again at a big, scary crossroads, one you never saw coming. The only thing to do then is to remember who you are, and with that knowledge, take a step forward in what feels like the truest direction. If you get it wrong, you can always turn another way.

ACKNOWLEDGMENTS

I have tremendous gratitude for so many people, all of whom have supported me in this endeavor in different ways, including:

My wonderful editor at Heliotrope, Naomi Rosenblatt, for selecting this book for publication, and editing it with great insight, intelligence, and compassion. My agent, Mel Flashman, for supporting this project even during the years when I was floundering, and too terrified to make significant progress. Shannon Barr, for her smart copy edits.

Memoirist, friend, and unofficial mentor Beverly Donofrio, for her encouragement and smart feedback. Susan Piperato, for her encouragement and helpful notes.

Eva Tenuto and Julie Novak, for starting TMI Project, where the kernels of some of these pieces were born, and bringing me on board—and Eva for being a wonderful, supportive creative partner for many years.

Mike Dang, who originally edited and published pieces that first appeared on The Billfold, and others, later, on Longreads. Krista Stevens, who thoughtfully edited some of the pieces that first appeared on Longreads. Danielle Jackson, Dana Snitzky, Michelle Weber, and Katie Kosma, who also offered valuable feedback on some of those pieces. Mark Armstrong, the founder of Longreads, who changed my life immeasurably by bringing me on board there.

Casey Scieszka and Steven Weinberg, owners of the wonderful Spruceton Inn, who granted me an artists' residency there to work on this in 2017. Omega Institute's Women's Leadership Center, which thrice granted me their Juno Cottage residency.

Writer friends Sara Eckel, Jen Doll, and so many other members of the Kingston writers' community, with whom I often talked shop about this project, and others.

Melissa Febos, who has enriched and enlightened me with her work, and always encouraged me. Emily Gould, whose writing I very much admire, and who has been supportive and generous to me over many years, in more ways than I can count.

Sue Shapiro, a supportive teacher and role model whose essay workshop all those years ago sparked earlier versions of a couple of pieces in here, and helped me get my essay writing mojo back when I desperately needed it.

Jami Attenberg, for her brilliant "1000WordsOfSummer" accountability program/Substack newsletter, which helped me to generate early drafts of a couple of these pieces.

Brian Keane, for effectively rewiring the connection between my heart and my brain.

My mother, father, and sister, for their encouragement, and their patience as I was deeply absorbed in this project.

Above all, Brian Macaluso, the most supportive partner I could ever ask for, in this life, and all my creative endeavors.

AUTHOR BIO

SARI BOTTON is a writer and editor living in Kingston, NY. Her work has appeared in the *New York Times*, the *Guardian*, and elsewhere. She is a contributing editor at Catapult, and the former Essays Editor for Longreads. She edited the award-winning, bestselling anthologies *Goodbye to All That: Writers on Loving and Leaving New York* and *Never Can Say Goodbye: Writers on Their Unshakable Love for New York*. She teaches creative nonfiction at Wilkes University, Catapult, Bay Path University, and Kingston Writers' Studio. She publishes the newsletters Oldster Magazine, Memoir Monday, and Adventures in Journalism. @**saribotton**

CPSIA information can be obtained
at www.ICGtesting.com
Printed in the USA
BVHW041407120722
641927BV00011B/580

9 781942 762997